PORTLAND

URBAN
TAPESTRY
SERIES
TOWERY

SPIRIT
OF THE EASTERN SEABOARD

INTRODUCTION BY SENATOR GEORGE J. MITCHELL • ART DIRECTION BY BOB KIMBALL

SPONSORED BY THE GREATER PORTLAND CHAMBERS OF COMMERCE

CONTENTS

By Senator George J. Mitchell

Portland is a city of historic charm and new technology, with a proud past and a bright future. It is big enough to offer its residents and visitors all that the largest cities provide, yet small enough to permit close and personal connections. With good reason, Portland is widely regarded as one of the best places in America to live.

Portland's long and colorful history dates back to 1632, when George Cleeve and Richard Tucker settled in the area then known as Falmouth. What is now the center of the city of Portland—a peninsula jutting eastward into the Atlantic Ocean—was the part of Falmouth known as The Neck.

The town grew slowly. Commercial activity concentrated on The Neck, especially in the port area. Then the area's settlers became entangled in a conflict that stretched halfway around the world.

In the 17th century, what is now Maine was part of the frontier in the long struggle for control of North America. South from Maine lay the English colonies; to the north was the French-controlled Canada. Along this frontier, Indians allied with the French engaged in constant skirmishes with English settlers.

In 1676, and again in 1690, the settlement at Falmouth was destroyed. A survivor of the second battle, Captain Sylvanus Davis, later wrote: "They [the French and Indians] fought us five days and four nights, in which time they killed and wounded the greatest part of our men, burned all the houses, and at last we were forced to parley with them." ▶

For many years, the area lay desolate and uninhabited. But slowly, the settlement re-formed and, with lumber as the foundation of its economy, it again grew and prospered. Providing masts for ships built for the British Royal Navy became a large and prosperous business. Between 1768 and 1772, more than 1,000 masts, averaging some three tons each, were shipped to England.

To help pay for the huge cost of the French and Indian wars, the British Parliament imposed a series of taxes on its colonies. This brought the British government into conflict with the very people on whose behalf it was ostensibly prosecuting the wars, and fueled the drive for American independence. Despite their close economic ties to the mother country, most of Maine's inhabitants strongly supported independence.

The Stamp Act of 1765 aroused such widespread protest that it had to be repealed. When word of the repeal reached Falmouth, a local citizen confided to his diary that "our people are mad with drink and joy; bells ringing, drums beating, colors flying . . . a bonfire, and a deluge of drunkenness." Despite the repeal, so many disagreements remained that war was inevitable. With it came yet another destruction of Falmouth.

On October 17, 1775, five British warships entered Falmouth Harbor. The following morning, following an evacuation of local residents, the warships unleashed a daylong bombardment of the town. Late in the day, British seamen went ashore to burn down the remaining buildings. The destruction of Falmouth was widely condemned. The French foreign minister denounced it, and George Washington called it "an outrage exceeding in barbarity and cruelty every hostile act practiced among civilized nations." Instead of intimidating the rebellious Americans, it steeled their resolve. ▶

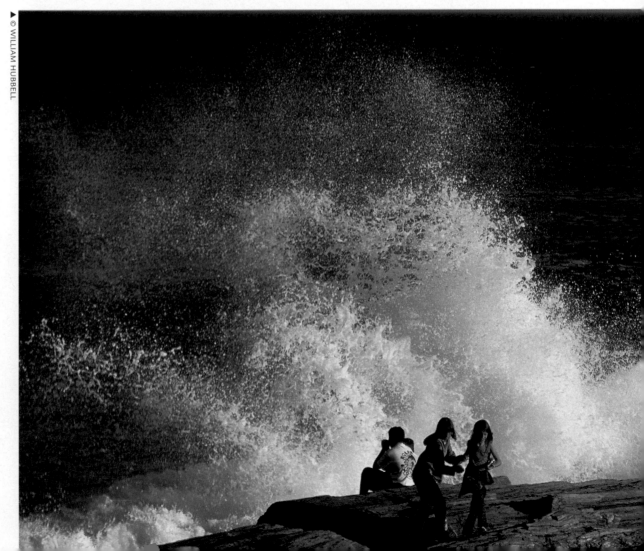

But once again Falmouth, especially the section known as The Neck, lay in ashes. Of the town's 500 buildings, 414 had been destroyed. This time, however, the rebuilding began immediately and was accompanied by a renaming. As the economy grew, so did the divergence of interests between The Neck and the rest of Falmouth. So on July 4, 1786, Independence Day, the city of Portland was born, with its commercial center located on the peninsula, where it has remained to this day.

There is no consensus among historians as to why the name Portland was chosen. The most likely explanation is that the entrance to the harbor reminded the citizens of the town by that name in England.

Portland grew rapidly, with its economy based on the sea. The port was captured in words by one of Portland's greatest native sons—and one of our nation's most esteemed poets—Henry Wadsworth Longfellow, who wrote in "My Lost Youth":

> I remember the black wharves and the slips,
> And the sea-tides tossing free;
> And Spanish sailors with bearded lips,
> And the beauty and mystery of the ships,
> And the magic of the sea.

Longfellow's home on Congress Street, the main thoroughfare in Portland, is now a museum housing the Maine Historical Society. It is a prime attraction for history-minded visitors, as is the large bronze statue of Longfellow that graces the square named for him, also on Congress Street.

As the Civil War neared, Maine was a hotbed of antislavery sentiment. On a per capita basis, Maine provided more men for the Union forces than any other state. Some 5,000 of them came from Portland, although

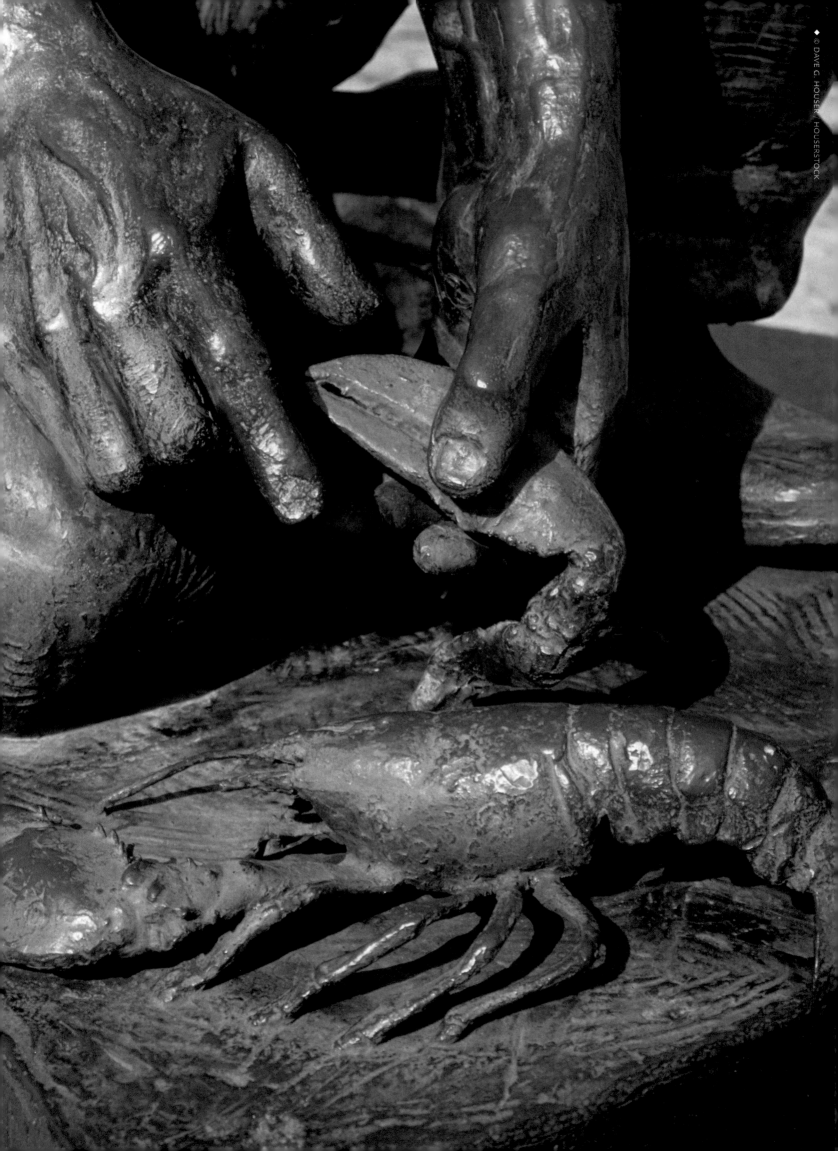

it was still a relatively small town. Victory in the Civil War was a cause for great celebration—too much so during Independence Day festivities on July 4, 1866, the year after the war ended. What is believed to have started as a small fire in a boatyard was whipped by strong winds into a raging inferno. City Hall, the post office, the customhouse, hotels, churches, businesses—everything in the fire's path was burned to the ground as the blaze swept across the peninsula. Nearly 2,000 buildings were destroyed, and thousands of people were left homeless.

Out of the devastation a new, more modern city arose. Atop a new bank was a huge carving of the phoenix, the legendary bird that rose from the ashes to live again. When the Indians and the British had destroyed Portland, the city had rebuilt itself. Portland residents were confident they could rebuild once again. Eventually, Portland rose to become the graceful city it is today.

Throughout the 19th and 20th centuries, Portland was ably represented in the political life of Maine and the nation. Many of the state's leaders lived or worked at some time in their lives in Portland, including Hannibal Hamlin, who served as Lincoln's vice president from 1861 to 1865, and James G. Blaine, who served as secretary of state and was the Republican nominee for president in 1884. Nathan Clifford was the attorney general of the United States and a justice of the Supreme Court. William Pitt Fessenden was a senator of uncommon integrity, and was praised by John F. Kennedy in his book *Profiles in Courage*. Thomas Brackett Reed served in the House of Representatives for nearly a quarter of a century, including several years as one of the most powerful Speakers in our nation's history. ▶

No two men better exemplified Portland's community spirit than James Phinney Baxter and his son, Percival. Through a rare combination of energy, vision, and business skill, James Baxter became wealthy at an early age. He then devoted his life to public service and philanthropy in Portland, creating parks and boulevards that to this day bear his name. Percival Baxter did the same thing on a broader scale. As a young legislator, and then as governor, he tried to persuade the state legislature to acquire for public use uninhabited land in northern Maine around Mount Katahdin, the highest peak in the state. The legislature refused, so Baxter did it by himself. Over the next 50 years, he personally purchased more than 200,000 acres of land, which he then gave to the people of Maine as Baxter State Park, a magnificent wilderness area that remains, at his request, forever wild. Baxter also donated land and money to enable the state to construct its first school for the deaf. When he died in 1969, at the age of 92, Percival Baxter left an inspiring legacy of public service and community spirit.

In recent years, Portland has experienced a significant renewal. In the downtown area, buildings long empty have been refurbished and are now occupied. L.L. Bean's decision in 1996 to open a store on Congress Street was heralded as a new beginning for the retail community. The Portland Public Market, which opened in 1998, treats those visiting the city to an indoor market full of produce, fish, and meats, as well as other items from local vendors.

Portland's rebirth isn't just about bricks and mortar. The city is a burgeoning technology center as well. Maine Medical Center has long offered cutting-edge medical care; it is a leading center for cardiac care, and its research institute conducts sophisticated medical research. Resort Sports Network, based in Portland, offers in-resort television

networks and information to travelers worldwide. A recent addition, Clareon, provides global, business-to-business payment networks. And companies such as GoFish.com now sell the day's catch on-line.

Even as fish is sold over the Internet, Portland's working waterfront remains, in some ways, the same as it was 100 years ago. Lobstermen still head out to check their traps before dawn each morning. One recent year, the fleet of working fishing boats registered in Portland brought in 23 million pounds of fish and lobster. Portlanders and tourists alike enjoy sitting on the decks at DiMillo's Floating Restaurant—a former car ferry that has been converted into a restaurant and quite literally floats at the dock while its guests dine—to watch the boats return to the harbor at day's end.

Large cruise ships come into Portland each year. In 2000, the fishing boats and cruise ships were joined by tall ships, as OpSail 2000 made its way to Portland Harbor. Nearly half a million people thronged the shoreline to watch these magnificent vessels come in under full sail. And, to further highlight our ocean proximity, the Gulf of Maine Aquarium is preparing to open its doors within the next few years. The aquarium—which will feature native species and sponsor educational programs, as well as housing a significant oceanographic research center— is truly an exciting addition to the city's offerings.

As much as Portland has to offer those who live or visit here—including Homer and Wyeth exhibits at the Portland Art Museum, concerts by the Portland Symphony Orchestra, and a multitude of shops and restaurants in the Old Port area—it is marked by a sense of community as much as by business and cultural opportunities. ▶

When I speak with young people, I stress the importance of giving back to their community. I urge them to spend time working on issues larger than their self-interest, to reach out to do what needs to be done in their schools and towns. In Portland, there is a tremendous sense of community that comes from that reaching out and giving back. Each year, United Way conducts its annual campaign. More than 800 major businesses and organizations, along with thousands of individuals, donated more than $8.4 million in 2000 to provide support to programs ranging from the East End Children's Workshop and Youth Alternatives to the AIDS Project and Pine Tree Legal Assistance.

The Boys and Girls Clubs in Portland have offered programs for area youth since 1930. An organization called Stone Soup provides culinary training to homeless individuals, and then puts them to work at two locations, cooking and serving a variety of soups and stews each day. The Area Agency on Aging helps to meet the needs of the elderly poor. The Portland Partnership acts as a clearinghouse for businesses and individuals who wish to volunteer in the Portland school system, providing mentoring, tutoring, and classroom help in schools through-out the city. These are but a few examples of programs that make a difference in the lives of Portland's citizens, and that mark the high level of commitment to community.

Portland has long been home to a diverse population of emigrants from all continents. A century ago, those emigrants were mostly Irish, Italian, and Russian. In recent years, families have come from other parts of the world: Somalia, Ethiopia, Cambodia, and Vietnam, to name a few. Children at the Reiche Elementary School speak a total of 30 different languages.

When I'm in Portland, I often think of my service there as a federal judge, before I entered the U.S. Senate. The most enjoyable of my

responsibilities was to preside at what are called naturalization ceremonies. They are citizenship ceremonies, of course. A group of people who had come from other parts of the world, and who had gone through the required procedures, gathered before me in the federal courthouse. There, I administered to them the oath of allegiance to the United States, and made them Americans.

It was always an emotional experience for me because my mother was an emigrant from Lebanon, and my father the orphaned son of Irish emigrants. My father had little education; my mother, none. He worked as a janitor; she on the night shift in a textile mill. But because of their efforts and, more important, because of the openness of American society, I, their son, was able to become the majority leader of the U.S. Senate.

After every naturalization ceremony, I spoke with the new citizens. Their devotion to—and enthusiasm for—the country of their choice was inspiring. I asked them why they had come, how they had arrived here, what they had hoped to find in this country. Their answers were as different as their countries of origin. But through them ran a common theme best expressed by a young man from Asia who, when I asked why he had come, answered slowly, in halting English: "I came because here in America everybody has a chance." That young man, who had been an American for only a few minutes, summed up the meaning of our country in one sentence. America is freedom and opportunity.

In the heart of Portland's financial and business district lies Monument Square, a lovely plaza dominated by a large memorial to men and women who served in our nation's armed forces during the Civil War. It is a powerful reminder of the history of Portland. ▶

When I speak with young people, I stress the importance of giving back to their community. I urge them to spend time working on issues larger than their self-interest, to reach out to do what needs to be done in their schools and towns. In Portland, there is a tremendous sense of community that comes from that reaching out and giving back. Each year, United Way conducts its annual campaign. More than 800 major businesses and organizations, along with thousands of individuals, donated more than $8.4 million in 2000 to provide support to programs ranging from the East End Children's Workshop and Youth Alternatives to the AIDS Project and Pine Tree Legal Assistance.

The Boys and Girls Clubs in Portland have offered programs for area youth since 1930. An organization called Stone Soup provides culinary training to homeless individuals, and then puts them to work at two locations, cooking and serving a variety of soups and stews each day. The Area Agency on Aging helps to meet the needs of the elderly poor. The Portland Partnership acts as a clearinghouse for businesses and individuals who wish to volunteer in the Portland school system, providing mentoring, tutoring, and classroom help in schools through-out the city. These are but a few examples of programs that make a difference in the lives of Portland's citizens, and that mark the high level of commitment to community.

Portland has long been home to a diverse population of emigrants from all continents. A century ago, those emigrants were mostly Irish, Italian, and Russian. In recent years, families have come from other parts of the world: Somalia, Ethiopia, Cambodia, and Vietnam, to name a few. Children at the Reiche Elementary School speak a total of 30 different languages.

When I'm in Portland, I often think of my service there as a federal judge, before I entered the U.S. Senate. The most enjoyable of my

When I left the Senate, I created a scholarship institute to help talented and needy students—160 of them each year. Many are first-generation college students, as I was. All are from families with modest resources. But they are fortunate, as I was, to have parents who believe deeply in the importance of education. The institute—located in a small, second-story office—looks out over Monument Square. The view from my office windows provides a nice counterpoint between the courage that built this country and the courage that, for me, represents its future.

For example, one of the Mitchell Scholars—Lien Le—symbolizes the kind of courage and desire that has come to characterize the new Portland. Le came to this country from Vietnam at the age of 12. She is as different from Portland's first settlers as the America of today is from that of the 17th century. But she has this in common with them: a desire for freedom and a fierce determination to succeed in a new land. Le is free and is well on her way to success.

When Le arrived, she spoke no English. Six years later, she was the valedictorian of her class at Portland High School. She graduated with honors from Bates College, is now finishing her first year at Dartmouth Medical School, and hopes to eventually work in pediatrics with immigrant and refugee children.

I hope Le will practice medicine in Portland. The city already has a thriving arts community, including an excellent symphony orchestra and dance company; first-class institutions of higher learning in the University of Southern Maine and the University of Maine School of Law; world-class restaurants; a busy, beautiful harbor; the ocean a step to the east; and mountains and forests minutes to the west. Add to that—as a symbol of a new Portland—a pediatrician born in Vietnam and raised in Portland, caring for young immigrants following in her footsteps. Percival Baxter, looking down upon his native city, will be able to smile and say, "The spirit of Portland lives on." ■

COMMANDING ATTENTION FROM any angle, Portland's stately City Hall is reflective of the beauty that still flowers downtown.

POST OFFICE SQUARE

S ELECTED IN 2000 TO BE MAYOR of Maine's largest city, Cheryl A. Leeman (LEFT) previously served for 13 years on the Portland City Council. Angus S. King Jr. (OPPO- SITE), Maine's 71st governor, holds the distinction of being one of the few independent governors in the nation and was first elected in 1994.

Portland

THE COBBLED STREETS AND RED-brick sidewalks of Portland's offbeat Old Port district are easily traversed by pedestrians, as well as by four-wheeled, two-wheeled, and occasional single-wheeled vehicles. The area features art galleries, specialty shops, and a plethora of charm.

S INCE DROPPING ANCHOR IN THE city's Old Port in 1999, China Sea Marine Trading Co. and proprietors Steve Bunker (RIGHT) and Sharon Bondroff have found a ready market for their colorful maritime curiosities. The shop's cargo includes nautical instruments, naval apparel, and sea-themed art.

Still an operational light-house, the Portland Head Light at Cape Elizabeth (LEFT) also guides inquisitive visitors through part of the area's history with a museum in the former keepers' quarters. As president of D. L. Geary Brewing Co., the first brewery to open in New England, David Geary (OPPO-SITE) lights the way for the thirsty with his celebrated, British-style ales.

NATURE DOESN'T ALWAYS SMILE on Portland's Peaks Island (BACKGROUND). When the weather is less than friendly, the Spring Point Ledge Light steers watercraft clear of the treacherous Spring Point Ledge, as it has since it was first lit in 1897.

Wᴇʟᴄᴏᴍᴇ ᴀʙᴏᴀʀᴅ: Tʜᴇ ᴄʀᴇᴡ at DiMillo's Floating Restaurant on Portland Harbor serves up some of the area's prime seafood and Italian fare. A landmark establishment, the upscale eatery is family owned and operated.

Captain's Log

WELCOME ABOARD

DiMillo's
SINCE 1954

FLOATING RESTAURANT

STANDING RESOLUTE IN THE
face of the elements, the region's
lobstermen, ships' captains, and
U.S. Postal Service foot soldiers
understand perfectly what Walt
Whitman meant when he wrote:
"O Captain! my Captain! our fear-
ful trip is done! / The ship has
weathered every wrack, the prize
we sought is won."

Portland

MORE THAN 200 FIREFIGHTERS and paramedics make up the Portland Fire Department. This roster allows the department to respond to tens of thousands of calls each year, both on land and on water.

Spirit of the Eastern Seaboard

F ALLING SNOW MAY BE DIFFI-
cult news to shovel during the
winter months, but Bill Nemitz
(OPPOSITE) can cull a story from it
anyway. Nemitz's columns appear
regularly in the *Portland Press Herald*
and *Maine Sunday Telegram*.

CALLING ALL CARS: Neighbor-hood businesses and city agencies team up with the Portland Police Department to help keep the area's streets and sidewalks safe for residents and visitors.

G OING TO THE HEAD OF THE class takes on a whole new meaning at the Cliff Island School, a one-room schoolhouse on a tiny strip of land just off the Portland coast. Island native Stephanie Villacci (ABOVE) teaches kindergartners through sixth-graders; older students boat over to the mainland to continue their educations.

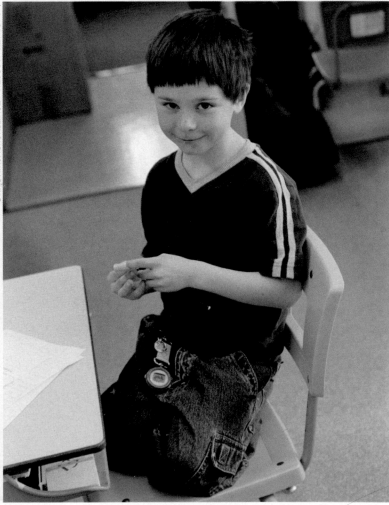

AMONG ITS MILLIONS OF MANU-
scripts, maps, and pieces of
printed matter, the Center for
Maine History in Portland houses
a complete set of signatures from
those who once put their pens to
the Declaration of Independence.
Center historians, including Herb
Adams (OPPOSITE), preserve the
past for visitors to the facility's
research library, Maine History
Gallery, and historic Wadsworth-
Longfellow House.

Portland

THE SOLDIERS AND SAILORS Monument, depicting and dedicated to those who fought in the Civil War, was erected on Portland's Congress Street in 1891, and the spot known as Market Square was redesignated Monument Square. Standing proudly atop the monument, the bronze *Our Lady of Victories*—designed by Maine native Franklin Simmons—represents the triumph of the Union Army.

PORTLAND
TO HER SONS WHO DIED
FOR THE UNION

Portland

HISTORY AS A BACKDROP
for the present: Reenactors
around the city acknowledge New
England's participation in the Civil
War. Tributes include a re-creation
of the 54th Massachusetts Regiment, the country's first all-black
infantry regiment (OPPOSITE).

Portland

THE TALL SHIP AND PORTLAND have a three-masted history that is in evidence all over town. OpSail Maine 2000 (ABOVE) docked in Portland for several days in July. Bringing with it a fleet of tours, exhibits, and races, the event left a wave of excitement in its wake.

Spirit of the Eastern Seaboard

OR DECADES, THE ANNUAL Old Port Festival has paraded through the district's streets for the single-day June event. The carnival-like atmosphere includes plenty of food and scheduled entertainment, with a colorful assortment of hands-on children's games and exhibits.

THE YARMOUTH CLAM FESTIVAL is well worth the scenic, 15-mile drive north from Portland. Held during the third weekend in July, the celebration's traditional clams and pie à la mode taste best in conjunction with live music and contests that include races and a firefighters' muster competition.

Portland

Sunbursts of brilliant color greet visitors to the Portland region, whether they're encountered in the middle of a field, at Deering Oaks Park (OPPOSITE), or during a quiet nature walk at Sebago Lake State Park (PAGES 64 AND 65), about a half hour's drive from the city.

DECEMBER MAY BE CALLED THE
dead of winter, but icicles can
spring to life on every available surface in the city. On sunny winter
days, the snow covering the open
spaces downtown often blooms blue
in imitation of the sky (PAGES 68
AND 69).

Spirit of the Eastern Seaboard

ADULTS IN THE AREA MAY NOT look forward to the work a heavy snowfall can cause, but children often have a different slant on the issue. Sledding with family or friends—or the chance of a weather-related school closing—gives Portland's youth something to shout about.

THE SKY'S THE LIMIT IN THE Portland region, where skiing has been refined to an art form. Whether skiing cross-country or downhill, on their own or at one of the resorts that dot the landscape, enthusiasts universally acknowledge the lift the sport offers.

I T IS A WELL-KEPT SECRET THAT Portlanders are watched over by angels in a variety of guises. Some adopt traditional stone poses as cemetery guardians; others wave magic wands from more sheltered perches.

Portland

U NDER THE AUSPICES OF THE Preble Street Resource Center in Portland, the Stone Soup culinary arts training program helps give financially underprivileged residents the ingredients for a new life. Working to bolster participants' professional and social abilities, Executive Director Mark Swann and trainer Teddi Reed (OPPOSITE, FROM LEFT) ensure that their students learn everything from food preparation and garnishing to kitchen sanitation. The program also offers job counseling and assistance with résumés and interviewing skills.

VOLUNTEERS AT WORK
JOIN US · FCS · 865-3985

Helping hands: The bronze figures of Thomas Kennedy's *The Ascent* (above) bear mute testimony to the Portland area's giving spirit. Some 25 miles north of the city, Freeport Community Services (opposite) operates a number of volunteer programs that assist residents of Freeport and nearby Pownal with donations of food, medical supplies, and other aid.

THE HEART OF THE COUNTRY: Gene Burchill (OPPOSITE), a past commander of the Maine division of AMVETS, still works to represent veterans' interests in areas including employment, health care, and benefits. The organization is open to all veterans and current servicemen and -women who have served honorably in the U.S. Armed Forces, Reserves, or National Guard.

FROM PREPAREDNESS PARADES during the Great War to memorials marking the individual tragedies produced by any war, Portland as a city has never shied away when called to its country's aid.

Portland

THE PORTLAND REGION'S ROLL-ing beaches provide ample evidence that it's easier to be footloose and fancy-free in a sundress and sand than in a sweeping skirt and sidewalk squall.

Fʀᴏᴍ ʙᴏᴀᴛ ᴅᴇᴄᴋs ᴛᴏ ᴅᴇᴄᴋ chairs, catching some rays is a breeze in the Portland area. The M/S *Scotia Prince* (ʟᴇꜰᴛ) cruise ship crosses the Bay of Fundy daily during the warmer months, making its 11-hour trip from Portland to Yarmouth, Nova Scotia. Those who prefer to remain on terra firma can pack up a towel and head to one of the region's myriad beaches, including Higgins Beach (ᴏᴘᴘᴏsɪᴛᴇ), just south of the city.

Portland

PORTLAND'S WORKING WATER-front is home to numerous business enterprises, including Merrill's Marine Terminal, an international cargo transportation center that unloaded its first shipment in 1982 and has long supported improvement and modernization of the waterfront.

Portland

WHETHER VIEWED FROM THE land, sea, or air, Portland and the surrounding area present a sight for travel-sore eyes. The sky's no limit at the Portland International Jetport, where eight passenger and two express-freight carriers take wing on a daily basis.

Tʜᴇʀᴇ'ꜱ ᴍᴏʀᴇ ᴛʜᴀɴ ᴏɴᴇ ᴡᴀʏ to get directions: When Portland's street signs are insufficient guides, seagulls may help provide some grounding for visitors. Apart from the friendly guidance of a feathered friend, however, a map is always a good backup plan.

Portland

THE OLD PORT AREA IS BUILT on a solid foundation of architecturally magnificent landmarks, including the United States Custom House (OPPOSITE) on Fore Street. The French Renaissance-style building was completed in 1871.

Bᴜɪʟᴛ ᴅᴜʀɪɴɢ Gᴇᴏʀɢᴇ Wᴀsʜ-ington's presidency, Portland Head Light is the oldest of Maine's extant lighthouses, and is also the oldest functioning—and most-often photographed—lighthouse in the country.

BRICK BY BRICK AND LEAF BY leaf, Portland's landscapes and artscapes contribute equally to the city's visual appeal.

Portland

THE HISTORY OF THE WORLD IS on display at Portland's many museums. At the not-for-profit Museum of African Tribal Art (LEFT)—the only New England facility of its kind—visitors can view a collection of tribal masks and other cultural artifacts spanning some 1,000 years. The holdings of the Portland Museum of Art (OPPOSITE) feature works by American and European artists, from Winslow Homer and Andrew Wyeth to Mary Cassatt and Edgar Degas.

Spirit of the Eastern Seaboard

Portland

THE PLAYGROUND FORMALLY known as the Children's Museum of Maine is filled with interactive, imaginative exhibits for kids of all ages. There is no maximum-age restriction at the museum, and grown-ups are encouraged to attend.

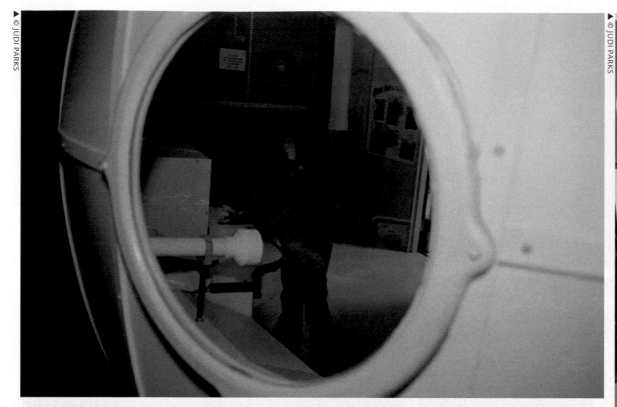

ORTLAND RESIDENTS AND VISI-
tors get around: Overlooking
the harbor, the Porthole Restaurant
(ABOVE) serves up everything from
lobster rolls to hamburgers. Guests
at the Children's Museum of Maine
(OPPOSITE TOP) and the Portland
Museum of Art (OPPOSITE BOTTOM)
get different views of the world.

Becky's Diner on Commercial Street is as unpretentious as its name. Specializing in plentiful portions of fresh food—rather than expensive ambience—the celebrated restaurant has been featured in *Gourmet* magazine.

B EAN COUNTERS: BURNHAM &
Morrill Company (B&M),
founded in 1867, has long been a
landmark at its Casco Bay location.
Over the years, B&M has received
numerous national and international awards for its traditional New
England baked beans and other
products.

Portland

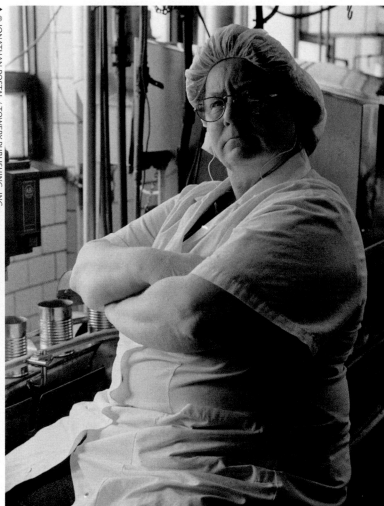

Spirit of the Eastern Seaboard

Bingo magic: That lucky streak is just around the corner at Four Seasons Bingo in Westbrook. Hundreds of card-carrying bingo lovers, including many couples and families, crowd the game hall each week in hopes of being the first to give the winning shout.

T HERE'S NOTHING LIKE A FLEA market to get bargain hunters out of the woodwork and into the truck. Goods—and shoppers—of every description fill local markets, where half the fun is in the looking.

Portland

On Portland's Commercial Street, artist Pat Plourde's armillary sphere stands as a well-rounded tribute to Maine (LEFT). DeLorme's Map Store (OPPOSITE) in Yarmouth holds the earth within its walls. Home to the largest rotating and revolving globe in the world, the shop proves that atlases and maps help make the world go round.

THE TAIL ENDS OF SOME EXPEDI-
tions are sweeter than others.
At the conclusion of a long day's
journey through the office, some
may gravitate toward establishments
like The Bitter End (RIGHT) or
Popeye's Ice House (OPPOSITE) to
help ship their troubles out on the
next available flight.

Portland

My true love gave to me

Spirit of the Eastern Seaboard

The nonprofit Center for Cultural Exchange (CCE) hosts hundreds of events each year that link artistic expression to the diverse nature of American culture at large (RIGHT). The CCE's Longfellow Square building also houses Café Culture, which serves up music as well as food. The stage is the chosen cup of tea for Portland actress Monique Raymond (OPPOSITE), whose credits include parts in local productions of *Electra* and *The Elephant Man*.

THE PORTLAND PUBLIC MARKET provides a feast for the senses. Vendors offer everything from just-caught fish to freshly picked flowers in the spacious building, and customers come from around the region to indulge their personal tastes.

COMMISSARY, A RESTAURANT LO-
cated at the Portland Public
Market, is the brainchild of owner
and Maine native Matthew Kenney
(OPPOSITE). Kenney, who also owns
several restaurants in New York
City, designed Commissary's menu
to feature ingredients available at
the market.

Portland

W HOLE LOTTA FISHIN' GOING
on: The Portland Fish Ex-
change hooks sellers and buyers
into its seafood auctions five days
each week. More than 20 million
pounds of fish pass through the
exchange's portals annually, and
purchasers may bid on lots ranging
in weight from one pound to more
than half a ton (PAGES 126-131).

© FRED J. FIELD

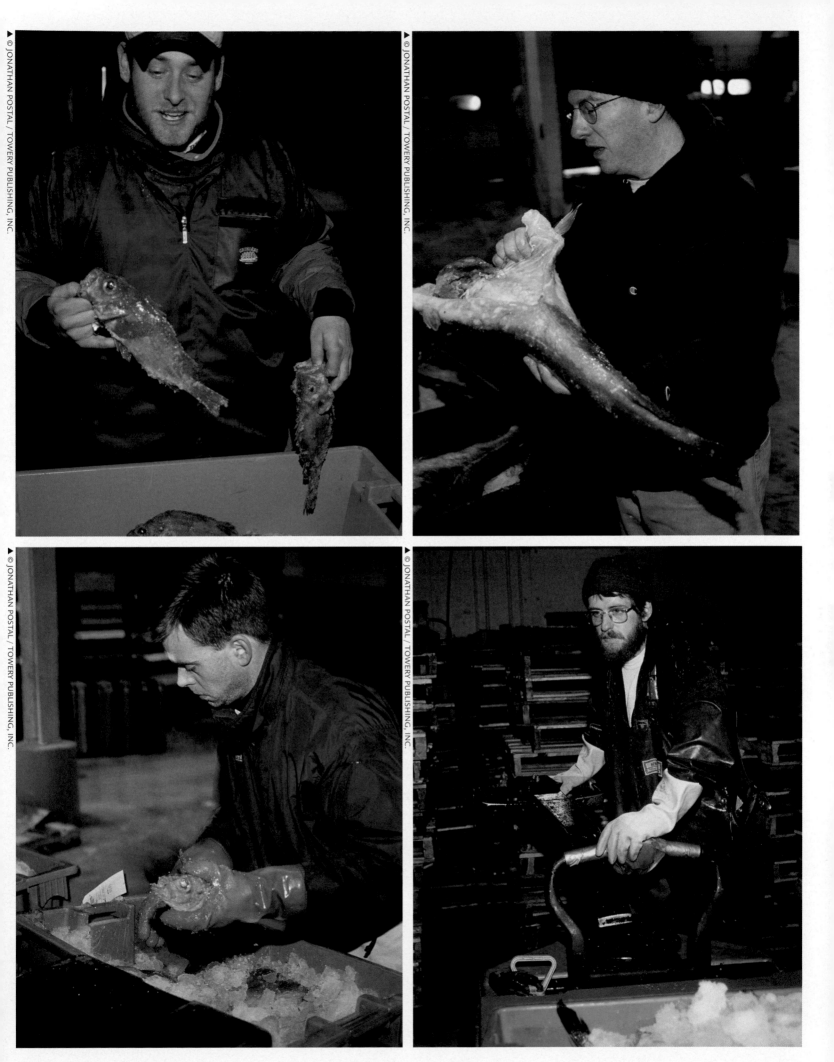

Spirit of the Eastern Seaboard

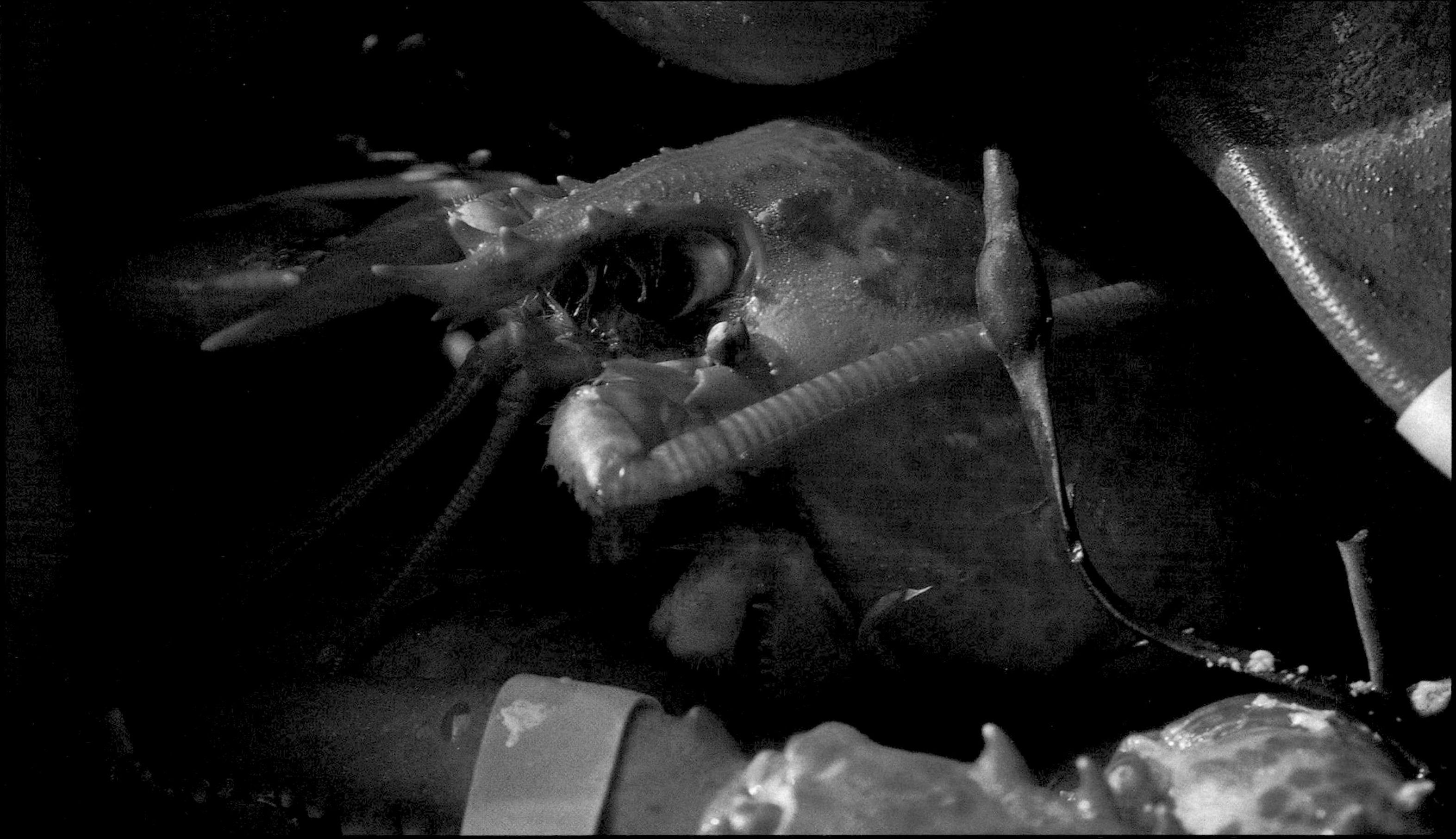

▲ © BRUCE E. BURNHAM

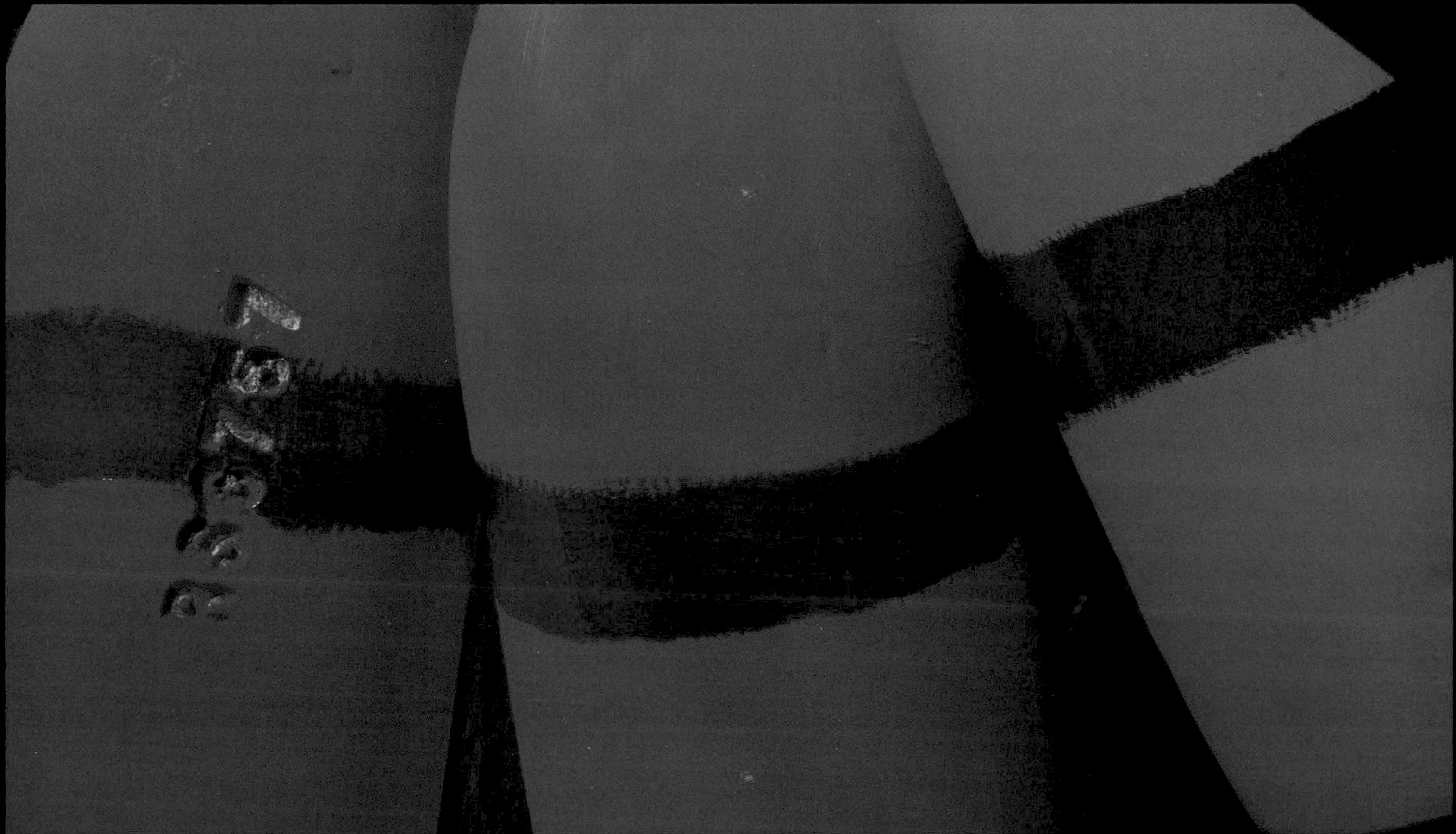

▲ © NANCE S. TRUEWORTHY

Spirit of the Eastern Seaboard

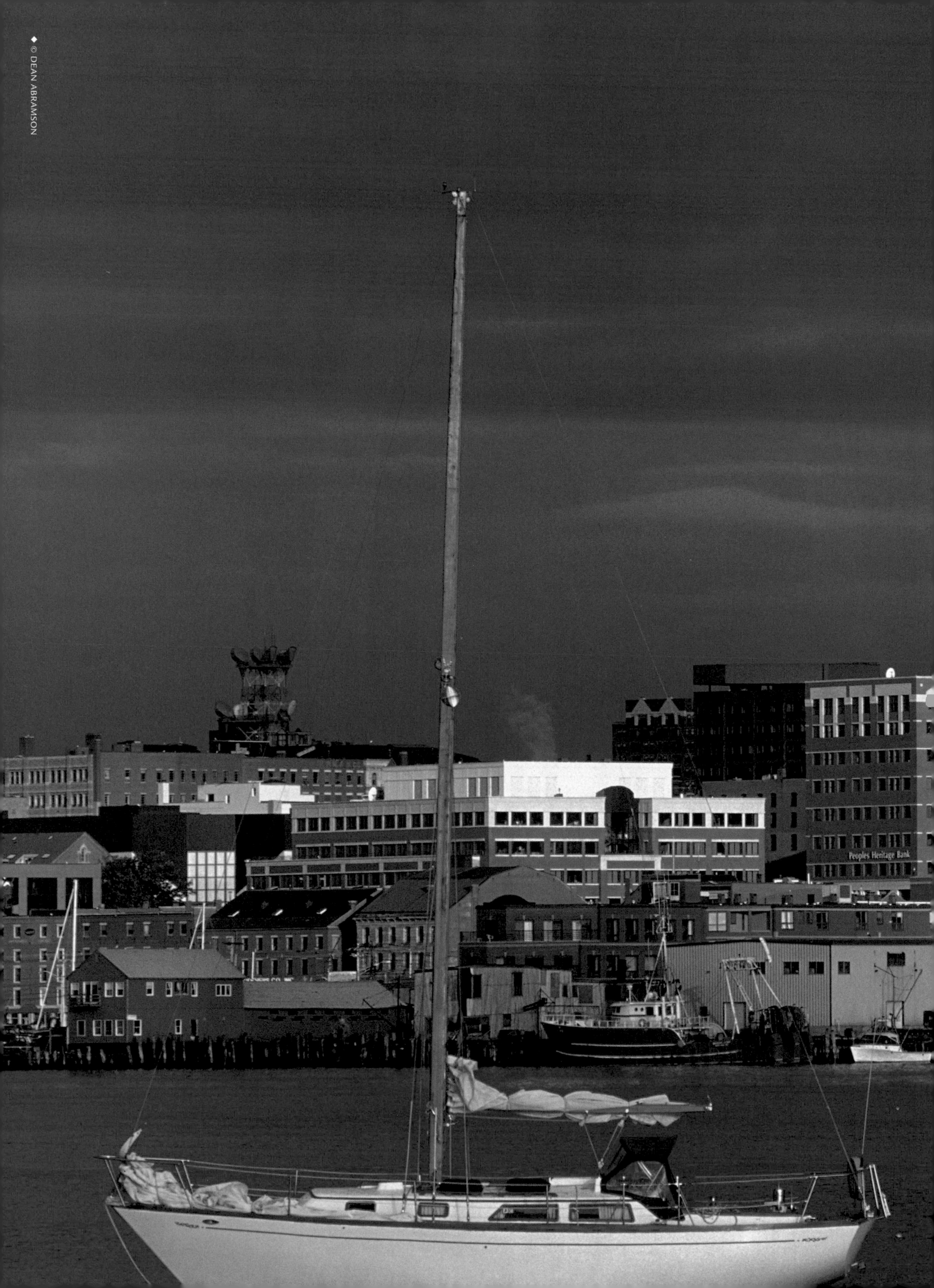

© DEAN ABRAMSON

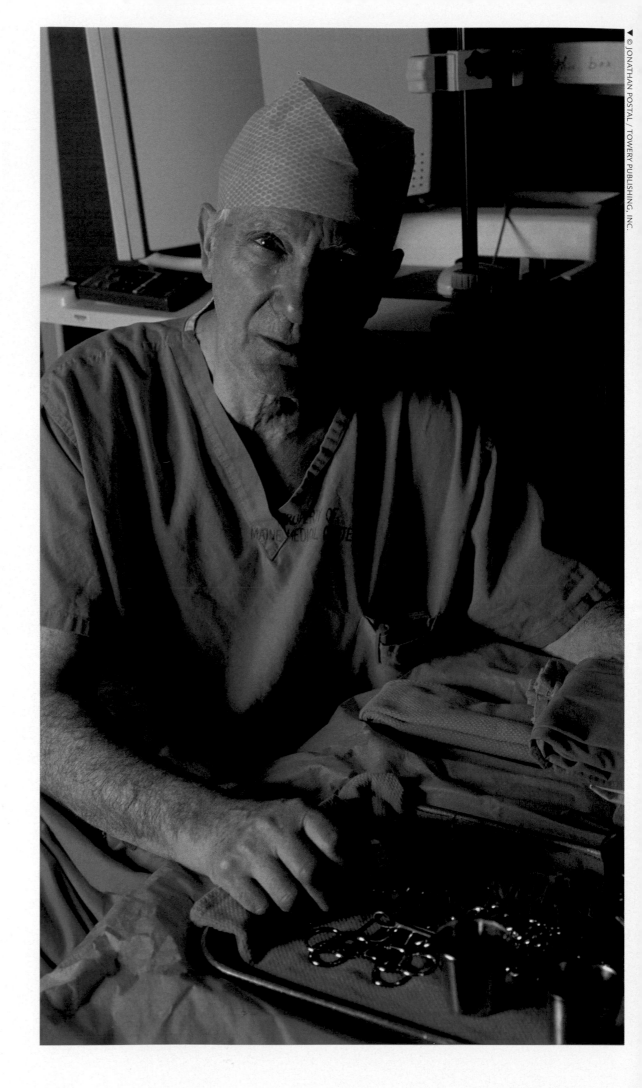

Portland

Tʜᴇʀᴇ'ꜱ ᴠᴇʀʏ ʟɪᴛᴛʟᴇ ᴛʜᴀᴛ can't be accomplished with a needle and thread. Dressmaker Amy Curtis (ʟᴇꜰᴛ) cobbles her creations together from whole cloth. As chief general surgeon at Maine Medical Center, Dr. Walter Goldfarb (ᴏᴘᴘᴏ-ꜱɪᴛᴇ) uses his skills to ensure that a stitch in time can save a life.

Portland

THE GLASS OF FASHION: Port-land's eclectic retail establish-ments offer everything from offbeat hats and hair-coloring tips to an excuse for temporarily escaping a snowy street.

Portland

IN 1994, BRUCE HANGEN (LEFT) and a small group of area opera lovers founded the Portland Opera Repertory Theatre (P.O.R.T). Now the organization's artistic and general director, Hangen conducts all P.O.R.T. performances at Merrill Auditorium. Artist George Lloyd (OPPOSITE) uses bold brushwork and bright colors to create his own visual symphonies.

Spirit of the Eastern Seaboard

I T'S NO ACT: MICHAEL CHITWOOD (LEFT), chief of police of the Portland Police Department, is serious about upholding and enforcing the law in his city. On a lighter note, Portland Opera Repertory Theatre singers Malcolm Smith and Margaret Yauger (OPPOSITE) stage crime for their audiences on a regular basis.

Portland

PORTLAND'S DOWNTOWN ARTS scene isn't limited to the visual. Clubs like the Skinny, owned by husband-and-wife team Johnny and Mellow Lomba (TOP), and the Old Port's Industry (BOTTOM) move to the beat of the city's nightlife. DJ Moshe (OPPOSITE) and his hip-hop crew kNOw Complex perform regularly at venues like the State Theatre.

AT THE CROSSROADS OF SKA AND funk live the Rustic Overtones (ABOVE), whose infinite musical elasticity draws a diverse audience. The Portland-based Munjoy Hill Society (OPPOSITE) quartet has built its reputation—and its first release, *Bon Voyage*—on its jazzy, Latin-lounge sound.

Education by the ocean: Portland is rich with opportunities for higher learning such as those at the Maine College of Art (LEFT AND OPPOSITE TOP), which offers undergraduate and graduate programs to its budding and established visual artists; the University of Southern Maine (OPPOSITE BOTTOM), comprising the largest of the University of Maine System's seven campuses; and Southern Maine Technical College, a publicly supported two-year college. Private, four-year institutions near Portland include Bowdoin College in Brunswick; Colby College in Waterville; and Bates College, located in the Lewiston-Auburn area.

KENNELED AT HADLOCK FIELD, the Portland Sea Dogs—the Eastern League, Double-A affiliate of the Florida Marlins—sink their teeth into every game they can get their paws on. Die-hard fans raised to a wild pitch by baseball fever and the team mascot, Slugger, guarantee that a good part of every season is sold-out.

Portland

UNDER THE DIRECTION OF manager Rick Renteria (TOP RIGHT), the Sea Dogs pack the stands at Hadlock Field with cheering crowds. Many of the team's biggest little admirers use their heads when it's time to get a favorite player's autograph.

Portland

Bᴇᴡᴀʀᴇ ᴛʜᴇ Aᴍᴇʀɪᴄᴀɴ Hᴏᴄᴋᴇʏ League Portland Pirates, who captured the coveted Calder Cup in their inaugural season, 1993-1994. The team, led by head coach Glen Hanlon (ᴏᴘᴘᴏsɪᴛᴇ ʟᴇꜰᴛ), embraces the possibility of more championships as both a short- and a long-term goal.

THE PORTLAND BOXING CLUB puts its best fist forward with contenders like regional light heavyweight Golden Gloves champion Lee Lamour (RIGHT) and New England heavyweight champion Anthony Reed (LEFT). Trainers Bobby Russo and Skip Neales (OPPOSITE, FROM LEFT) fight to keep their athletes prepared for every bout.

THERE'S NO FOILING NANCY Becker (TOP), a competitive fencer at the national level and owner of the Portland Fencing Center in Westbrook. Olympic swimmer Ian Crocker (BOTTOM) brought his gold medal home to Portland—and to what was immediately designated Ian Crocker Day—from the 2000 Olympic Games in Sydney, Australia. At Chuck's Pro Shop on Congress Street, owner and personal trainer Chuck Allen (OPPOSITE) helps customers find their inner strength.

SHIPBUILDING HAS BEEN AN integral part of the area's life since the end of the 18th century. Some 20 miles north of Portland, in the town from which it takes its name, the Bath Iron Works upholds this tradition, designing and constructing naval ships.

Descendants of William Frost—designer of the prototypical Jonesport lobster boat—the unsinkable Jamie and Joe Lowell (ABOVE, FROM LEFT) preside at the helm of Even Keel Marine Specialties, Inc. in Yarmouth.

Portland

ISLAND LIVING DOESN'T NECES-sarily mean isolation. Casco Bay Lines' mail boats make regular runs to and from Cliff Island and other small coastal islands, ferrying everything from people and postal services to boxes of bottles between outlying communities and the mainland (PAGES 162-165).

Portland

IT DOESN'T MATTER WHETHER the path is paved or pine; from the breathtaking vistas of Cadillac Mountain (LEFT) to the rocky promontory at the Marshall Point Lighthouse (OPPOSITE), it sometimes seems that all of coastal Maine's roads lead to the ocean.

Spirit of the Eastern Seaboard

Portland

THE MAINE NARROW GAUGE Railroad Co. & Museum is right on track when it comes to preserving antique railroad equipment. The nonprofit organization, run by volunteers like Peter Eastman (OPPOSITE BOTTOM), conducts daily tours—aboard original narrow gauge accoutrements—that run along Casco Bay (PAGES 170-173).

Spirit of the Eastern Seaboard

WHETHER GOING OUT FOR a performance of Vivaldi's *Four Seasons* at Merrill Auditorium or taking in the changing leaves on Falmouth's 100-acre Mackworth Island, Portland area residents and visitors can make a clean sweep of recreational activities year-round.

Aᴌᴛʜᴏᴜɢʜ ᴛʜᴇ Pᴏʀᴛʟᴀɴᴅ Sʏᴍ-phony Orchestra (PSO) has undergone several name changes since it was founded in 1924, its commitment to bringing musical masterworks to the Portland region remains undiminished. Noted PSO music director and conductor Toshiyuki Shimada (ᴏᴘᴘᴏsɪᴛᴇ)— who has recorded with and served as guest conductor for orchestras worldwide—guides the acclaimed organization through its perfor-mances at Merrill Auditorium (ᴀʙᴏᴠᴇ).

The Maine State Ballet (MSB) makes a point of working with the Maine State School for the Performing Arts in training its talented dancers. Artistic Director Linda MacArthur Miele (RIGHT), a former student of George Balanchine, has choreographed and added contemporary pieces to the company's traditional repertoire of one-act and full-length ballets.

Portland

Each year, perennial favorite *The Nutcracker* dances its way into the hearts of Portlanders, as the Maine State Ballet ushers in the winter season with spectacular performances at Merrill Auditorium.

MAINE BANK

Portland

PORTLAND COMES ABLAZE WITH lights during the winter holidays, when ornaments and decorations brighten everything from trees to festive window displays.

Poet Henry Wadsworth Longfellow, a native son of Portland, described the city as "the beautiful town seated by the sea" (PAGES 186 AND 187). A sculpture of the writer, now enthroned at Longfellow Square (OPPOSITE), adds holiday presents to the lasting gift of his work.

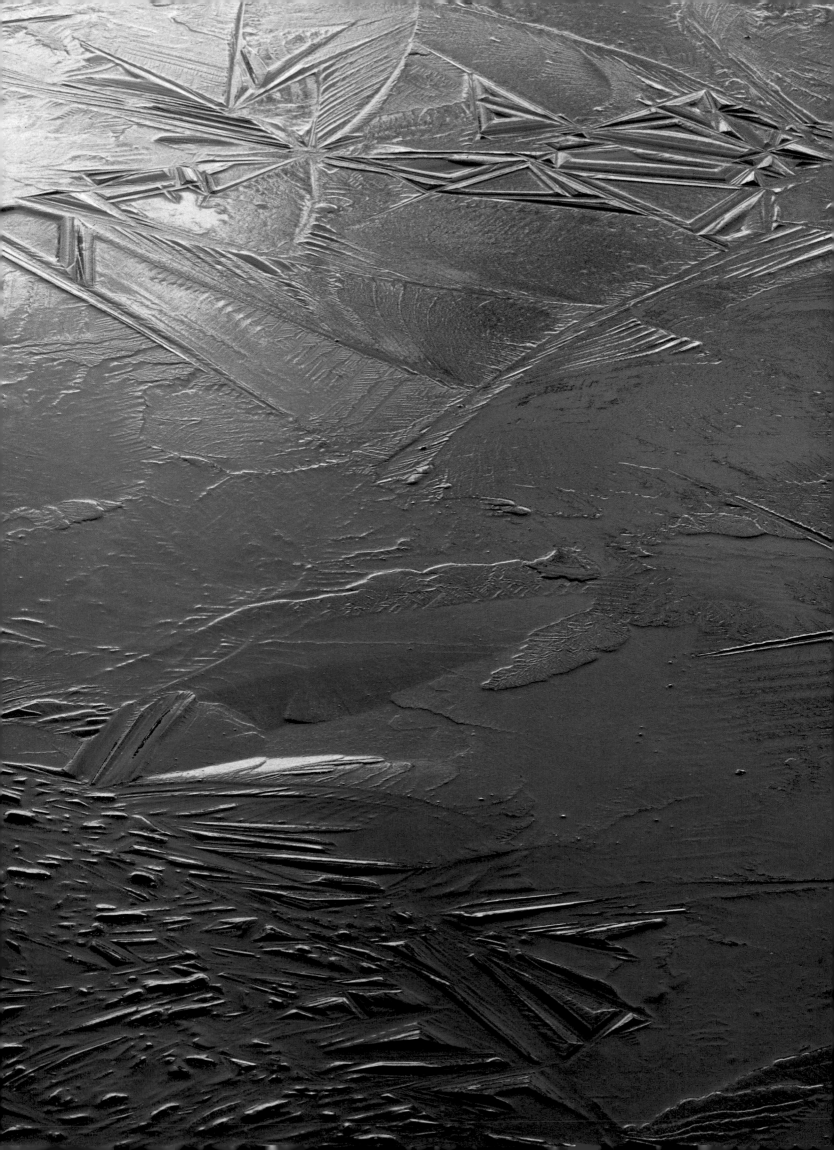

SOMETIMES SHAPED BY HUMAN-
ity, and in other instances
crafted by wind and water, ice
sculptures lend an incandescent
brilliance to their surroundings.

Portland

IN STANDISH, JUST A CATWALK away from Portland, Carol Pedley (ABOVE) owns Le Beau Minu, where she breeds Maine Coon cats both for shows and as pets. Veterinarian Dr. Debra Givin (OPPOSITE) makes the fur fly at The Cat Doctor, the first animal hospital in the state devoted entirely to the care and treatment of felines.

DOG DAZE: WESTERN CEMetery, once a favorite place for dog owners to walk their pets, was declared off-limits to dogs in 2001. These days, for unleashed affection, many make a run to Fetch, a Congress Street pet supply store dedicated to all things canine.

FONT OF JUSTICE: JUST A FEW blocks from Monument Square, the Cumberland County Superior Court renders its verdicts behind the tranquility of a fountain and lush, shady grounds.

P ALATIAL RESIDENCES AND houses of worship line Portland's roads, from the historic Stroudwater section of town (RIGHT) and the George C. West House on the Western Promenade (LEFT) to the well-tended Eastern Promenade (OPPOSITE), which features some two miles of bicycle and pedestrian paths.

AT THE INTERNATIONAL CHRIS-tian Fellowship in Portland, it's spirit that matters, not age or gender or race. The organization's doors and arms are always open, both to newcomers and to regulars.

Spirit of the Eastern Seaboard

Founded by Frannie Peabody (bottom) and situated in Portland's Western Promenade neighborhood, Peabody House is a residential care facility for people living in advanced stages of AIDS. The facility provides around-the-clock nursing care and works to help residents—and their families and friends—cope with the daily and long-term issues created by the disease.

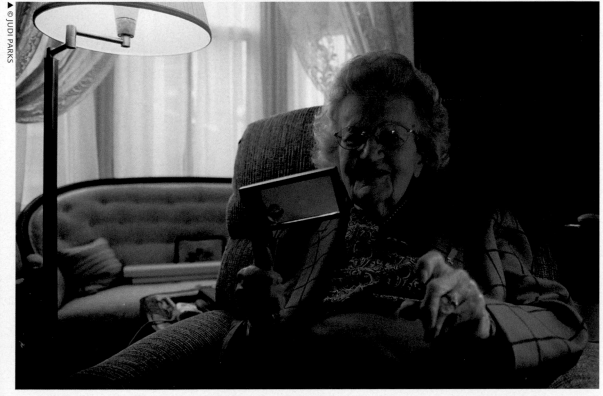

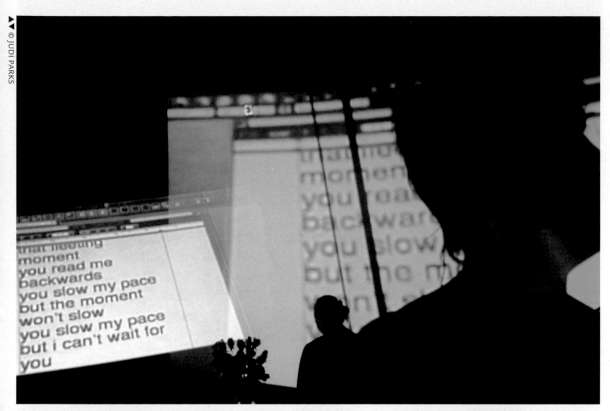

THE WRITTEN WORD EXERTS A powerful grip on some Portlanders. From poetry and beneficent wishes to simple, unadorned declarations, the city says it all with style.

A REAL MAINE TOURIST TRAP

Enjoy it here or take* it with ya!

* SMALL FEE REQUIRED

Exemplifying the spirit of the eastern seaboard, Portland offers a welcoming hand and an invitation to explore. From any angle, during any season, this seaside metropolis' zest for living makes it an intriguing place to work, to visit, and especially to call home (PAGES 204-209).

Profiles in Excellence

A look at the corporations, businesses, professional groups, and community service organizations that have made this book possible. Their stories—offering an informal chronicle of the local business community—are arranged according to the date they were established in Portland.

Albin, Randall & Bennett ■ Allied/Cook Construction Corp. ■ Auto Europe ■ Barber Foods ■ Berry, Dunn, McNeil & Parker ■ Black Point Inn ■ Blue Rock Industries ■ Bowdoin College ■ Brown Construction, Inc. ■ Casco Bay Weekly ■ Central Maine Power Company ■ Cheverus High School ■ DiMillo's Floating Restaurant ■ Drummond Woodsum & MacMahon ■ The Eastland Park ■ Fairchild Semiconductor International ■ Granger Northern, Inc. ■ Greater Portland Chambers of Commerce ■ Greater Portland Municipal Credit Union ■ Hannaford Bros. Co. ■ H.M. Payson & Co. ■ IDEXX Laboratories, Inc. ■ I-many, Inc. ■ Intelligent Controls, Inc. ■ Lebel & Harriman, LLP ■ L.L. Bean, Inc. ■ Maine Aviation Corporation ■ The Maine College of Art ■ Maine Employers' Mutual Insurance Company ■ Maine Historical Society ■ Maine Medical Center ■ Maine Turnpike Authority ■ MBNA ■ Merrill's Marine Terminal ■ Moon Moss ■ National Semiconductor ■ The Nelson Group, Ltd. ■ OEST Associates, Inc. ■ Orthopaedic Associates of Portland ■ Overhead Door Company of Portland ■ Pape Chevrolet ■ Perkins, Thompson, Hinckley & Keddy ■ Pierce Atwood ■ Port City Life Magazine, LLC ■ Portland International Jetport ■ Portland Pipe Line Corporation ■ Portland Press Herald/Maine Sunday Telegram ■ Portland Public Schools ■ Portland Regency Hotel ■ Portland Tugboat and Ship Docking Co., Inc. ■ Portland Water District ■ Portland's Downtown District ■ Preti Flaherty Beliveau Pachios & Haley, LLC ■ PricewaterhouseCoopers LLP ■ Princeton Properties ■ Scotia Prince Cruises Limited ■ Senator George J. Mitchell Scholarship Research Institute ■ Southern Maine Technical College (SMTC) ■ SYSCO Food Services of Northern New England, Inc. ■ Troiano Waste Services, Inc. ■ UBS PaineWebber Inc. ■ The University of Maine ■ University of Southern Maine ■ UnumProvident Corporation ■ Verrill & Dana, LLP ■ WBACH ■ WCSH 6 ■ WMTW Broadcast Group, LLC ■ Wright Express LLC ■

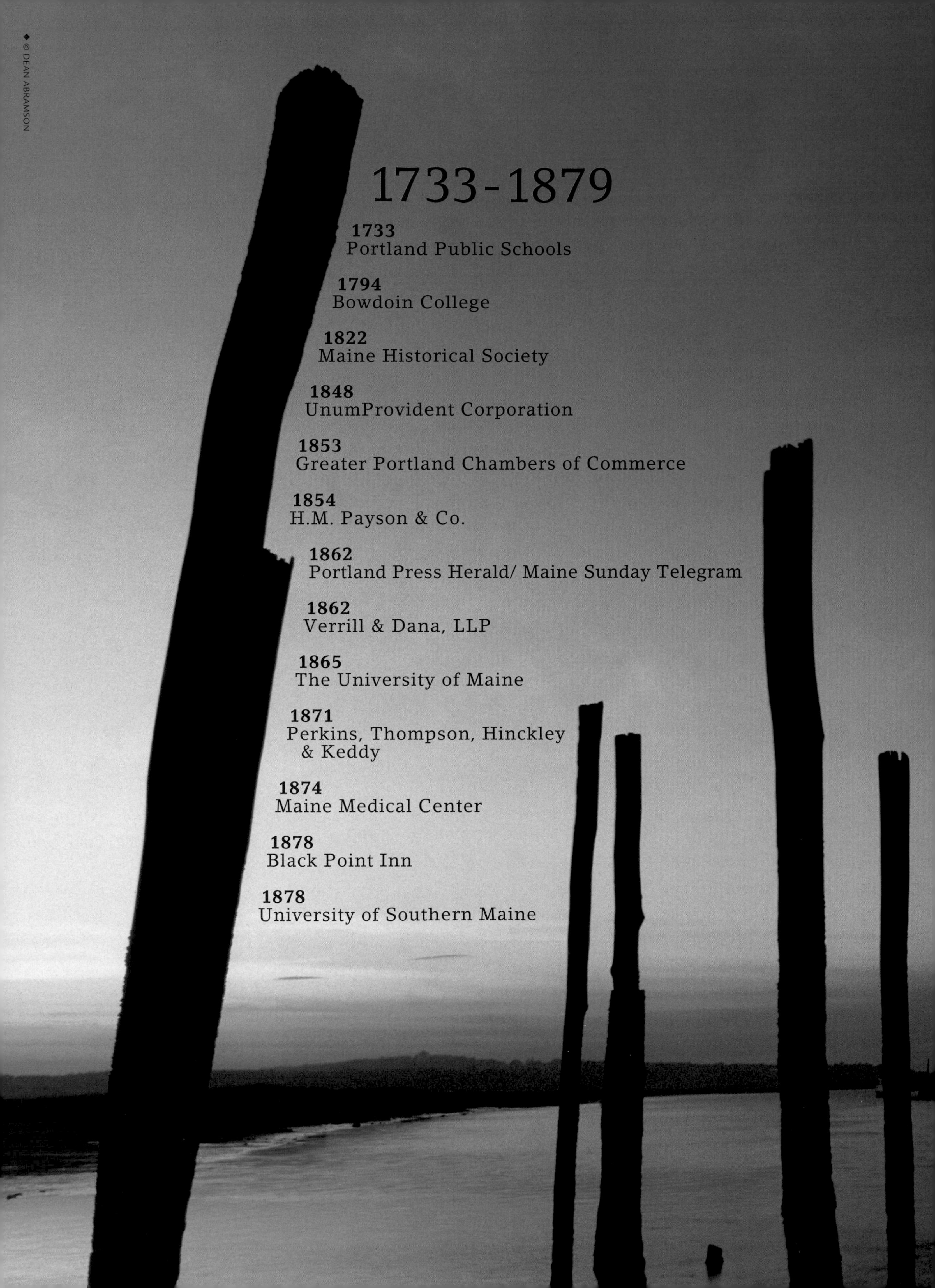

© DEAN ABRAMSON

1733-1879

1733
Portland Public Schools

1794
Bowdoin College

1822
Maine Historical Society

1848
UnumProvident Corporation

1853
Greater Portland Chambers of Commerce

1854
H.M. Payson & Co.

1862
Portland Press Herald/ Maine Sunday Telegram

1862
Verrill & Dana, LLP

1865
The University of Maine

1871
Perkins, Thompson, Hinckley & Keddy

1874
Maine Medical Center

1878
Black Point Inn

1878
University of Southern Maine

PORTLAND'S FUTURE IS SITTING IN THE CLASSROOMS OF ITS SCHOOLS TODAY. PORTLAND PUBLIC SCHOOLS—THE LARGEST SCHOOL SYSTEM IN MAINE—IS DEDICATED TO "ASSURING THAT ALL STUDENTS ARE LEARNING FOR THEIR FUTURE." THE ORGANIZATION TAKES SERIOUSLY THE REALITY THAT THE FORTUNES OF PORTLAND'S CHANGING COMMUNITY RIDE WITH ITS STUDENTS' FUTURES. ■ THE ORIGINAL PORTLAND SCHOOL DISTRICT WAS OFFICIALLY ESTABLISHED IN 1733, WHEN THE

city hired Robert Bailey as its first public school teacher. Portland High School opened in 1821. Today, Portland High School is the second-oldest continuously existing public high school in the nation.

Annually, Portland Public Schools educates some 7,700 students in 19 schools, with two of the schools on islands in Casco Bay. The system's 12 elementary schools have student populations ranging from seven to 624. The city has two high schools—Portland and Deering—and also sends students to the regional Portland Arts and Technology High School.

Results for Every Child

Mary Jo O'Connor, Portland Public Schools' superintendent, implements the district's mission statement in programs that find the means to get results for every child—no small feat in an era of rising pcr-pupil costs mixed with declining state revenue. The superintendent's upbeat perspective is

COURTESY OF PETER GRIBBIN

PORTLAND HIGH SCHOOL HAS BEEN RE-BUILT SEVERAL TIMES SINCE ITS FOUNDING IN 1821.

PORTLAND'S 12 ELEMENTARY SCHOOLS REFLECT THE CITY'S NEIGHBORHOODS, FROM THE DOWNTOWN PENINSULA TO QUIET, RESIDENTIAL AREAS TO THE ISLANDS OF CASCO BAY.

NANCE TRUEWORTHY

expressed in the overarching factors that define the district, including professional and personal development, as well as its cost-revenue ratio and growing multiculturalism.

Portland Public Schools' above-average performance in Maine Educational Achievement testing is one proof of the district's progress in pursuing its mission. Portland students in grades four, eight, and 11 usually average one to three points above the statewide level. The district's leaders appreciate that level of success, yet constantly seek improvement.

Portland Public Schools provides an array of educational opportunities that is unmatched in the state. The district's 12 neighborhood schools feature a variety of teaching styles and such options as looping—remaining with the same teacher or teachers for more than one year—and multiage classes. The district has made a major investment in foreign language instruction by beginning French and Spanish classes in the third grade.

Portland's secondary students can choose between the district's two high schools or, at Portland Arts and Technology High School, they can

enroll in programs ranging from horticulture to architectural drafting, dancing, and many other fields. Portland Public Schools' middle schools are organized into houses that create opportunities for individual participation, as well as for integration of varied content. Throughout the district, schools offer an instrumental music program, athletic teams, theater groups, and a rich diversity of other extracurricular activities.

Broad Range of Programs

Portland Public Schools is, perhaps, the primary local institution managing the impact of the city's role as a refugee resettlement community. This impact is as broad as the sounds of 53 different languages being spoken in the city's schools, and as intensely personal as serving the needs of a 12-year-old to whom English is a secondary language. The system's multilingual program has secured, on average, $1 million a year in competitive grants since the mid-1990s. Among the program's innovations is the creation of seven parent advisory councils for each of the major language groups in Portland.

Portland Public Schools' Portland Adult Education program offers academic classes, enrichment courses, and job-training programs developed in cooperation with local businesses. Thanks to the efforts of the Portland Partnership, Portland has the highest total volunteer hours and the greatest number of business partners of any school district in northern New England.

Portland Public Schools invests imaginative and persistent efforts in seeking to supplement the district's conventional revenues. Federal grants totaling more than $4 million helped fund Project Safe and Smart, an after-school and summer school program; Reading Excellence at Peninsula Schools; and Project Success, supporting the multilingual programs at Portland High School and Portland Arts and Technology High School.

The operating principles of Portland Public Schools place learning at

the center, and good teaching as the prime vehicle. The district's principles specifically avoid the all-too-frequent attempts in the education field to find the quick fix, the formula that will be a shortcut to excellence.

Consequently, the district pursues ongoing professional development at all levels—certainly for teachers, but also for all of its personnel. For example, Portland Public Schools works extensively with principals because of their role as links between classroom teachers and the resources represented by the central office. The district has established detailed performance

standards for all, including teachers, principals, and administrators.

In the broad context of schools defining the community, Portland Public Schools sees pupils as adding value to the future for their community, as well as for themselves, through their education. The district seeks to protect that investment by getting the maximum value from the economic resources available to it.

Portland Public Schools is focused on providing the best educational value for each area child, while understanding the district's obligation in the broader context. "The more people understand that Portland has something to offer, the more people will add to its value," says O'Connor. "The more people move into Portland because of the schools, the better it is for the community and the economy." ●

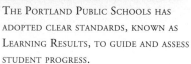

THE PORTLAND PUBLIC SCHOOLS HAS ADOPTED CLEAR STANDARDS, KNOWN AS LEARNING RESULTS, TO GUIDE AND ASSESS STUDENT PROGRESS.

STUDENTS IN THE PORTLAND PUBLIC SCHOOLS USE THE COMMUNITY AS THEIR CLASSROOM WHILE WORKING ON SERVICE PROJECTS SUCH AS WATER MONITORING AND TRAIL BUILDING (LEFT).

PORTLAND ADULT EDUCATION CLASSES TEACH ENGLISH AND OTHER ACADEMIC SUBJECTS TO THE CITY'S GROWING IMMIGRANT POPULATION (RIGHT).

BOWDOIN COLLEGE, A SMALL, COEDUCATIONAL, HIGHLY SELECTIVE LIBERAL ARTS INSTITUTION NESTLED WITHIN THE TOWN OF BRUNSWICK, 30 MINUTES FROM PORTLAND, HAS A LONG AND DISTINGUISHED HISTORY OF PRODUCING SOME OF THE BEST AND BRIGHTEST IN AMERICA. ITS GRADUATES INCLUDE LITERARY GIANTS NATHANIEL HAWTHORNE AND HENRY WADSWORTH LONGFELLOW, PRESIDENT FRANKLIN PIERCE, AND CIVIL WAR HERO JOSHUA L. CHAMBERLAIN, WHO

would later be president of Bowdoin and governor of Maine. In the modern era, graduates include former U.S. Secretary of Defense William Cohen, former U.S. Senate Majority Leader George Mitchell, and Olympic gold medalist Joan Benoit Samuelson.

Whether they go on to become famous or not, all Bowdoin graduates walk a tree-lined campus that has been described as one of the most beautiful in New England. More than 90 college buildings reflect a variety of architectural traditions, from Registered Historical Landmarks and classic McKim, Mead, and White structures to award-winning work by well-known contemporary architects.

MEMORIAL HALL CONTAINS BOWDOIN COLLEGE'S 600-SEAT PICKARD THEATER AND THE NEW, BLACK-BOX WISH THEATER (TOP).

THE WALKER ART BUILDING, WHICH HOUSES THE BOWDOIN COLLEGE MUSEUM OF ART, ANCHORS ONE SIDE OF A BEAUTIFUL AND HISTORIC QUADRANGLE (BOTTOM).

A Full Range of Liberal Studies

The prominence of many Bowdoin graduates is a direct result of the college's care in maintaining a strong teaching faculty committed to individual attention to the student. The student-faculty ratio at Bowdoin is 10-to-1, and class sizes for advanced-level courses generally range from four to 20 students; many larger courses include labs and discussions, allowing for more individualized instruction even at the introductory levels.

Bowdoin College offers 30 departmental majors, seven interdisciplinary majors, and a coordinate major. While there are courses in the full range of liberal studies, that is just the beginning of academic exploration at Bowdoin. Students are offered opportunities for nearly limitless exploration—in such interdisciplinary pursuits as Africana Studies and special academic programs as Arctic Studies, or through actual travel to Italy and other countries to dig for ancient artifacts. The college also offers 31 varsity sports, five club sports, a tremendously popular intramural sports program, and more than 20 physical education courses.

In addition to Bowdoin's extensive new and newly renovated laboratories for the natural sciences, the social sciences, and foreign language study, the college's electronic resources allow both students and faculty access—

from virtually anywhere on campus—to a world of information. All campus buildings have network access to the Web-based library gateway.

A new president, Barry Mills, was chosen in January 2001 to succeed Robert H. Edwards, who had been president for 11 years. Mills, a 1972 Bowdoin graduate, holds a doctorate in biology from Syracuse University and a law degree from Columbia University.

Civilizing the Frontier

Bowdoin was founded in 1794 to serve Maine families who did not want to send their sons all the way to Harvard, 150 miles away in Massachusetts. A broader description of the college's history appears in *A Small College in Maine: Two Hundred Years of Bowdoin*: "In the decade after the Revolution, the District of Maine rapidly increased in population as newcomers pushed the line of settlement beyond the coastline and into the densely wooded interior. In the eyes of 'the great and the good'—the propertied and the pious—such a frontier region needed civilizing institutions, notably a college. . . . In 1794, a college was chartered by the General Court in Boston and named for the statesman-scientist James Bowdoin II."

Today, about 93 percent of Bowdoin's some 1,600 students live on the campus. The college maintains a

carefully planned residential system, College Houses, which Bowdoin instituted as it phased out fraternities, beginning in 1996. The system is the base of volunteer activities, fund-raising for charitable causes, social events, and, for some students, residence in the houses. Bowdoin's students hail from nearly every state and more than two dozen foreign countries, and the college both seeks and encourages diversity. Bowdoin became fully coeducational in 1971.

A New Century

A major advancement in the current and future strength of the college was the unprecedented success of the New Century Campaign for Bowdoin that took place in the 1990s. From its inception, and in every facet, the campaign strengthened the academic fiber of the institution, and its success in raising funds greatly enhanced Bowdoin's campus and educational vitality.

Donations to the New Century Campaign enabled Bowdoin to devote resources to an improved program and facilities for the natural sciences. The campaign contributed significantly in other ways as well, providing support to an annual operating budget that grew from $55 million to $72 million, and raising the college's endowment from $185 million to $370 million. Today, the endowment is nearing $500 million.

Though it can stabilize the underpinnings of an institution, a substantial endowment is a poor measure of a college's impact on the lives of its students, alumni, and the surrounding community. The deeper meaning of a Bowdoin education is underlined in an anecdote told by Cohen, Class of 1962, as he—then serving as secretary of defense—accepted the 2000 Bowdoin Prize.

As a Bowdoin student and captain of the basketball team, Cohen had resisted a class assignment to write a sonnet. He acquiesced when confronted with the prospect of failing the course. "I tell you this story because it was one of the most important and transforming moments in my education," Cohen told the Bowdoin audience. "Professor Greason, by insisting that I comply with the rules, forced me to open up my mind. And from that point on I became a student of literature, of poetry. . . . That experience forced me to think about art and about this education in a different way." ●

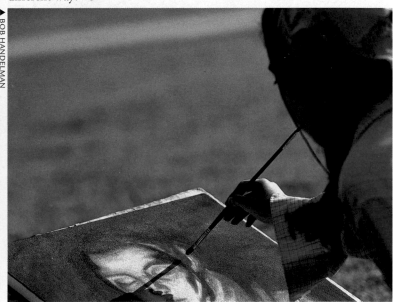

CLOCKWISE FROM TOP LEFT: BOWDOIN'S TREE-LINED CAMPUS IS A HOME AWAY FROM HOME FOR ITS STUDENTS.

MOST BOWDOIN CLASSES ARE SMALL, AND STUDENTS HAVE THE OPPORTUNITY TO WORK DIRECTLY WITH FULL PROFESSORS.

BOWDOIN'S STUDENTS TAKE ADVANTAGE OF THE MAINE OUTDOORS FOR ACADEMIC AS WELL AS RECREATIONAL PURSUITS.

MASSACHUSETTS HALL IS BOWDOIN'S FIRST BUILDING.

THE MAINE HISTORICAL SOCIETY ESTABLISHED A PERMANENT HOME IN PORTLAND IN 1901 WHEN ANNE LONGFELLOW PIERCE BEQUEATHED HER FAMILY'S BRICK RESIDENCE ON CONGRESS STREET AS A TRIBUTE TO HER FAMOUS BROTHER—THE POET HENRY WADSWORTH LONGFELLOW—WITH THE PROVISION THAT THE SOCIETY CONSTRUCT A LIBRARY ON THE GROUNDS IMMEDIATELY ADJACENT TO THE HOME. THE HOME, ALONG WITH ITS ADJACENT GARDEN, IS NOW THE ONLY

CLOCKWISE FROM LEFT:
THE WADSWORTH-LONGFELLOW HOUSE—HOME TO THE MAINE HISTORICAL SOCIETY—WAS BUILT IN 1786 BY GENERAL PELEG WADSWORTH, GRANDFATHER OF POET HENRY WADSWORTH LONGFELLOW.

HENRY WADSWORTH LONGFELLOW IS ONE OF AMERICA'S MOST FAMOUS 19TH-CENTURY POETS.

THE MAINE HISTORICAL SOCIETY RESEARCH LIBRARY, BUILT IN 1907, IS LOCATED IN THE LONGFELLOW GARDEN, AN OASIS OF QUIET IN DOWNTOWN PORTLAND.

surviving 18th-century residence in downtown Portland.

Built in 1907, the Maine Historical Society Research Library, now with more than 125,000 books and some 2 million manuscripts, serves as the primary research facility in the state for the study of Maine history by students, scholars, genealogists, businesses, and the media. The society's one-acre campus in the heart of Portland's downtown district also includes a museum gallery, a lecture hall, a museum store, and administrative offices.

The Story of Maine

Maine Historical Society's exhibition program brings Maine history to life and permits regular public access to the institution's exceptional collection of paintings, sculpture, decorative arts, costumes, and textiles, as well as its extraordinary rare books, manuscripts, architectural and engineering drawings, maps, photographs, and ephemera. The society's exhibitions have included *Take Me Out to the Ballgame*, which chronicled the history of baseball and explored the question, "Was baseball really invented here?"; *First Light*, which featured Maine daguerreotypes and early photography; and *Rum, Riot, and Reform*, which explored the history of drinking in Maine, the first state to institute Prohibition. A 2001 exhibition, *Henry Wadsworth Longfellow: The Man Who Invented America*, profiles the famous poet who defined America's national identity through such American legends as *The Courtship of Miles Standish*, *The Midnight Ride of Paul Revere*, and *Hiawatha*.

Dynamic and Expansive Programs

The Maine Historical Society's mission is to honor, preserve, and animate the rich history of Maine through exhibitions, lectures, research, field trips, events, and educational programs. Nearly 20,000 visitors, including more than 5,000 children from 60 area elementary schools, tour the society's facilities each year. Current exhibits and programs are featured on the organization's Web site at www.mainehistory.org. The society's new, Web-based virtual museum, the Maine Memory Network, provides on-line access to thousands of images and documents, and opens the door to historical treasures for every school, library, and Internet-ready home in the state. For thousands of visitors throughout Maine and from around the world, the rich associations of the Wadsworth-Longfellow House and the society's extensive collections offer visitors a gateway to the past and promote a reverence for history. ●

I N 1854, PORTLAND BUSINESSMAN HENRY MARTYN PAYSON FOUNDED AN INVESTMENT BANK SPECIALIZING IN THE FINANCING OF PUBLIC WATER COMPANIES. THE COMPANY THAT BORE HIS NAME BECAME WELL KNOWN AS AN UNDERWRITER OF AMERICA'S GROWING INFRASTRUCTURE. WITH TIME, THE FIRM'S SERVICES EVOLVED TO MEET THE MORE COMPREHENSIVE NEEDS OF ITS CLIENTS. SOME 150 YEARS LATER, H.M. PAYSON & CO. IS KNOWN THROUGHOUT NEW ENGLAND AS A TRUSTED STEWARD OF FINANCIAL ASSETS. THE COMPANY'S LONGEVITY IS A

testament to its investment philosophy, discipline, and commitment.

H.M. Payson & Co. provides investment advisory and trust services to a variety of individuals and institutions. To its clients, the firm brings a combination of qualities rarely found in the financial services marketplace: a complete team of experienced professionals; a rigorous, independent research effort; and highly personalized service.

Wealth Management

The term wealth management has become increasingly common, but the delivery of such services varies. At H.M. Payson & Co., wealth management means creating a framework for the management of financial assets that carefully considers multiple long-term objectives and constraints, while ensuring effective implementation of the client's planning strategies.

The framework begins with a close working relationship with tax and estate-planning advisors. In addition, the firm's professional staff is comprised of experienced individuals trained in a diverse set of disciplines. Through these relationships and in-house expertise, portfolio managers can effectively incorporate their clients' planning strategies into the investment management process.

Wealth planning strategies often involve the creation of trusts. H.M. Payson & Co. has managed trust accounts for more than 40 years, and as a state-chartered trust company can provide the same trust services offered by larger institutions, with a more personalized approach.

Taxes can have a significant impact on investment returns. H.M. Payson & Co. has a long tradition of managing taxable accounts in a tax-sensitive manner. Portfolio turnover and realized gains are generally quite low. In addition, overall tax liabilities can be further reduced by judiciously managing an investment

portfolio in concert with outside tax considerations.

Research

Successful long-term investing requires not only access to information, but the experience, skills, and discipline to interpret and employ it effectively. Although financial market data is ubiquitous today, an understanding of the impact of investor behavior on securities prices is essential.

H.M. Payson & Co. maintains a research facility dedicated to upholding an independent perspective. When the company's work finds it at odds with consensus thinking, H.M. Payson & Co.'s commitment to its investment process gives the firm the discipline to stay the course and act on its convictions.

Team Approach

At H.M. Payson & Co., clients work closely with a seasoned portfolio manager, who works in concert with in-house planning experts and research analysts to formulate investment policies and discuss portfolio strategies. As a result, clients benefit from a unique combination of personalized service and

investment expertise. Although the financial services industry looks vastly different than it did a century and a half ago, H.M. Payson & Co.'s steadfast commitment to the judicious stewardship of its clients' assets has remained unchanged. ●

H.M. PAYSON & CO.'S INVESTMENT PROFESSIONALS, SKILLED IN A VARIETY OF DISCIPLINES, WORK AS A TEAM IN IMPLEMENTING INVESTMENT STRATEGIES (TOP).

H.M. PAYSON & CO. ANALYSTS EMPLOY STATE-OF-THE-ART INFORMATION TECHNOLOGIES IN BRINGING AN INDEPENDENT PERSPECTIVE TO ACCOUNT MANAGEMENT (BOTTOM).

UNUM CORPORATION, A DISTINGUISHED MAINE COMPANY WITH A LONG HISTORY OF INNOVATION AND COMMUNITY SERVICE, JOINED WITH PROVIDENT COMPANIES, INC., A LIKE-MINDED TENNESSEE FIRM, IN JUNE 1999 TO FORM UNUMPROVIDENT CORPORATION, A WORLD LEADER IN INCOME PROTECTION, COMPLEMENTARY LIFE, SPECIAL RISK, AND LONG-TERM CARE INSURANCE COVERAGE. THROUGH ITS SUBSIDIARIES, UNUMPROVIDENT OFFERS A COMPREHENSIVE, INTEGRATED PORTFOLIO

of products and services that protect the rewards of customers' hard work: their paychecks, assets, and lifestyles.

By putting together these leading disability organizations, UnumProvident created a unique company with a powerful leadership position and the economies of scale necessary to support the creation of innovative products, services, and resources dedicated to returning people to work and productive lives. The company's core competencies are unmatched in its industry, and include extensive data and distribution resources; a focused, flexible infrastructure; a sustainable business plan; and tremendous human and intellectual capital.

UNION MUTUAL LIFE, A PREDECESSOR TO UNUMPROVIDENT CORPORATION, WAS PROVIDING INSURANCE AS EARLY AS 1848 (TOP).

TODAY, UNUMPROVIDENT IS HEADQUARTERED IN PORTLAND (BOTTOM) AND CHATTANOOGA, TENNESSEE.

19th-Century Roots

Union Mutual Life Insurance Company, the predecessor to Unum Corporation and one of the oldest insurance companies in the United States, was founded in 1848. In 1986, Unum was one of the first major U.S. mutual insurance companies to convert to public ownership.

The broad strategy used by Unum evolved into one with a clear focus on disability and special risk products. Through its subsidiaries, Unum became a world leader in group income protection, group life, and special risk insurance. Through its subsidiary Colonial Life & Accident Insurance Company, Unum became a leader in the voluntary benefits market.

Provident Life and Accident Insurance Company dates back to 1887. Originally founded as a life, health, and accident insurance company, Provident evolved into one of the largest individual disability insurers in the world, pioneering new ways to help disabled individuals return to work. In 1997, the company further enhanced its leadership position through the acquisition of the Paul Revere Life Insurance Company and its subsidiaries.

Community Support and Involvement

Today, UnumProvident has offices around the world, but devotion to its home community continues to be its hallmark. The character of the company's commitment has been demonstrated time and again by its employees and the corporation itself. Guided by a conscious philosophy of community involvement, the company's giving has been significantly above the median level for insurance companies. In recent years, UnumProvident's Portland-based employees donated, on average, 75,000 hours a year as volunteers and leaders in the communities of the Greater Portland area.

UnumProvident believes in investing in leadership, as illustrated by the instrumental role the company played in helping to launch the Maine Coalition for Excellence in Education, which since 1990 has focused on and fueled educational reform in Maine. UnumProvident has continued its support over the past 10 years, donating almost $250,000 to the coalition's operating expenses and programs.

UnumProvident has also given major support to the Maine Aspirations Foundation, University of Maine Leadership Consortium, University of Southern Maine (USM) College of Education, and Barbara Bush Children's Hospital at Maine Medical Center. The generous support of UnumProvident is recognized throughout the Portland community, especially in the many cultural organizations that make up the Downtown Arts Corridor.

The spirit of corporate giving is further evidenced through UnumProvident's 3,600-plus Portland-based employees, who are frequently involved in volunteer efforts that support the community. These employees are involved in everything from serving breakfast at the Preble Street Resource Center, donating blood, serving as mentors, delivering holiday baskets and gifts, and helping in local schools, to building homes with Habitat for Humanity and pitching in during the annual United Way Day of Caring.

A Business Strategy with a Personal Touch

Similarly, UnumProvident's guiding business strategy has a strong people orientation with three main elements. The company focuses on the human element in providing integrated product choices for income and lifestyle protection; benefits management that emphasizes returning people to work and an independent lifestyle; and innovative services that complement the company's products, while emphasizing the ease of doing business.

"We realize the value of providing financial support for customers during a time of work disruption due to accident or illness," says J. Harold Chandler, chairman, president, and CEO. "In addition to financial support, we provide return-to-work services that help restore our customers' confidence and ability to enjoy a more independent and productive lifestyle."

UnumProvident Corporation values its role in helping to make Portland the vibrant, caring, progressive community it is. Through both its corporate relations philosophy and its position as a world leader, UnumProvident works to provide services backed by industry-leading return-to-work resources and disability expertise. ●

UNUMPROVIDENT'S 3,600-PLUS PORTLAND-BASED EMPLOYEES ARE FREQUENTLY INVOLVED IN VOLUNTEER EFFORTS THAT SUPPORT THE COMMUNITY.

A REGIONAL UMBRELLA ORGANIZATION COMPOSED OF FIVE COMMUNITY CHAMBERS—FALMOUTH/CUMBERLAND, PORTLAND, SOUTH PORTLAND/CAPE ELIZABETH, SCARBOROUGH, AND WESTBROOK—THE GREATER PORTLAND CHAMBERS OF COMMERCE HAS SOME 1,300 MEMBER BUSINESSES AND NONPROFIT ORGANIZATIONS THAT INCLUDE MORE THAN 57,000 EMPLOYEES, ALL OF WHOM CAN PARTICIPATE IN CHAMBER EVENTS AND ENJOY ALL THE BENEFITS OF MEMBERSHIP. ■ THE CHAMBER HAS BEEN

shaping Greater Portland's business scene since 1853, but President W. Godfrey Wood prefers to emphasize recent accomplishments and a long list of new challenges. The chamber attracts and rewards members by building communities and the regional economy, calling on a full-time professional staff to concentrate on member support. The chamber organizes mutual efforts in expense control programs such as energy aggregation, exclusive discounts, and group health insurance, and sponsors major public affairs programs—often in collaboration with universities and other organizations. It operates through the local boards of the community chambers that focus on city and town governmental affairs and community betterment, and pursues regional

THE PORTLAND PUBLIC MARKET PROVIDES RESIDENTS AND VISITORS WITH FRESH LOCAL PRODUCE, ORGANIC MEATS, SPECIALTY BAKED GOODS, CHEESES, AND, OF COURSE, FRESH FISH (TOP).

THE COAST GUARD CUTTER *EAGLE* LED A PARADE OF TALL SHIPS FROM AROUND THE WORLD INTO PORTLAND HARBOR IN JULY 2000 (BOTTOM).

STUDIO 1 PHOTOGRAPHY

issues through local, regional, and state legislative channels.

"The Chambers of Commerce will play an essential role in keeping and attracting business in, and to, Greater Portland. In so doing, we will work to build stronger bonds with neighborhoods and to advance cultural, artistic, and recreational opportunities. We will be at the forefront of initiatives to make this a region where more people want to live, work, and raise their children, and where our children are educated and inspired for today's top careers—a region where they can find great jobs without leaving Maine," reads the chamber's vision statement.

Recent Accomplishments

In recent years, the chamber has had several noteworthy accomplishments. The chamber has actively advocated for widening the Maine Turnpike, reforming the State's Workers' Compensation System, and developing the cruise ship business in Portland Harbor. The rapid increase in cruise ship stops over the last several years brought the 1999 total to 45 ships and $38 million in estimated revenue. It has also supported infrastructure improvements, including passenger rail service from Boston; lobbied aggressively for development of the Bath Iron Works site as a world-

class passenger ship terminal; and supported, over many years, the development of the Gulf of Maine Aquarium on the waterfront.

Forging an alliance with the Maine State Chamber to merge activities in health insurance, energy aggregation, and other purchases, the chamber has also made state chamber membership affordable to small-business members, so they can reap the benefits of its advocacy activities. The chamber also stepped boldly to the plate when the United States Postal Service planned to move its regional distribution center to Lewiston-Auburn, educating the postal service and the public about the attendant losses to the Portland area. In addition, the chamber is tackling the issue of health care cost and availability, working with innovative people in the industry on an entirely new model for health care delivery in the state.

The Future

Where does the Greater Portland area go from here? The chamber has plenty of ideas. It will implement a strategy to create, attract, and grow a critical mass of technology-based businesses so technical workers have a broad base of employment here.

On the supply front, it will work to have the state government, university

system, and related institutions provide education and training to match tomorrow's job opportunities. It also will try to inspire middle school students and high school students to continue on to higher education, and make sure they have jobs in the state after college. Workforce development, says the chamber, will mean solving the labor shortage through education, training, technology, outreach, and support of the Workforce Investment Act.

Continuous communication with businesses and their employees will underline the importance of voting for public officials who are supportive of business. As a key part of that process, the chamber will provide its members with candidates' records on business-related issues.

The chamber will pursue its all-out effort to build a world-class convention facility in Portland, thus bringing in tremendous numbers of new visitors whose spending will increase tax revenue. In cooperation with a statewide committee, the chamber will work to develop an array of such facilities throughout the state where there is demonstrated demand.

The chamber's relationship with Portland International Jetport will continue, demonstrating to national low-cost airlines that the area can support such service to Florida and other major destinations, since 40 percent of travelers depart from loca-

tions outside Portland, in search of improved service and price. This is not only a major cost consideration for those companies already here, but is a business attraction issue. Reducing Maine's overall tax burden will also remain a priority, while ensuring tax policy is current, equitable, and favorable to business attraction.

As the Greater Portland Chambers of Commerce works for the future, it will continue to fulfill its essential purpose, actively focusing on local and regional opportunities—including public policy advocacy, business growth, community improvement, quality of life, and economic development—for the benefit of its members. ●

CLOCKWISE FROM TOP LEFT: TODAY, PORTLAND HEADLIGHT LIGHTS THE WAY INTO PORTLAND HARBOR AS IT HAS FOR CENTURIES.

THE UNIVERSITY OF SOUTHERN MAINE, SHOWN HERE IN AN AERIAL VIEW OF PORTLAND, INCLUDES A SCHOOL OF LAW AND AN ACCREDITED BUSINESS SCHOOL.

CUNARD'S *QUEEN ELIZABETH II* VISITS PORTLAND ANNUALLY.

THE PORTLAND MUSEUM OF ART EXHIBITS WORLD RENOWNED COLLECTIONS, INCLUDING WORKS BY HOMER AND WYETH, AND ATTRACTS VISITORS FROM AROUND THE GLOBE.

I N THE *Portland Press Herald/Maine Sunday Telegram*, READERS SEE THE REPORTER'S TELEPHONE AND E-MAIL ADDRESS AT THE END OF THE ARTICLE. THIS IS A NEWSPAPER THAT IS IN TOUCH WITH ITS READERS AND THEIR COMMUNITIES—AND HAS BEEN FOR MANY DECADES. TODAY, THE PAPER IS NATIONALLY KNOWN FOR ITS HIGH-QUALITY JOURNALISM AND ITS PIONEERING WORK TO INVOLVE THE PUBLIC IN THE COVERAGE AND DISCUSSION OF IMPORTANT ISSUES. ■ MONDAY THROUGH SATURDAY, THE *Portland Press Herald*

A MECHANICAL SCOREBOARD ON THE FEDERAL STREET SIDE OF THE *PORTLAND PRESS HERALD/MAINE SUNDAY TELEGRAM* BUILDING GIVES BASEBALL FANS THE PLAY-BY-PLAY ACTION AS THE NEW YORK YANKEES SWEEP THE PITTSBURGH PIRATES IN OCTOBER 1927 (TOP).

THE EDITORIAL AND BUSINESS OFFICES OF THE *PORTLAND PRESS HERALD/MAINE SUNDAY TELEGRAM* AT THE CORNER OF CONGRESS AND EXCHANGE STREETS ARE IN THE HEART OF THE CITY, ACROSS THE STREET FROM CITY HALL AT THE TOP OF THE BUSTLING OLD PORT AREA (BOTTOM).

serves the most heavily populated area of Maine with a primary circulation area that stretches along the coast from York County to Knox County. The Sunday edition, the *Maine Sunday Telegram*, is distributed statewide. The on-line version of the *Press Herald* is available, along with many other information-oriented sites, at MaineToday.com, the newspaper's nationally recognized affiliate.

Contributing Focus

Tracing its roots back to 1862, the *Portland Press Herald/Maine Sunday Telegram* is read by hundreds of thousands of Maine residents every week. Its news staff of more than 100 reporters, photographers, and editors operates from main offices on Congress Street in Portland; four regional bureaus located in Sanford, Biddeford, Brunswick, and Augusta; and a bureau in Washington, D.C.

In addition to its news staff, the newspaper's around-the-clock, seven-day-a-week operation includes nearly 500 other employees in advertising, circulation, production, finance, marketing, information technology, and human resources. The newspaper is printed every night of the year at a state-of-the-art printing and distribution facility in South Portland, using environmentally friendly, water-based inks. In addition, all of the company's newsprint waste is returned for recycling.

Along with the daily news, editorial, sports, and classified sections, the newspaper provides a different special focus each day, giving readers expanded coverage of topics such as business, food and health, arts and entertainment, the outdoors, real estate, and religion. Throughout the year, the newspaper publishes a variety of special sections, including popular seasonal guides that promote Maine as a vacation destination for visitors and year-round residents alike, as well as an annual holiday shopping guide.

Guy Gannett Era

The thriving Portland newspaper of today took form in 1921 when Guy Gannett, son of the publisher of the nationally circulated *Comfort* magazine, purchased the *Portland Daily Press* and the *Portland Herald*, and combined them into the single publication known today. Construction of the seven-story Press Herald building at Exchange, Federal, and Market streets began the next year, and in 1925, Gannett bought the *Evening Express*, which ceased publication in 1991, and the *Portland Sunday Telegram*, renamed the *Maine Sunday Telegram* in 1968.

In 1954, as he was adding radio and television to his newspaper holdings, Gannett died, thrusting leadership of the growing company into the hands of his daughter, Jean. Jean Gannett Hawley presided over major growth during the next 40 years. Major developments under her tenure include continued expansion into television, as well as construction of a multimillion-dollar, state-of-the-art printing and distribution facility in South Portland in 1988. Following Hawley's death in 1994, leadership of the company passed to Madeleine "Maddy" Corson, Gannett's granddaughter, and her uncle, John. In 1998, faced with growing uncertainty about the future of the company as a family-run enterprise, the owners put the company up for sale.

The Blethens Return to Maine

The sale of Gannett's newspapers attracted the interest of major media companies from around the country, but the successful suitor

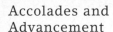

Accolades and Advancement

The *Portland Press Herald/Maine Sunday Telegram* has earned a reputation in Maine and elsewhere in the country for top-quality journalism, exceptional printing and design, and a commitment to the communities it serves. The newspaper supports a variety of cultural, performing arts, and social service and educational programs, including an extensive Newspaper in Education program, *Press Herald* in the Classroom, and its annual Bruce Roberts Toy Fund, which for more than 50 years has provided toys to thousands of deserving Maine children during the holidays.

The *Portland Press Herald/Maine Sunday Telegram* regularly wins Newspaper of the Year honors in the annual judging by the New England Newspaper Association, and has earned consistent recognition in various state, regional, and national competitions for investigative reporting, sports coverage, and community journalism. *Editor & Publisher*, a leading industry magazine, has cited the newspaper in its 10 That Do It Right list.

Maintaining a focus on quality journalism and community service, the newspaper has endured and prospered. As a result, the *Portland Press Herald/ Maine Sunday Telegram* continues to serve generations of loyal Maine readers and advertisers as a leading source of news and information. ●

was the Seattle Times Company, another fiercely independent, family-owned company with its own Maine roots. Alden Blethen, who was born in Waldo County, Maine, in 1854, and who once practiced law just down Exchange Street from the Press Herald/Telegram building, purchased the Seattle Times Company in 1896. Today, the company remains firmly in the hands of a fourth and a fifth generation of Blethens.

The Seattle Times Company established a new Maine company, Blethen Maine Newspapers, to publish and operate the *Portland Press Herald/ Maine Sunday Telegram* and its sister publications in Maine. The company also publishes the *Kennebec Journal* in Augusta and the *Morning Sentinel* in Waterville, both dailies, as well as the weekly *Coastal Journal* in Bath. In addition, the company owns MaineToday.com, a nationally recognized developer of on-line content and Web sites.

As part of Blethen Maine Newspapers, the *Portland Press Herald/ Maine Sunday Telegram* has remained close to its Maine roots while adopting its owner's four core values: to be the best newspapers and newspaper-owned Web site—in their size range—anywhere in the country; maximize the workplace satisfaction of the employees; be a leader in providing community service; and remain independent.

FOUNDED IN 1862, VERRILL & DANA, LLP HAS LONG BEEN ONE OF MAINE'S MOST PROMINENT AND RESPECTED LAW FIRMS. TODAY, THE FIRM'S PRACTICE RANKS AMONG THE LARGEST AND MOST SUCCESSFUL IN NORTHERN NEW ENGLAND. FROM OFFICES IN PORTLAND, AUGUSTA, AND KENNEBUNK, MAINE; KANSAS CITY; AND WASHINGTON, D.C., THE FIRM SERVES CLIENTS THROUGHOUT THE UNITED STATES AND INTERNATIONALLY, OFFERING SOPHISTICATED REPRESENTATION IN A WIDE VARIETY OF AREAS.

While Verrill & Dana celebrates its history and traditions of excellence and accomplishment, the firm takes even greater pride in its ability to help clients understand and meet the challenges of today's ever changing legal and economic environment. Over the years, Verrill & Dana has increased in size and strengthened its capabilities, while preserving and adapting the values that have served the firm and its clients so well. As a result, it is able to combine the resources and expertise of a large law firm with the individualized and responsive attention that clients expect and deserve. Today, Verrill & Dana's commitment to specialization enables it to handle the most complex legal issues as capably as firms that are much larger.

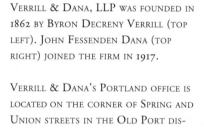

VERRILL & DANA, LLP WAS FOUNDED IN 1862 BY BYRON DECRENY VERRILL (TOP LEFT). JOHN FESSENDEN DANA (TOP RIGHT) JOINED THE FIRM IN 1917.

VERRILL & DANA'S PORTLAND OFFICE IS LOCATED ON THE CORNER OF SPRING AND UNION STREETS IN THE OLD PORT DISTRICT (BOTTOM).

Traditions of Excellence

On April 24, 1862, Byron Decreny Verrill was admitted to the Maine Bar. In the some 140 years since then, the name of Verrill has been one of the most important in the practice of law in Maine. In 1917, John Fessenden Dana joined the firm, beginning an association of the Dana family with the firm that has continued until recent years. The ideals for which these families stood are the foundations of the firm's excellence and reputation today. In recognition of the accomplishments of the Verrill and Dana families, the name of the firm was permanently changed to Verrill & Dana in 1977.

For generations, Verrill & Dana has been an important and influential part of Maine's legal, business, and political history. Many of Maine's most able and talented lawyers have practiced at the firm. Through their efforts, the firm has become counsel to some of the region's leading businesses, numerous local and state governmental entities, and countless individuals who have made important contributions to Maine and the New England region.

A number of the firm's lawyers have also gone on to distinguished careers in public service, ranging from elected and appointed positions in town and city government to important statewide and national positions. These have included numerous state legislators; two Speakers of the Maine House of Representatives (Robert Hale and Donald W. Philbrick); a Governor of Maine (John

R. McKernan Jr.); a U.S. Senator (Frederick Hale); three U.S. Congressmen (Frank M. Coffin, Robert Hale, and John R. McKernan Jr.); and a fourth member of Congress who became a legendary Speaker of the U.S. House of Representatives (Thomas Brackett Reed).

Verrill & Dana's lawyers have also made an indelible mark on the judiciary, where the names of Frank M. Coffin (U.S. Court of Appeals), Edward T. Gignoux (U.S. District Court), and Howard H. Dana Jr. (Maine Supreme Judicial Court) have become synonymous with the finest traditions of excellence, integrity, and public service that have been instilled in Verrill & Dana's lawyers from the firm's earliest days.

Commitment to Clients

Verrill & Dana applies exacting standards for quality and responsiveness, assuring that its clients receive effective legal representation that is thoughtful, timely, and cost-effective. The firm is committed to the principles of total quality, through which everyone at the firm works together not only to meet the immediate needs of clients and deliver legal services of the highest quality, but also to achieve the goal of continuous improvement in the quality of the firm's services.

MICHAEL L. SIDES

The firm is organized into a number of specialized practice groups, each of which includes lawyers with complementary skills and expertise. The groups evolve as the needs of the firm's clients require, but include a number of broad, traditional practice areas (business, real estate, litigation, estate planning and administration, regulatory matters, labor and employment, and legislative advocacy) and several highly specialized areas (environmental, employee benefits, insurance, intellectual property and technology, financial services regulation, non-profit and tax-exempt organizations, bankruptcy, sports, commercial lending, construction, utilities and energy, immigration, and land use).

By combining the breadth of experience and abilities available only in a large law firm with the depth of expertise available only in lawyers who are dedicated to a specialized area of the law, Verrill & Dana can respond to virtually every type of legal challenge that its clients may confront.

Commitment to Community

Commitment to public and community service has always been a cornerstone of Verrill & Dana's practice, and it is one of the guiding principles of the firm today. Both individually and collectively as a firm, Verrill & Dana's attorneys are engaged in active support of a wide variety of charitable, professional, and community causes, ranging from legal organizations and associations to the fine and performing arts, as well as to educational and other civic, social service, and professional organizations that make the communities of the region such desirable places to live and work.

Verrill & Dana, as a firm, is also deeply committed to being a leader in support for and participation in pro bono legal services. By providing close to $2 million worth of pro bono legal services since 1996 and through service by the firm's lawyers on governing boards of organizations such as Pine Tree Legal Assistance, the Maine Bar Foundation, Legal Services for the Elderly, the Maine Equal Justice Project, and the Muskie Fund for Legal Services, Verrill & Dana's lawyers have distinguished themselves in the quantity and quality of their pro bono work. The firm's lawyers have received several state and national awards in recognition of their commitment to promoting equality of access to the legal system.

Verrill & Dana, LLP—the law firm that arose from humble beginnings in the 19th century and grew to achieve great successes during the 20th century—stands poised today to assist its clients in meeting the challenges of the 21st century. ●

SETH BREWSTER AND JACKIE RIDER DISCUSS TRIAL STRATEGY OUTSIDE THE CUMBERLAND COUNTY COURTHOUSE (TOP LEFT). BOB PATTERSON REVIEWS DEVELOPMENT PLANS WITH CLIENT TOM DUNHAM (TOP RIGHT). JULIET BROWNE AND SEAN MAHONEY OF THE FIRM'S ENVIRONMENTAL LAW GROUP WORK ON A CASE (BOTTOM).

ESTABLISHED IN 1865 IN ORONO, THE UNIVERSITY OF MAINE (UMAINE) IS THE FLAGSHIP CAMPUS OF THE UNIVERSITY OF MAINE SYSTEM AND IS THE STATE'S LAND- AND SEA-GRANT INSTITUTION. LIKE THAT OF OTHER LAND-GRANT INSTITUTIONS ACROSS THE COUNTRY, THE UNIVERSITY'S MISSION IS EDUCATION, RESEARCH, AND SERVICE. ■ WITHIN THE UNIVERSITY SYSTEM, UMAINE HAS UNIQUE RESPONSIBILITIES. IN ADDITION TO PROVIDING HIGH-QUALITY UNDERGRADUATE PROGRAMS, THE UNIVERSITY MAINTAINS

graduate programs in a number of disciplines, carries out basic and applied research, and serves the public through its many outreach activities statewide. Of the some 3,800 accredited colleges and universities throughout the country, UMaine is one of only 148 schools to be classified by the Carnegie Foundation for the Advancement of Teaching as a Doctoral/Research University-Extensive, the highest classification available.

Distinctive Setting

UMaine is located north of Portland in the center of the state, between the Penobscot and Stillwater rivers and within close proximity to the ocean, lakes, and mountains. The campus offers an inspiring learning environment: more than 161 buildings on 660 acres overlooking the beautiful Stillwater River. Besides its many classroom buildings, dorms, athletic fields, and facilities, the university maintains miles of bike and cross-country ski trails, and recreation and athletic areas for use by students, faculty, staff, and the community.

At the heart of the university is its mall—an open, tree-lined quadrangle, beautifully landscaped and surrounded

by some of the most distinctive buildings on campus. Most prominent is the Raymond H. Fogler Library, the largest library in Maine, with collections and services that support the faculty, students, and staff of the university, as well as the residents of Maine.

Just off the university's mall, the UMaine Business School is housed in the Donald P. Corbett Business Building, which offers state-of-the-art teaching and learning facilities. Close by is the Class of 1944 Hall, which opened its doors to students in 1998 and was quickly recognized as one of the finest educational facilities for

performing arts in the Northeast. The hall is home to UMaine's School of Performing Arts.

UMaine maintains the look and feel of a traditional New England institution of learning while providing modern research facilities. Undergraduate and graduate educational offerings are built on a liberal arts and sciences foundation, as well as on profession-oriented education in a wide range of disciplines, many of which are found nowhere else in the state. The university's engineering, business, science, liberal arts, and natural resources programs have gained national and international respect.

CLOCKWISE FROM TOP: WINSLOW HALL IS HOME TO THE UNIVERSITY OF MAINE (UMAINE) GRADUATE SCHOOL AND THE COLLEGE OF NATURAL SCIENCES, FORESTRY, AND AGRICULTURE. IT IS ONE OF THE MOST HISTORIC BUILDINGS ON CAMPUS.

UMAINE HAS FIVE COLLEGES WITH STUDENTS FROM SOME 45 STATES AND MORE THAN 70 COUNTRIES. THE UNIVERSITY HAS THE LARGEST FULL-TIME STUDENT BODY IN MAINE.

FOGLER LIBRARY, THE CENTER OF STUDENT LIFE AND ACTIVITIES, IS IN THE HEART OF THE BEAUTIFUL UMAINE CAMPUS, AT THE APEX OF THE UNIVERSITY'S MALL. THE LIBRARY IS THE LARGEST IN THE STATE AND HOUSES MANY IMPORTANT COLLECTIONS.

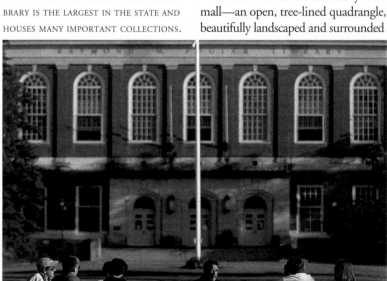

Noteworthy Faculty and Programs

UMaine's faculty members are internationally known for their research and academic credentials. More than 300 of the university's faculty members are engaged in externally funded research, and are creating new knowledge in areas as diverse as watershed and environmental research, speech and child development, climate studies, and sensor technology. Because of the faculty members' responsibility to teach, conduct research, and serve the public, they combine their knowledge with classroom activities. This often gives students hands-on experience in research activities. Students and faculty also provide business and community assistance, and perform public service.

As a public university, UMaine strives to offer programs and services of the highest quality, while remaining affordable and accessible. Even with one of the largest student bodies of any institution in the state, UMaine is still small enough to promote a sense of familiarity among members of the campus community. And with a low student-to-teacher ratio, the university has garnered a reputation for faculty members who are well known for their ability to inspire their students, helping to create active professionals and lifelong learners.

Cultural and Athletic Activities

Outstanding cultural and athletic programs and opportunities exist at UMaine for both active participants and spectators. The 1,600-seat Maine Center for the Arts attracts some of the world's top performers to the campus. UMaine's Museum of Art and Hudson Museum feature works

and artifacts of international renown.

The university's Alfond Sports Arena and surrounding athletic facilities house the state's only NCAA Division I athletics program, including the UMaine Black Bear hockey team—1993 and 1999 national champions—and the UMaine baseball and basketball teams. The 10,000-seat Alfond Stadium and Morse Field, both of which opened in September 1998, are home to UMaine's football and field hockey teams. In all, 20 varsity sports are represented at UMaine. These cultural and athletic programs enhance UMaine students' learning experiences, and

are immensely popular with the people of the area and the state.

In day-to-day activities, as well as in overall direction, UMaine exemplifies many of the values often identified with the state of Maine: a strong work ethic, community and state pride, self-reliance, and environmental sensitivity. The goals of the University of Maine include helping Maine and the nation solve their most pressing needs; generating and disseminating new knowledge; preparing students for life, work, citizenship, and change in the 21st century; and providing responsible stewardship of university resources. ●

CLOCKWISE FROM TOP LEFT:
AS THE STATE'S PUBLIC RESEARCH UNIVERSITY, UMAINE ASSISTS BUSINESSES, INDUSTRIES, ENTREPRENEURS, AND OTHER CITIZENS THROUGH BASIC AND APPLIED RESEARCH. HERE, STUDENTS TEST A CARBON FIBER BICYCLE FRAME FOR A MANUFACTURER IN MAINE.

STEVENS HALL, LOCATED ON UMAINE'S MALL, IS ONE OF THE MOST DISTINCTIVE BUILDINGS ON CAMPUS. THE HALL IS THE HOME OF THE COLLEGE OF LIBERAL ARTS AND SCIENCES. SOUTH STEVENS HALL HOUSES THE MAINE FOLKLIFE CENTER.

NAMED AFTER BENEFACTORS HAROLD ALFOND AND PHIL AND SUE MORSE, UMAINE'S NEW, PRIVATELY FUNDED STADIUM SERVES DIVISION I ATHLETICS, INTRAMURAL AND RECREATIONAL SPORTS, AND OTHER ACTIVITIES.

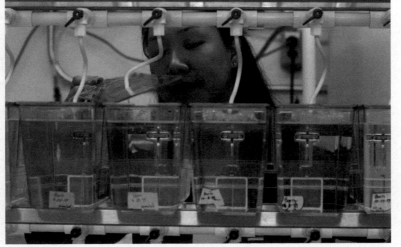

UMAINE BRINGS IN MILLIONS OF DOLLARS EACH YEAR TO THE STATE THROUGH GRANTS AND CONTRACTS MADE TO THE UNIVERSITY'S FACULTY. HERE, SCIENTIST CAROL KIM IS USING ZEBRA FISH TO STUDY DISEASE RESISTANCE. THE COMMON AQUARIUM FISH HAS BECOME A MODEL FOR BIOMEDICAL RESEARCH THAT MAY PROVIDE NEW WEAPONS IN THE FIGHT AGAINST INFECTION.

TRACING ITS ROOTS IN PORTLAND TO 1871, PERKINS, THOMPSON, HINCKLEY & KEDDY PROVIDES PROFESSIONAL LEGAL SERVICES IN FIELDS THAT INCLUDE BUSINESS TRANSACTIONS, TAXATION, BANKING, ESTATE PLANNING, REAL ESTATE, LITIGATION, AND EMPLOYMENT LAW. SINCE ITS FOUNDING MORE THAN 130 YEARS AGO, PERKINS THOMPSON HAS EMPHASIZED BUSINESS-ORIENTED COUNSELING, PROFESSIONALISM, AND INTEGRITY. THE FIRM REPRESENTS A WIDE ARRAY OF ESTABLISHED

businesses such as financial institutions, utilities, commercial real estate developers, forest products producers, health care providers, manufacturers, retailers, refiners, and distributors, in addition to nonprofit foundations, start-up companies, and individuals.

Experienced and large enough to handle even the most complex matters, Perkins Thompson prides itself on its ability to deliver individualized, personal service. The firm is one in which clients work closely with experienced counsel, and it is such personal attention that allows this midsize law firm of more than 25 attorneys to serve a select clientele.

Current in Outlook and Practice

Perkins Thompson dedicates itself to producing timely, top-quality legal services in a friendly and efficient manner. Its client service includes regular discussion of budgets for legal services and estimates of

probable charges for specific projects. The firm recognizes that constant communication with its clients is critical to success.

The firm's progressive outlook determines procedure as well as substance. Each of Perkins Thompson's lawyers fully integrates the latest in computer-based resources into his or her practice. The effective use of technology furthers the firm's demonstration that bigger is not necessarily better. The close attention to providing and using state-of-the-art technology produces client-sensitive efficiencies that level the playing field with the largest firms.

Recognizing that its clients face competitive and marketplace pressures to modernize, Perkins Thompson applies the same self-renewing processes to its own practice. From that comes the development of expertise in emerging fields, as well as ongoing adjustments in organization, staffing, and equipment with an eye to im-

proving efficiency and quality. The firm is equally committed to providing a friendly, professional working environment for its dedicated associates, assistants, and staff.

Perkins Thompson's strength is founded in its relationships: the collegial relationships among the firm's attorneys and staff; the professional relationships with its clients; and the many relationships with the community manifested through its attorneys' commitment to public service.

Established in History

While the firm is sensitive to modern tools and changing business dynamics, it is also comfortably established in history. For its first 100 years, Perkins Thompson maintained its offices at a building on Middle Street, near its current location. The firm has occupied the upper floors of One Canal Plaza, overlooking the heart of Portland's Old Port, since the building was constructed in 1973.

STRETCH TUEMMLER STUDIO

PERKINS, THOMPSON, HINCKLEY & KEDDY ATTORNEYS (FROM LEFT) BRUCE LEDDY, TIM BENOIT, AND MELISSA MURPHY CONFER ON TAX AND REAL ESTATE ISSUES FOR A MAJOR DEVELOPMENT.

PERKINS THOMPSON ATTORNEYS (FROM LEFT) JOHN UPTON, OWEN WELLS, AND ANDY CADOT REVIEW PLANS FOR PINELAND.

The firm's proudest public history is expressed in the achievements of its prominent partners and former partners, from the very beginning in 1871. Three of the firm's partners, including one of the founders, have served as justices of the Maine Supreme Judicial Court. D. Brock Hornby, current chief judge of the U.S. District Court for the District of Maine, is a former partner as well.

Franklin G. Hinckley served as chairman of Maine's first Board of Overseers of the Bar. Owen W. Wells, currently Of Counsel to the firm, is president of the Libra Foundation, a pioneer in economic philanthropy that has done much to revitalize downtown Portland and numerous Maine industries and institutions. Wells also has been a charter fellow of the Maine Bar Foundation, a trustee of the University of Maine System, board chairman of Maine Medical Center, and president of the Portland Museum of Art.

Various other members of the firm contribute to their communities through participation in local planning boards, school boards, and town councils. They have also served the wider community as court-appointed members of the Committee on the Future of Maine Courts; Maine School of Law adjunct professors; members of the Maine Board of Environmental Protection; trustees of Ronald McDonald House; and presidents of the Maine Bar Foundation, Maine Audubon Society, Cumberland County Bar Association, and Maine Trial Lawyers Association. The firm was a founding member of the Maine Bar Foundation's Coffin Fellowship Program, and lawyers in the firm have authored widely used treatises on Maine real estate law, probate practice, and civil remedies.

Service across the Board

Legal issues and client projects no longer stop at the state's borders. As Perkins Thompson's clients increasingly operate in multiple states and provinces, the firm now actively provides legal counsel and litigation services on matters of New Hampshire law and on legal issues in other New England states and eastern Canada. In addition to being licensed in Maine, Perkins Thompson's attorneys are licensed to practice in New Hampshire, Massachusetts, Connecticut, New Jersey, and New York.

On the firm's Web site, www.perkinsthompson.com, the firm lists many practice specialties, including mergers and acquisitions, bankruptcies and reorganizations, intellectual property, government relations, immigration, education, personal injury, product liability, antitrust, and environmental law.

Rooted in a tradition of excellence in the practice of law and growing with the changing legal profession, Perkins, Thompson, Hinckley & Keddy is certain to continue its leadership for generations to come. ●

FIRM MEMBERS (FROM LEFT) BILL SHEILS, JOHN RICH, AND PEGGY MCGEHEE CONDUCT LEGAL RESEARCH IN THE LIBRARY.

T

THEY COULD NOT HAVE KNOWN, THE 12 MEN WHO WROTE THE FIRST WORDS OF THE MAINE MEDICAL CENTER (MMC) STORY, HOW IT WOULD END. THEY COULD NOT HAVE KNOWN THAT THE GENERAL HOSPITAL THEY CONCEIVED IN 1868 WOULD BECOME A MEDICAL CENTER OF NATIONAL STATURE. THEY COULD NOT HAVE IMAGINED THAT A FUTURE PORTLAND WOULD BE HOME TO A MEDICAL AND SCIENTIFIC COMMUNITY OF A LEVEL FAR OUT OF PROPORTION TO THE CITY'S SIZE. ■ MMC'S STORY BEGAN IN A WORLD THAT HAD BEEN

irrevocably changed by the Civil War and the assassination of Abraham Lincoln, and in a city that had been largely destroyed by the Great Fire of 1866. Everything was on the mend, but there was no general hospital to serve the some 35,000 residents of Portland and 700,000 residents of Maine. So it was that the Maine General Hospital was created with private philanthropy and an act of the Maine legislature, and opened its doors in 1874.

Today's MMC is a unique resource for Portland and for Maine. It is the busiest community hospital in the state, and also offers services and specialties unavailable elsewhere in Maine and often in northern New England. The depth and breadth of care at MMC rivals that of major medical centers across the country, even those located in far larger cities in more populous states.

MAINE MEDICAL CENTER (MMC) HAS BECOME A HOSPITAL OF NATIONAL STATUS (TOP).

POSTGRADUATE PHYSICIAN TRAINING IS A KEY PART OF MMC'S MISSION (BOTTOM).

Comprehensive and Unique Services

Like any hospital, MMC offers routine medical and surgical care, childbirth, and outpatient services. Outpatient surgery, an option for many procedures, is offered at both the main campus and the Brighton SurgicalCenter. MMC's physician practices provide primary office care in the Outpatient Department at the main campus on Bramhall Street, the Family Practice Center on Munjoy Hill, the Falmouth Family Health Center in Falmouth, and Lake Region Primary Care in Windham.

MMC's Emergency Department is the most comprehensive in the region, and is the gateway to Maine's only Level I trauma service for the most serious injuries. MMC provides another option, Brighton FirstCare, for those with less serious injuries and urgent medical needs.

Specialty and subspecialty care sets MMC apart. The hospital has the facilities and staff to provide care for the most difficult pregnancies, as well as early or complicated deliveries. MMC's Maine Transplant Program is the only kidney transplantation program in Maine, and its results are among the best in the country.

MMC's cardiac surgery and angioplasty programs are among the largest in New England, and results, again, are among the best in the country.

Barbara Bush Children's Hospital

Maine's only children's hospital is The Barbara Bush Children's Hospital at Maine Medical Center. This hospital-within-a-hospital provides comprehensive inpatient and outpatient care for everything from well-child visits to the most serious cancer and heart disease cases, all with a special focus on the needs of children. The only pediatric cardiac surgeons in Maine practice at MMC, as do the only pediatric general surgeons.

MMC is a teaching hospital in the broadest sense. It provides a vast clinical experience for students of medicine, nursing, and allied health disciplines, and sponsors programs for students enrolled at affiliated academic institutions.

Postgraduate physician training programs are the hallmark of a tertiary care hospital. The presence of a teaching hospital is an important factor in bringing physicians to Maine, since most physicians remain in the area of their residency training. Also, teaching

hospitals attract the best physicians, who serve as faculty for the residents.

Research is another hallmark of a tertiary care hospital, and the Maine Medical Center Research Institute (MMCRI) is the largest hospital-based biomedical research facility in northern New England. Research brings leading-edge advances to Maine as early as possible, and has a direct impact on the care of patients.

The MMCRI receives major funding from the National Institutes of Health as a Center of Biomedical Research Excellence. Its work in blood vessel growth holds great potential for treating cardiac disease and cancer, two of MMCRI's focal areas. Other research areas include bone and mineral disease, psychosis, Lyme disease, and a vast number of pharmaceutical trials.

MMC is the flagship institution of MaineHealth, a family of health care providers serving southern, central, and western Maine. MMC is joined in MaineHealth by others who are committed to making their communities the healthiest in America through public education, health status improvement, and improved access to health care for all citizens.

As the largest employer in southern Maine and one of the largest in the state, MMC is a force for economic stability and development. The caregivers and support people MMC employs, along with the physicians who practice there, are a substantial portion of the region's taxpayers, consumers, sports fans, and patrons of the arts. Two out of every five people in southern Maine either work at MMC or know someone who does.

MMC has never defined its mission of community service as simply free care, although the hospital provides about 23 percent of all of the free care delivered in Maine. MMC's mission is evident in the variety of its support groups and special clinics, its model programs for people with disabilities, and its array of public education offerings.

Maine Medical Center was born of community need and has been sustained by community support. MMC's story, which began so many years ago, continues to grow far beyond anything its founders could have dreamed. ●

THE BARBARA BUSH CHILDREN'S HOSPITAL IS MAINE'S ONLY CHILDREN'S HOSPITAL (TOP).

THE QUALITY OF ITS HEALTH CARE TEAM MAKES MMC WHAT IT IS (BOTTOM LEFT AND RIGHT).

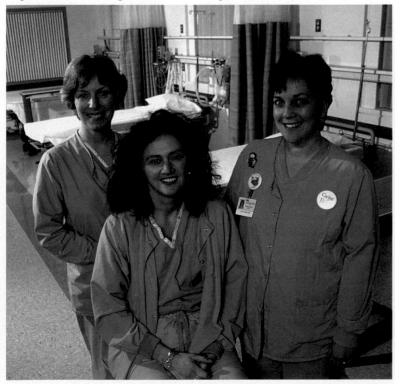

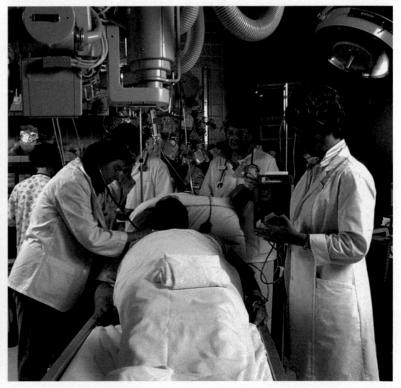

THE BLACK POINT INN, A MEMBER OF THE HISTORIC HOTELS OF AMERICA NATIONAL TRUST, PRESENTS BOTH THE GRACE OF ITS HISTORY AND THE HIGH-TECH AMENITIES ONE WOULD EXPECT FROM A 21ST-CENTURY ESTABLISHMENT OF ITS CLASS. AND, FOR THE FIRST TIME SINCE ITS FOUNDING IN 1878, THE INN REMAINED OPEN YEAR-ROUND IN 2000. ■ THE BLACK POINT INN IS BEAUTIFULLY SITUATED ON NINE ACRES ON A PRIVATE PENINSULA OVERLOOKING THE ATLANTIC OCEAN. IT IS A

GUESTS AT THE BLACK POINT INN CAN ENJOY IMPECCABLY DECORATED ROOMS, JUNIOR SUITES, OR TWO-ROOM SUITES WITH OCEAN OR GARDEN VIEWS.

THE MEALS OFFERED AT THE BLACK POINT INN PROVIDE THE SPECIAL TASTES OF MAINE, AND A VARIETY AND RICHNESS EQUALING THAT OF MANY OF THE FINEST RESTAURANTS IN THE COUNTRY.

half-hour from downtown Portland, 15 minutes from Portland International Jetport, and within easy reach of Boston. The inn serves as a popular destination for corporate and vacation clients from New York and Chicago.

The beauty and tranquility of the Prouts Neck area remain the same, and the guest service is carefully maintained at the caliber befitting such a place. However, the elegant old inn has been gently modified and modernized to take advantage of the conveniences and technology of the current era. The Black Point Inn has one of the first geothermal heating systems in Maine, for example, and the electronic infrastructure to permit guests to hook up their laptop computers in their rooms.

Offering meal plans and holiday weekend packages, the Black Point Inn welcomes guests who come to the area on business or leisure travel. The inn is a traditional New England resort that specializes in conferences as well. It has the staff and facilities to cater to corporate meetings, conferences, and retreats year-round, while providing the services of a quality resort very different from others typical of today. The meals provide the special tastes of Maine, and a variety and richness equaling that of many of the finest restaurants in the country.

A Pointed Name

Samuel de Champlain named the area Black Point because its pines presented a dark appearance from the sea. Even before Prouts Neck was colonized, Black Point was a summer retreat for Native Americans who would canoe downriver to the sea and spend the summer enjoying the ocean's bounty.

In the late 1800s, Prouts Neck experienced the boom that led to the construction of the Black Point Inn in 1878, as word spread about the desirability of summering at Black Point. Guests would arrive by train from Montreal and New York, disembarking at Scarborough Marsh for the ride by horse-drawn wagon down to the inn. The inn's guests would typically pass the entire summer swimming, sailing, and relaxing.

Traditions Preserved Throughout

Over the years, various owners of the Black Point Inn added cottages (originally built for the presidents of the Pennsylvania and Lackawanna railroads) and the first cocktail lounge after Prohibition ended in 1933, while maintaining the inn's history of a perfect balance of civility and a certain level of formality. In 1969, two gentlemen in short sleeves were asked to leave the cocktail lounge, since it was after 5:30 p.m. Little did it matter that they were the governors of Connecticut and Rhode Island.

In 1998, Eric Cianchette, a Maine native and Portland real estate developer, purchased the inn with a commitment to preserving its genteel history and traditions. Cianchette also owns the Portland Regency, a 95-room, luxury hotel in the Old Port District.

Cianchette's goal of making the Black Point Inn a year-round luxury destination has resulted in the institution of year-round service, as well as a winterization process that has included ongoing guest-room renovations and the addition of five guest rooms, to reach a total of 85.

Conference Facilities, Numerous Activities

The Black Point Inn's eight meeting and conference rooms—most with breathtaking views—can accommodate groups from a dozen people up to 200 in the main building and the five cottages on the grounds. Guests can enjoy impeccably decorated rooms, junior suites, or two-room suites with ocean or garden views.

As far as entertainment available to guests is concerned, there is much to do. At or near the Black Point Inn itself, there are two 1.5-mile sandy beaches, the beginning of the 1.75-mile Cliff Walk, and bird and nature sanctuaries. Bicycles and fishing gear are available, and guests can rent kayaks or play croquet. There are indoor and outdoor heated pools and Jacuzzis, two life-size chess and checker sets, and a fitness room.

Black Point Inn guests have access to the PGA-rated, 18-hole Prouts Neck Country Club golf course, as well as 14 clay tennis courts. Other golf courses in the area are Sable Oaks, Willowdale, and Nonesuch River. The Winslow Homer Studio is located at Prouts Neck and, in Portland, the inn's guests can explore the Narrow Gauge Railroad, Portland Museum of Art, Portland's Historic Old Port District, and historic mansions in every direction.

Among the other activities available to Black Point Inn guests are sailing on the *Palawan*, boat tours of Casco Bay that leave from Portland, deep-sea fishing, whale-watching trips, nearby horseback riding, and guided canoe trips with the Maine Audubon Society. The L.L. Bean shopping experience, including the countless designer outlets of Freeport, is available just down east along the coast. Two Lights State Park and Portland Head Light are minutes away. For the theatrically minded, there is Portland's Theater District, and in the other direction, Kennebunkport offers the Seashore Trolley Museum.

The Black Point Inn's ratings and reviews include AAA, four diamonds; Mobil, four stars; *Travel & Leisure* magazine, highly recommended; *New England Travel Guide*, best seaside resort; *Down East* magazine, Queen of Prouts Neck; *Golf Magazine* and *Country Inns Magazine*, recommended.

With numerous industry accolades and a growing lists of guests, the Black Point Inn has been able to stand the test of time. Promising fine accommodations in a prime location, the inn will continue to welcome travelers for years to come. ●

THE BLACK POINT INN IS BEAUTIFULLY SITUATED ON NINE ACRES ON A PRIVATE PENINSULA OVERLOOKING THE ATLANTIC OCEAN.

THE UNIVERSITY OF SOUTHERN MAINE (USM) PLAYS A SIGNIFICANT ROLE IN THE STATE—AND HAS AN EQUALLY IMPORTANT PLACE IN THE STATE'S EXPECTATIONS OF A BETTER FUTURE. GOVERNOR ANGUS KING HAS SAID, "THERE IS NO MORE IMPORTANT SINGLE PIECE TO THE ECONOMIC DEVELOPMENT FUTURE OF SOUTHERN MAINE THAN USM." ■ USM PRESIDENT RICHARD L. PATTENAUDE AGREES: "FROM ECONOMIC, CIVIC, CULTURAL, AND EDUCATIONAL PERSPECTIVES, OUR STATE IS POISED TO BE MORE PRODUCTIVE

than ever before. The University of Southern Maine is at the heart of this new vitality."

These statements connote the limitless future of Maine's largest institution of higher learning. Each year, some 1,200 university employees and 10,800 students participate in the continuing growth of USM, as do the nearly 80,000 people served by noncredit programs in business, the health care field, professional development, and personal enrichment. The university provides for its participants by holding classes on campuses in Gorham and Portland, as well as at its Lewiston-Auburn College.

Starting with Citizen Petition

USM's identification with the lives of citizens in the larger community has been true throughout its existence. In 1878, leading citizens of Gorham petitioned the state to create Western Maine Normal School to educate teachers who could offer the children of Maine the advantage of a formal education. Over the years, its mission broadened and, in 1945, the education facility became Gorham State Teachers College.

In the heart of the Great Depression, a coalition of Portland citizens met to discuss the creation of Port-

land Junior College. The college was affiliated with the Boston University School of Business Administration, and its focus was to educate and train local students—specifically, returning veterans—in business administration as a means for helping develop Portland businesses. In 1957, the school became the University of Maine at Portland-Gorham and, in 1978, the name was changed to University of Southern Maine.

Today, the University of Southern Maine is the most cosmopolitan and largest of Maine's institutions of higher learning. As an urban, comprehensive university, USM is a major educational force in the overall growth and improvement of the southern Maine area, a region often described as an integral part of the energetic and growing corridor stretching from Washington, D.C., through New York and Boston.

Growing and Expanding Programs

USM's direction for the first decade of the new millennium received important input from a 2000 report and subsequent recommendations by its Board of Visitors. Based largely on the results of numerous meetings with stakeholder groups, the report sought opinions from citizens and from representatives of businesses and institutions facing the knowledge-based global economy of the 21st century as to where and how USM could expand in the areas of technology and information. The primary message the Board of Visitors conveyed in their report was that USM must utilize the first 10 years of the century in an effort to become one of the top-ranked, public, regional, comprehensive universities in the United States in the quality, breadth, and accessibility of its academic programs.

To meet this goal, USM offers a variety of classes to meet any need. USM's eight academic units are the College of Arts and Sciences; the

THE GLICKMAN FAMILY LIBRARY PROVIDES AN EXCELLENT RESEARCH AND STUDY CENTER FOR THE STUDENTS OF THE UNIVERSITY OF SOUTHERN MAINE (USM).

School of Applied Science, Engineering, and Technology; the School of Business; the College of Education and Human Development; the College of Nursing and Health Professions; Lewiston-Auburn College; the Edmund S. Muskie School of Public Service; and the University of Maine School of Law.

In the late 1990s, the university initiated the development of Senior College, which provides intellectually stimulating opportunities and special activities for students 55 years of age or older. USM also has Weekend

College, Summer Session, Winter Session, a National Student Exchange Program, and a Lifeline Center for Fitness, Recreation, and Rehabilitation to address the broad range of interests of its students and the community. Courses are offered over the Internet, as well as at off-campus centers throughout the state.

USM's leadership in biotechnology research and information technology has emerged with state and legislative support. The university has added and expanded programs, upgraded its laboratories, strengthened computer

capacity, and attracted additional faculty in biotechnology and information technology. Key areas for distinguished contributions are molecular biology, immunology, microelectronics, and information technologies, all with important potential for evolving industries.

Giving Back to the Community

Besides its powerful contribution to the social and cultural vitality of the state and the professional careers of its citizens, USM has an enormous economic impact on the Cumberland County economy. The total economic impact generated through USM's purchase of goods and services is significant to the county alone, while income and sales taxes paid by students, faculty, and staff benefit the entire state.

The University of Southern Maine, born and built in response to requests from citizens and civic leaders, is now in an era of physical and academic renewal and enlargement. The future is bright for such a prized institution, and even brighter for the regional community that depends so heavily upon it. ●

USM PLAYS AN ESSENTIAL ROLE IN DEVELOPING MAINE'S FUTURE.

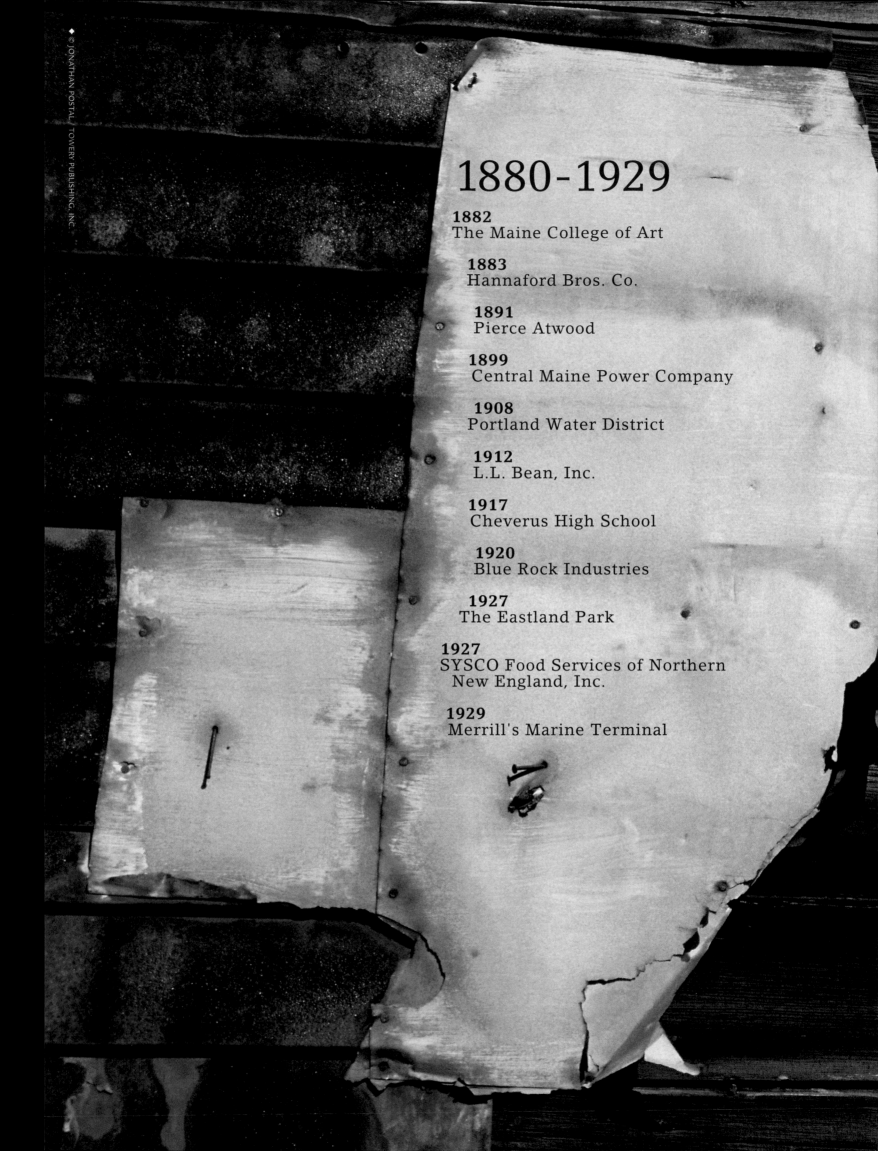

1880-1929

1882
The Maine College of Art

1883
Hannaford Bros. Co.

1891
Pierce Atwood

1899
Central Maine Power Company

1908
Portland Water District

1912
L.L. Bean, Inc.

1917
Cheverus High School

1920
Blue Rock Industries

1927
The Eastland Park

1927
SYSCO Food Services of Northern
New England, Inc.

1929
Merrill's Marine Terminal

THE MAINE COLLEGE OF ART (MECA) AWARDS BACHELOR'S AND MASTER'S FINE ART DEGREES, AND HAS MORE THAN 400 DEGREE STUDENTS. IT ALSO OFFERS A WIDE VARIETY OF EDUCATIONAL OUTREACH PROGRAMS TO MORE THAN 2,500 ADULTS AND CHILDREN EACH YEAR. ■ MECA'S FIVE BUILDINGS IN DOWNTOWN PORTLAND—INCLUDING THREE THAT ARE LISTED ON THE NATIONAL REGISTER OF HISTORIC PLACES—ARE WITHIN AN EASY WALK OF ONE ANOTHER. ITS PURCHASE AND ONGOING RENOVATION OF THE

landmark Porteous Building on Congress Street has been a key ingredient in the revival of Portland's city center. All of these things serve to introduce the oldest and largest arts educational institution in Maine.

MECA sees its mission as multifunctional: to provide for the highest quality, professionally oriented education in the visual arts and related studies in art history and liberal arts for degree and non-degree students; to support artistic excellence; to foster an environment that will stimulate the resources of creative expression; and to develop and enhance public understanding of the arts.

ADORNED FOR THE HOLIDAYS, MAINE COLLEGE OF ART'S (MECA) LANDMARK PORTEOUS BUILDING HAS RECEIVED NATIONAL ATTENTION AS A MODEL OF URBAN RENEWAL (RIGHT).

Visual Literacy Approach

At the heart of MECA's Bachelor of Fine Arts (BFA) degree program are the nine studio majors offered to the growing body of undergraduates. The designated majors are ceramics, graphic design, new media, metalsmithing and jewelry, painting, photography, printmaking, sculpture and self-designed studies. Required courses in liberal arts and art history constitute fully one-third of the curriculum.

MECA emphasizes visual intelligence and visual literacy. Its Foundation Program provides rigorous

training in the fundamentals of drawing, design, color, and form prior to the declaration of the studio major. Its curriculum is based on the traditional fine arts, while reaching out into modern forms such as new media. A 10-to-1 student to faculty ratio allows for the kind of individual attention that is the hallmark of a quality visual arts education. Students have 24-hour access to studios for their work.

New media was introduced as a studio major in 2001. MECA has developed new computer classrooms and a state-of-the-art New Media

Studio to support work in the exploding fields of digital art. MECA's Baxter Building, a unique example of Romanesque architecture, will be renovated into MECA's New Media Center to house the departments of photography, graphic design, and new media.

Landmark in Arts District

MECA's Porteous Building is a landmark former department store at the center of Portland's thriving Arts District that is being transformed into some of the finest art making facilities in the country. An example of the Beaux-Arts style, the five-story building features spacious, light-filled classrooms and studios with panoramic views of Casco Bay and historic Congress Street. The downtown campus includes another historic building, the Clapp House, and two residence halls, all within a four-block area of the city.

The Institute of Contemporary Art (ICA) at MECA is one of the college's unique contributions to Maine. It is a professional gallery, open to the public free of charge, and brings leading-edge national and international contemporary art to Maine year-round. It is considered

THE COLLEGE'S 10-TO-1 STUDENT TO FACULTY RATIO PROVIDES THE INDIVIDUAL ATTENTION THAT IS THE HALLMARK OF QUALITY EDUCATION IN VISUAL ART AND DESIGN.

one of the finest exhibition spaces in the Northeast for contemporary art.

While acknowledging that contemporary art can sometimes be difficult for audiences to understand, ICA Director Mark H. C. Bessire sees audience participation as an essential ingredient of much work made today. Besides its crucial role as a resource for MECA students and faculty, the ICA plays a significant part in the larger artistic community of Portland and New England through programming that emphasizes social, aesthetic, and material diversity.

Recent Growth and Developments

MECA has developed dramatically during the 12-year tenure of President Roger Gilmore, which began in 1989. Among important initiatives was the creation of a unique, 24-month Master of Fine Arts (MFA) degree program, which includes nationally renowned artists among its visiting faculty.

There has been significant enroll-ment growth at MECA, from 300 degree students in 1996 to more than 400 at the turn of the century. In 1999-2000, MECA enrolled the largest first-year class in its 118-year history. Students come from 32 states and 16 other countries.

During Gilmore's tenure, many changes have been made to the school. The institution changed its name from the Portland School of Art to the Maine College of Art. The purchase and renovation of the Porteous Building was begun in 1993. An Art In Service program was launched to provide service learning opportunities for students. MECA's new media program was developed, and opportunities for interdisciplinary study were expanded. And an international exchange program was developed with the Hanoi Fine Arts College, the first such arrangement between American and Vietnamese art colleges. MECA is poised to build on Gilmore's legacy under the leadership of Christine J. Vincent.

MECA's Future and its Community

MECA will continue to play a leading role in the educational and art communities with a wide variety of programs that serve important needs in the region. Programs include the Saturday School for children in grades 4-12; Early College for high school students; the Scholastic Art Awards for middle and high school students throughout Maine; Continuing Studies classes for adults; the Maine Summer Institute in Graphic Design, the only program of its kind in the country for professional designers; and the statewide Art Honors gala, which recognizes excellence, leadership, and community service in the arts.

MECA's future will reflect its commitment to the highest quality visual arts education, whether in its nationally respected BFA and MFA degree programs or in its myriad community and public programs. MECA and its strong reputation put the spotlight on art-making at the heart of Maine's largest city, in a state famous for its rich legacy in the visual arts. ●

NEW STUDIO AND CLASSROOM FACILITIES AT MECA FEATURE SPACIOUS, WELL-EQUIPPED STUDIOS AND STUNNING VIEWS OF CASCO BAY (LEFT).

MECA OFFERS A BACHELOR OF FINE ARTS DEGREE IN NINE STUDIO MAJORS AND AN INNOVATIVE MASTER OF FINE ARTS DEGREE PROGRAM (RIGHT).

ONE OF THREE CAMPUS BUILDINGS ON THE NATIONAL REGISTER OF HISTORIC PLACES, MECA'S BAXTER BUILDING WILL BE RENOVATED TO HOUSE MECA'S CENTER FOR NEW MEDIA (LEFT).

THE INSTITUTE OF CONTEMPORARY ART AT MAINE COLLEGE OF ART IS CONSIDERED ONE OF THE FINEST EXHIBITION SPACES IN THE NORTHEAST FOR LEADING EDGE CONTEMPORARY ART (RIGHT).

MELVILLE MCLEAN

T

HE CORNERSTONE OF SUPERMARKET LEADER HANNAFORD BROS. CO. DURING ITS MORE THAN 117 YEARS OF OPERATION HAS BEEN INNOVATION—A RELIANCE PROVED BY THE COMPANY'S ENDURING STABILITY AND CONTINUING GROWTH. IN THE FIRST DECADE OF THE NEW CENTURY, THE COMPANY'S NEW HANNAFORD STORES ARE DISTINGUISHED BY THE TRADEMARK COMBINATION OF QUALITY, SERVICE, VALUE, AND VARIETY THAT FULLY JUSTIFY THE PHRASE "A SHOPPING EXPERIENCE."

While the Hannaford stores introduced in 2000 were cutting edge in the industry, they carried on the tradition of pioneering new customer service ideas that have marked Hannaford throughout its history.

Tending to Business and Looking Ahead

Arthur Hannaford started the business by selling fresh produce from his family's farm in Cape Elizabeth. He sold from the back of a cart for several years before being joined by his younger brother Howard. In 1883, the two set up shop in a warehouse on the Portland waterfront, and in 1898, the Hannaford brothers' storefront was selling more produce than their father, Albert, could produce on the farm. Products such as poultry, butter, and eggs also were added. By 1902, Arthur had left to pursue other ventures, and Howard had begun working with brother Edward; together, they incorporated the company as Hannaford Bros.

THE HANNAFORD BROS. CO. SEAFOOD DEPARTMENT IS EASILY IDENTIFIED BY ITS AQUARIUM-STYLE DÉCOR. A HIGHLIGHT OF THE DEPARTMENT CAN BE FOUND IN ITS VARIETY, INCLUDING EXOTIC WHOLE FISH NOT FOUND IN ANY OTHER SEAFOOD MARKET IN MAINE (TOP).

THE PRODUCE DEPARTMENT IS LOCATED IN AN ATRIUM SETTING WITH NATURAL LIGHTING, TREES, AND PUSHCART-STYLE DISPLAYS. APPROXIMATELY 800 ITEMS ARE OFFERED FROM THE TRADITIONAL TO THE TROPICAL AND EXOTIC (BOTTOM).

Edward Hannaford—a prescient businessman with a knack for predicting changing market trends—became president of the company in 1906, and kept Hannaford in touch with the American shift away from an agricultural to an urban economy. Hannaford anticipated the exploding demand for produce and groceries as people left the farm to live in the city.

The company continued to add to its product offerings, and enlarged its corps of regional and city salespeople. Orders were now being shipped by railroad and steamboat as far north as Bangor and as far south as Boston. Hannaford's one-horse cart was replaced by a Model T Ford.

By 1918, Hannaford had established itself as a leading fruit and produce wholesaler. Throughout those years, the company moved to a series of ever larger quarters to accommodate its steady growth. In 1927, its line of fruits, vegetables, and other farm products expanded to include a full range of modern grocery items.

Through the hard times of the 1930s, Hannaford persevered through shrewd business decisions by Edward Hannaford and his protégé, future president Stewart Taylor. By the end of the Great Depression, Hannaford had not only survived, but had managed to turn a modest profit.

A New Idea in Retailing

In 1940, Hannaford expanded services to retailers to include advertising, sign making, displays, and retail accounting. IBM machines were leased to help tabulate inventory, and the company ventured into retailing for the first time in 1944, when it began helping finance new supermarkets

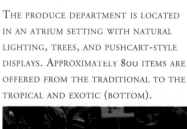

under a unique equity partnership arrangement. Each individual supermarket that partnered with Hannaford held up to a 49 percent share of the partnership, while Hannaford held 51 percent or more. Over the years, Hannaford would be associated with a variety of retail names, including Clover Farm, Red & White, Sampson's, Shop 'n Save, and, most lately, Hannaford Food and Drug Superstores.

In 1945, in anticipation of a growing and changing market, the company added meat and frozen food departments, a first in the wholesale food business. Hannaford's executives also realized that chain store operations based outside the state represented the greatest threat to continued growth. With that in mind, Hannaford made the dramatic decision in the 1950s to shift its primary focus from wholesale to retail.

To support its transition to a retail food distributor, Hannaford acquired the T.R. Savage Co. in Bangor, and in the 1960s, built a 200,000-square-foot food distribution center in Rumery Industrial Park in South Portland and purchased Progressive Distributors, a specialty food distributor in Winthrop, Maine. By 1971, the company owned or controlled 59 supermarkets in Maine, New Hampshire, and Vermont, and served 43 other wholesale accounts.

Always on the leading edge, Hannaford responded to customer needs during the recession of the 1970s as the first company in its trading area to offer lower-priced, simply packaged "no-brand" products. The company introduced Operation Price Watch in competition with the new warehouse-type stores, promising consumers that Hannaford would not be undersold on national brand items by any local competitor. The firm also introduced two innovative technologies in the late 1970s: an electronic ordering device and a computerized scanning checkout system, which improved accuracy and reduced checkout time.

The Modern Business

Hannaford's technological and customer-service leadership was to continue through the following decades. The growth that resulted was substantial by any measure. Hannaford began selling common stock in 1971, the same year the company's net earnings reached $1 million. In 1986, Hannaford stock was listed on the New York Stock Exchange, and in 1987, sales were $1 billion for the first time.

Hannaford continued its steady growth, expanding into Massachusetts and New York in the late 1980s, and into Virginia, North Carolina, and South Carolina in the mid-1990s. Sales totaled $2 billion in 1991, $3 billion in 1997, and $3.5 billion in 1999.

In 2000, Hannaford sold a majority interest in its growing E-commerce business, HomeRuns.com, and merged with Delhaize America, allowing Hannaford to operate as a separate business while being part of a $14 billion company with more than 1,400 stores from Maine to Florida. Delhaize America was—at the time of the merger—the fifth-largest grocery retailer in the nation.

The future promises a continued record of growth and innovation for Hannaford Bros. Co. The company continues to make one simple promise: A Hannaford store will never be either just a place or just a service; it will be a shopping experience. ●

THE MEAT DEPARTMENT FEATURES A 360-DEGREE DESIGN, INCLUDING A 40-FOOT BUTCHER SHOP. IT OFFERS FOUR DIFFERENT GRADES OF BEEF AS WELL AS A VARIETY OF SPECIALTY ITEMS (LEFT).

IN ADDITION TO A BREAD CAPTAIN, HANNAFORD OFFERS ARTISAN BREADS AND TWO CERTIFIED ORGANIC BREAD LINES. THERE IS ALSO A CAKE DECORATING STATION WHERE CUSTOMERS CAN OBSERVE THEIR CAKES BEING CUSTOM DECORATED (CENTER).

NATURE'S PLACE, HANNAFORD'S NATURAL AND ORGANIC FOODS DEPARTMENT, FEATURES 32 FEET OF BULK PRODUCT, INCLUDING SPICES, PASTA, NUTS, DRIED FRUITS, BEANS, RICE, AND VARIOUS GRAINS. ONE OF THE HIGHLIGHTS OF NATURE'S PLACE IS THE HEALTH NOTES KIOSK THAT PROVIDES INFORMATION TO CUSTOMERS ABOUT HERBAL REMEDIES AND NUTRITION SUPPLEMENTS (RIGHT).

A FEATURE OF THE DELI DEPARTMENT, THE STATE-OF-THE-ART FIREWORKS ROASTERY OFFERS FRESHLY PREPARED CHICKEN, TURKEY BREAST, AND OTHER ITEMS. A COMPUTERIZED DELI ORDERING SYSTEM HAS BEEN DESIGNED TO PERMIT CUSTOMERS TO COMPLETE THEIR SHOPPING AND THEN PICK UP THEIR DELI ORDERS.

SINCE 1891, PIERCE ATWOOD HAS FORGED A STANDARD OF LEGAL PRACTICE THAT CARRIES THE WEIGHT OF ACHIEVEMENT AND THE WARMTH OF FAMILIARITY. AN ENDURING TRADITION OF EXCELLENCE AND A COMMITMENT TO TOTAL CLIENT SATISFACTION INFORM EVERY TRANSACTION WITHIN THE FIRM, FOSTERING AN ENERGETIC, COLLABORATIVE SPIRIT AMONG PIERCE ATWOOD'S NEARLY 100 ATTORNEYS. ■ PIERCE ATWOOD'S ROOTS ARE AS A FULL-SERVICE COMMERCIAL LAW FIRM. THE FIRM'S SIZE, STRUCTURE, AND

legal philosophy enable its attorneys to develop strategic relationships with their clients, resulting in creative, innovative solutions to the most challenging legal problems. Pierce Atwood's expertise is highly portable, as the firm has grown from its Portland and Augusta, Maine, offices into neighboring New Hampshire and Massachusetts.

Beyond its extensive statewide and regional practice, Pierce Atwood serves national and international clients. The firm's attorneys have managed matters throughout the world, including Central and South America, Australia, South Africa, several dozen countries in Europe, and many countries in Asia.

A Century of Distinctions

For more than a century, the attorneys at Pierce Atwood have helped to shape the history of Portland and the state of Maine. Even as it adapts for the future, the firm points with pride to its record of leadership in public life, the practice of law, and community affairs.

Firm founder Joseph Symonds set a standard of achievement from the outset. Hailed by the *Portland Sunday Telegram* in 1911 as "one of the soundest and ablest judicial minds in Maine," Symonds earned early distinction by becoming the youngest person of his time to be appointed a justice to the Maine Supreme Judicial Court.

Leonard Pierce, who joined the firm in 1920, practiced corporate law. Among Pierce's most prestigious clients was Central Maine Power Company, the state's largest utility; the company is still among the firm's most prominent clients. Sigrid Tompkins, the first woman to be admitted to any Portland law

firm, joined Pierce Atwood in 1953. Another member of the firm, Charles Allen, is remembered for his long and vital support of the Maine Civil Liberties Union.

Pierce Atwood has made contributions at the national level as well. In 1952, Fred C. Scribner left the firm to serve as general counsel for the Republican National Committee, ultimately becoming general counsel for the U.S. Department of the Treasury and undersecretary of the Treasury in the Eisenhower administration before returning to Pierce Atwood in 1961.

Since 1992, the U.S. Supreme Court has appointed five special masters to preside over original jurisdiction interstate disputes. Pierce Atwood holds four of these appointments, made to present-day litigation attorneys Vincent L. McKusick and Ralph I. Lancaster Jr. McKusick is a former Maine

▼ JACK KENNEALY

PIERCE ATWOOD IS THE MAJOR TENANT OF ONE MONUMENT SQUARE, WHICH OVERLOOKS THE HEART OF PORTLAND'S DIVERSE DOWNTOWN DISTRICT.

formed a public policy consulting subsidiary in 1997. Pierce Atwood Consulting provides a broad range of community and governmental relations, issues management, and diversity recruiting and training services. Former City of Portland Mayor George N. Campbell is a principal with Pierce Atwood Consulting.

Community involvement takes many forms at Pierce Atwood, including contributions and individual involvement in numerous charities and nonprofits. As part of their practice, the firm's attorneys are encouraged and recognized for pro bono service. Pierce Atwood is a founding member of—and continues to support—the Frank M. Coffin Family Law Fellowship, and participates in the Volunteer Lawyers Project, the Legal Services Response Team, and other legal outreach programs.

The potential for a sophisticated practice at Pierce Atwood, along with the attractive Greater Portland region, continues to draw top-tier legal talent from the nation's best schools and law firms. Finding ways to accommodate today's busy lifestyles is yet another facet of the progressive culture at Pierce Atwood, whose Saturday day care program has been featured in the *American Bar Association Journal.* ●

PIERCE ATWOOD REPRESENTS AQUABIO PRODUCTS SCIENCES LLC, A MAINE-BASED MARINE BIOTECHNOLOGY COMPANY THAT OPERATES INTERNATIONALLY. AQUABIO CREATES AND LICENSES BREAKTHROUGH TECHNOLOGIES THAT USE NATURAL PROCESSES TO INCREASE THE PRODUCTIVITY OF SAFE AND HEALTHY AQUATIC FOOD SOURCES.

chief justice whose tenure on the bench is distinguished by significant reforms in Maine's courts. Lancaster is a past president of the American College of Trial Lawyers and a former federal independent counsel.

dominate commerce, members of the firm work with both start-ups and established businesses in expanding their use of Web technology.

Long supportive of local economic development initiatives, the firm

Integrated Services for Today's Challenges

Pierce Atwood's client base is best characterized by its diversity, and includes New England-based businesses, Fortune 500 companies, multinational development organizations, public utilities, health care and financial institutions, venture capital interests, and entrepreneurs.

The firm's services cut across a wide spectrum of legal disciplines, with particular strengths in complex litigation, taxation, labor and employment, environmental, commercial, and energy and utilities representation. Pierce Atwood was an early leader in establishing—among its 25 practice groups—the largest intellectual property and emerging technologies practice in northern New England. The firm uses a team concept to draw from and integrate any relevant area of practice and outside alliances to provide the best solution for each client and its business strategy. As information technologies increasingly

FAIRCHILD SEMICONDUCTOR IS A GLOBAL LEADER IN THE DESIGN AND MANUFACTURING OF HIGH-PERFORMANCE SEMICONDUCTORS. PIERCE ATWOOD SERVES AS OUTSIDE IMMIGRATION COUNSEL TO FAIRCHILD AND PROVIDES A BROAD ARRAY OF OTHER LEGAL SERVICES.

STARTING AS A 100-CUSTOMER VILLAGE HYDROELECTRIC COMPANY IN 1899, CENTRAL MAINE POWER COMPANY (CMP) HAS GONE THROUGH SEVERAL NAMES AND MANY OTHER CHANGES TO REACH ITS STANDING TODAY AS THE DELIVERER OF ELECTRICITY TO MORE THAN 540,000 CUSTOMERS IN CENTRAL AND SOUTHERN MAINE. ■ OVER THE YEARS, CMP HAS BUILT UP A RELIABLE NETWORK OF POWER LINES AND GENERATORS. THE UTILITY ENTERED THE GREATER PORTLAND AREA AND YORK COUNTY MARKETS

FROM LEFT:
FROM METER READERS AND LINEMEN TO SYSTEM OPERATORS AND CUSTOMER-SERVICE SPECIALISTS, MORE THAN 1,400 CENTRAL MAINE POWER COMPANY (CMP) EMPLOYEES WORK TO DELIVER ELECTRICITY TO MORE THAN 540,000 CUSTOMERS.

MORE THAN 100 SKILLED CMP LINE CREWS MAINTAIN AND REPAIR MORE THAN 20,000 MILES OF POWER LINES IN A SERVICE AREA COVERING MORE THAN ONE-THIRD OF MAINE.

MAINTAINING TRANSMISSION FACILITIES— THE SUPERHIGHWAYS OF ENERGY DELIVERY— IS A TOP PRIORITY FOR CMP CREWS.

with its 1942 acquisition of Cumberland County Power & Light Co. After dozens of expansions, CMP's service area has grown from the village of Oakland to cover 11,000 square miles of Maine—more than one-third of the state's area and home to more than three-fourths of its population.

In the course of its 100-year presence in Maine, CMP has worked through booms, wars, and depression. Great technological changes have swept the industry as well. Meter readers' notepads and pencils have given way to hand-held electronic data recorders. Line crews can view and process work orders transmitted to notebook computers in their trucks. Customers can pay bills over the Internet.

But the greatest change of the past century came from public policy, as Maine law redefined CMP's role. Following a 1997 mandate, CMP sold its power plants for $846 million (retiring debt and financing a rate cut

in the process), and became strictly an energy delivery company as of March 1, 2000. With energy supply deregulated and removed from CMP's control, the company focused on operating and maintaining the more than 20,000 miles of power lines and scores of substations needed to move electricity to the homes, businesses, and other customers that need it.

The divestiture of CMP's power plants sharply reduced its state-authorized revenue level. To recover economies of scale and reduce pressure on prices, CMP's parent company, CMP Group, sought a merger partner. With the approval of shareholders and regulators, CMP and its affiliates became units of Energy East Corporation on September 1, 2000. Energy East companies serve more than 2 million electric, gas, and energy services customers in the Northeast. The new structure leaves CMP a Maine-based, -managed, and -regulated utility.

A Catastrophe Overcome

The supreme test of CMP's commitment to service began January 7, 1998, as a fierce ice storm struck the Northeast and Quebec. Governor Angus King and President Bill Clinton declared emergencies, and CMP called in extra crews from as far away as Nova Scotia and North Carolina to put more than 2,000 workers in the field. More than 425,000 outage reports were dealt with in the following three weeks–punctuated by a second ice storm before damage from the first was completely repaired—requiring replacement of 3,000 broken poles, 2,000 transformers, and miles of line. The restoration drive directed by Sara Burns, now president of CMP, and completed without a single electrical injury, led to an unprecedented 91 percent "favorable" rating in surveys of CMP customers' opinions.

Today, Central Maine Power Company operates within a new organizational structure and under new Maine regulations. But the company retains its traditions of reliable energy delivery as it moves into a second century of service. ●

THE 21ST CENTURY OPENED WITH YOUNG WOMEN ATTENDING CHEVERUS HIGH SCHOOL FOR THE FIRST TIME, ONE GREAT CHANGE AMONG MANY IN WHAT HAD BEEN THE CATHOLIC BOYS' SCHOOL OF PORTLAND SINCE 1917. ■ THE 420-MEMBER STUDENT BODY OF 2000 WITH 25 GIRLS IS TO BE 700 STRONG BY 2007, WITH 40 PERCENT WOMEN. ALSO BY THEN, THERE ARE TO BE NEW AND EXPANDED BUILDINGS AND FACILITIES FOR AN INSTITUTION THAT VIGOROUSLY EMBRACES THE PRESENT AS IT VENERATES THE PAST AND THE FUTURE.

Cheverus High School—Catholic and Jesuit—is a college-preparatory secondary school. The Reverend John W. Keegan, president, describes Cheverus as value based, distinguished by the hallmarks of Jesuit education: focus on the individual and the expectation of excellence.

Change and Continuity

For its first 25 years, Cheverus was a diocesan school, staffed by parish priests. In 1942, the priests and brothers of the Society of Jesus (Jesuits) were asked to take over the growing institution to relieve the diocesan priests of the double burden.

A change in the times is illustrated by the religious-to-lay ratio on the faculty: In 1976, there were 20 Jesuits and five lay teachers; by 2000, there were three priests and 30 laypeople.

Through the auspices of Time-Warner, Cheverus had the state's first high school computer lab with high-speed cable access. The school's library catalog is completely on-line, and all faculty and students have security clearances and e-mail access to advanced research databases.

The continuous expansion of classrooms, plus new gym space and a theater, will not cramp the present site. Cheverus occupies a 25-acre campus overlooking the city's Back Cove. However, it is what goes on in the classroom, and the community, that is the prime concern at Cheverus.

A People Philosophy

Cheverus is not so much a 'what,' but a 'who,'" says Keegan. "It's the people—the students, faculty, parents, alumni, and friends." The school's philosophy includes a sense of service to people outside its immediate circle. "Students are educated not just so they can go out and get a job," says Keegan. "We're preparing them to be part of a community in which they take responsibility."

One highly representative example of that preparation occurs at the end of the students' senior year: The final month of each student's high school career is devoted to providing 120 hours of community service. The student is placed by the school in a hospital, an institution, or an elementary school to work in some capacity such as tutoring or visiting.

While final exams are taken early to allow for the service program, the school maintains supervision both at school and at the service site. At the end of the program, each student writes a reflection piece about the experience. Returning alumni speak movingly about the impact the service program has had on them.

With this dedication to the community, plus gender diversity and physical expansion, Cheverus High School will retain its focus on excellence. The school is backed by its place in a Jesuit network of 46 high schools and 25 colleges and universities, as well as by the order's educational tradition. ●

CHEVERUS HIGH SCHOOL'S BLEND OF ACADEMIC, SOCIAL, AND ATHLETIC PURSUITS MAKES FOR WELL-ROUNDED STUDENTS.

THE FIRST WATER SERVICE IN PORTLAND WAS TURNED ON THANKSGIVING DAY 1869, AN APPROPRIATE OCCASION FOR A CITIZEN-INITIATED IMPROVEMENT. PRIVATE WELLS WERE NO LONGER SUFFICIENT FOR DOMESTIC AND FIRE-PROTECTION USE IN THE GROWING AREA. THE CONCERN WAS WELL PLACED: THE GREAT FIRE OF 1866 DESTROYED 1,800 BUILDINGS IN DOWNTOWN PORTLAND AND LEFT 10,000 PEOPLE HOMELESS. MUCH HAS HAPPENED OVER THAT LONG HISTORY, THE GREATER PART OF WHICH

is utterly unknown by the end users whose apathy towards this vital resource is perhaps the highest tribute to the quality of the service the Portland Water District has delivered.

Today, the Portland Water District services more than 189,000 people through more than 46,000 household and business services in 11 communities of Greater Portland. The source of water is Sebago Lake, which is clean enough to be exempt from the expensive filtration process required with most surface water sources.

A History of Growth

The original water service organization sprang from a group of citizens who first gathered in 1862 to form the Portland Water Company. In 1908, Portland Water District bought the Portland Water Company and the Standish Water and Con-

struction Company. Initially serving water to the cities of Portland and South Portland, the Portland Water District later acquired the Gorham Water Company and the Falmouth Water Company. In the succeeding decades, the Portland Water District charter was amended to include Cumberland, Falmouth, Windham, Scarborough, Gorham, Westbrook, Cape Elizabeth, and the islands of Casco Bay.

Over the next half-century, as Portland grew to be the industrial and financial hub of the state, as well as an ever-larger population center, the demands on the district increased. From the 1970s on, Portland Water District added wastewater treatment to its services and constructed plants in a number of communities. Since the 1990s, greater governmental attention to environmental concerns

has required construction and major modifications to meet the paired needs of growing volume demand and cleaner water.

In recent years, the internal processes of the Portland Water District have undergone significant change, much of it springing from an efficiency goal adopted in the 1990s. Technological innovations and organizational development efforts resulted in rate reductions in recent years.

Independent Operation

The Portland Water District is an independent, regional municipal corporation. It operates under a charter from the State of Maine, with its own board of trustees publicly elected from the member communities. The district delivers water service to South Portland, Scarborough, Standish, and Falmouth. It provides both water and wastewater service to Portland, Cape Elizabeth, Westbrook, Gorham, Windham, and Cumberland.

Portland Water District owns and controls more than 2,500 acres of land around the water intakes at the southern end of Sebago Lake, and it leads a number of environmental protection efforts, including community outreach, school projects, and lake monitoring programs. The lake, 16 miles north of Portland, is 12 miles long and 995 billion gallons in volume.

For protection of the water source, the district maintains a two-mile "no-bodily-contact" zone and a 3,000-foot no-trespassing zone around the intakes. It also treats and disinfects the lake water at the Sebago Lake Water Treatment Facility, the first free-standing ozonation plant in New England.

As the water travels through the district's some 1,000 miles of water mains, it is protected by a small amount of chloramine to retain disinfection. Corrosion inhibitors are added to prevent lead and copper

THE PORTLAND WATER DISTRICT'S EAST END WASTEWATER TREATMENT facility, CONSTRUCTED IN 1979, HAS BEEN INSTRUMENTAL IN THE CLEANUP OF CASCO BAY.

MICHELLE CLEMENTS

from leaching into the water from home plumbing. Fluoride is added to promote dental health.

Significant Technology Upgrades

One important technology tool for the Portland Water District is Geographic Information Systems (GIS), a modern mapping of the entire system. GIS supports better ongoing maintenance of the system as well as faster response to emergencies. Traditionally, much of the information and knowledge about the physical system has resided in archived paper records and the memories of long-term employees, described by Public Relations Manager Michelle Clements as "our walking maps."

Other technology investments have improved plant operations, water system monitoring, customer relations, finance, and asset management. When Portland Water District employees attend conferences, they often find themselves in the forefront of the field.

The Portland Water District recognizes that a service affecting so many lives should not be one that no one ever hears from or about. The Portland Water District maintains a strong customer relations program, ensuring customers have the information they need to make decisions about their water.

Measures of Progress

The Portland Water District takes customer service seriously. Annual goals are set in such areas as customer satisfaction, water quality, reliable and prompt service, reasonable price, and employee satisfaction and work environment.

The fact that all the measurements—those that reach goal and those that do not—are published is a true sign of a commitment to excellence. This measure of progress is also strong support for the expectation that the Portland Water District, the quiet utility, will continue doing such a superior job that the public will continue to show tremendous confidence in it. ●

L

.L. BEAN, INC. IS A LEADING DEVELOPER AND RETAILER OF QUALITY APPAREL, FOOTWEAR, SPORTING EQUIPMENT, AND HOME PRODUCTS FOR PEOPLE WHO LOVE THE OUTDOORS. THE COMPANY IS HEADQUARTERED IN FREEPORT, MAINE. ■ THE FIRM WAS FOUNDED IN 1912 BY LEON LEONWOOD "L.L." BEAN, A MAINE OUTDOORSMAN WHO WAS TIRED OF COMING HOME WITH SORE, WET FEET FROM THE HEAVY LEATHER WOODSMAN'S BOOTS OF HIS DAY. BEAN DECIDED TO INVENT A NEW KIND OF BOOT

that combined lightweight leather tops with waterproof rubber bottoms, incorporating the best features of both materials.

The practical advantages of his new Bean Boots were readily apparent, and Bean soon sold 100 "guaranteed" pairs through the mail to fellow sportsmen. Unfortunately, 90 pairs were sent back when the stitching gave way. But Bean was true to his word: he refunded his customers' money and started over with an improved boot.

Bean's products were originally sold only through the mail. Because of his avid interest and expertise in the outdoors, his merchandise soon filled more catalog pages. Since many people dropped by his Freeport workshop to purchase items, Bean opened a showroom in 1917.

THE BEAN BOOT HAS BEEN A MAINSTAY OF L.L. BEAN, INC. SINCE ITS INCEPTION.

A Continuous Focus on Quality

Over the years, L.L. Bean's high-quality products and excellent service became legendary. In 1951, Bean announced, "We've thrown away the keys"—opening his Freeport retail store 24 hours a day, 365 days a year to accommodate sportsmen who'd appear at the store at any hour of the day or night en route to their favorite fishing hole or hunting ground. In 1954, the product line was expanded to include a women's department and, by 1960, sales had exceeded $2 million a year. Bean, who attributed his long life and good health to an interest in active, outdoor sports, was 94 years old when he died in 1967.

Soon after Bean's death, Leon A. Gorman, his grandson, was named president of the company. If Bean had been the driving force behind the creation and identity of the company, it is Gorman who transformed L.L. Bean, Inc. into what is now regarded as one of the world's preeminent retail brands. Gorman built upon the company's reputation for integrity and trustworthiness through his investment in catalog marketing, state-of-the-art operations, and an unrelenting focus on the inherent value of delivering quality products and services to people who share L.L. Bean, Inc.'s focus on the outdoors. "Superior personal service has always been, and will always be, a hallmark of L.L. Bean," says Gorman. "Our long-standing commitment to treating customers like

L.L. BEAN WAS FOUNDED IN 1912 BY LEON LEONWOOD BEAN (LEFT). TODAY HIS GRANDSON, LEON A. GORMAN (RIGHT), SERVES AS CHAIRMAN OF THE BOARD.

Summer 1986

human beings differentiates L.L. Bean in the marketplace."

Today, L.L. Bean's reputation as a catalog industry leader has reached into its expanding e-commerce and retail channels. In 2000, total company net sales exceeded $1.1 billion. The firm distributed approximately 200 million catalogs to its customers in 2000, and handled more than 15 million toll-free telephone calls, while its Internet business nearly doubled.

Gorman is an outdoor enthusiast and is committed to maintaining L.L. Bean's reputation as an authentic source for high-quality outdoor apparel and equipment. He is a strong advocate for people-powered outdoor recreation, and actively supports conservation and preservation efforts such as the Nature Conservancy's St. John River project. An avid outdoorsman himself, Gorman frequently tests L.L. Bean products on trips, most notably during an ascent to the base camp of the 1990 Mount Everest International Peace Climb, an effort sponsored by the company in observance of Earth Day. Gorman has also climbed Mount Rainier and Mount Kilimanjaro. In 2001, he was named chairman of the board, turning over his responsibilities as president and CEO to Chris McCormick.

Expanding the Business

L.L. Bean's 120,000-square-foot, flagship retail store is still located on Main Street in Freeport. Along with Acadia National Park, the store is one of the most visited destinations in Maine, attracting 3.5 million visitors annually. In addition to full-price stores in Maine, Virginia, and Maryland, the company also has off-price factory stores in Maine, New Hampshire, Delaware, Maryland, Virginia, and Oregon, as well as nine stores in Japan. Through its stores, catalogs, and Web site, L.L. Bean now offers more than 16,000 products across seven product divisions.

In founding the company, Bean had a rule by which he did business: "Sell good merchandise at a reasonable profit, treat your customers like human beings, and they will always come back for more." Despite the passage of time and changing technology, Bean's golden rule remains the founding principle upon which L.L. Bean, Inc. conducts all of its affairs. ●

L.L. BEAN IS A LEADER IN THE CATALOG INDUSTRY (TOP).

THE ORIGINAL L.L. BEAN SHOWROOM WAS OPENED IN FREEPORT IN 1917 (BOTTOM LEFT). TODAY, THE COMPANY'S 120,000-SQUARE-FOOT, FLAGSHIP RETAIL STORE IS ONE OF THE MOST VISITED DESTINATIONS IN MAINE, ATTRACTING 3.5 MILLION VISITORS ANNUALLY (BOTTOM RIGHT).

A GLORIOUS PAST AND A MAGNIFICENT FUTURE COMPRISE THE HISTORY AND PROMISE PROUDLY DISPLAYED BY EASTLAND PARK, PORTLAND'S GRANDE DAME HOTEL. THE EASTLAND IS THE HOTEL WHOSE BUILDER, AFTER SPENDING THE PRESENT-DAY EQUIVALENT OF $250 MILLION ON THE CONSTRUCTION PROJECT IN 1927, THREW A SET OF THE BUILDING'S KEYS INTO CASCO BAY TO SYMBOLIZE HIS COMMITMENT THAT THE HOTEL WOULD NEVER CLOSE. ■ UPON ENTERING THE HOTEL, VISITORS ARE ENVELOPED IN A

sense of understated elegance created by taste and artistic sensitivity, deluxe decor, and a dignified style of customer service rarely seen in the 21st century. The guest rooms are beautifully appointed, the public areas are rich with services as well as imaginative elements, and the range of guest amenities is broad.

The Eastland has 204 luxurious guest rooms and suites; 15 extended-stay suites with kitchens; a Concierge Club level with an executive lounge;

a business center; a fitness center; and valet parking. In addition, other amenities include Internet hookups in the guest rooms, the latest audio-visual equipment in the meeting rooms, and fully up-to-date plumbing and electronic fixtures everywhere.

The Dignity of Elegance

In recent years, steps have been taken to return the Eastland Park to its original grandeur. A $4 million, top-to-bottom refurbishing completed

in 2001 was focused on restoration, reviving the Top of the East rooftop lounge, luxury rooms, and meeting and eating areas. This involved removing the less-desirable interior features that had been added through the decades, as well as building and installing reproductions of long-gone details that represent the dignity of the premier hotel.

The renovation was completed under the direction of Heather Strauss, general manager, a veteran of grand hotel resurrection. Strauss' enthusiasm for history, art, and community sensibility matches her clarity and energy in directing the restoration work itself.

The concept of the Eastland, while honoring history, enthusiastically embraces the fresh and creative. Artist Scott Potter worked with the new owners on the decoration of the new restaurant, named Decoupage in recognition of the art form Potter employed. The hotel also opened the new Eastland Gallery for displays of art. The renovation included the basics of upgrading all the public areas, guest rooms, and elevators, as well as replacement of many of the windows. Adjacent to the public areas, the new owners emphasized varied and upscale retail space over administrative offices.

Near the lobby entry is a prominent display of historic photographs and captions that tell the story of the hotel as a landmark and an important feature of Portland's social and economic life for its many decades. On occasion, the hotel displays memorabilia such as menus from past wedding celebrations.

Facilities and Attractions

The Eastland Park features three styles of guest rooms: concierge, deluxe, and standard. Its 18,000 square feet of conference space includes 13 adaptable meeting rooms accommodating groups from 10 to

THE EASTLAND PARK HAS BEEN A PORTLAND LANDMARK SINCE 1927.

200, and banquet facilities for up to 400 people. The stately, 6,500-square-foot Eastland Ballroom, with its balcony overlooking the dance floor, is one of the most elegant and historic in Maine; the ballroom can accommodate 750 people in comfort and style. The Top of the East is a magnet for evening relaxation and panoramic views. Decoupage offers fine dining with its European flair and a focus on table-side service.

The hotel is located in the heart of downtown Portland's acclaimed arts and shopping district, close to the Children's Museum of Maine and the Portland Museum of Art. Short blocks away is the famed Old Port District, with fine shopping, quaint galleries, and superb restaurants. Portland is rumored to be second only to San Francisco in the number of restaurants per capita, and most of them are superb.

Equally accessible downtown are theaters, the Cumberland County Civic Center, the Henry Wadsworth Longfellow Home, numerous historic mansions, the Portland Observatory, and the Eastern and Western promenades, with breathtaking views of the harbor, the working waterfront, and, on occasion, magnificent cruise ships entering or anchored in the bay. During most of the year, the Maine Narrow Gauge Railroad Co. & Museum operates along the harbor under the Eastern Promenade, its three-mile ride enhanced by a light show during the holiday season.

The view from the Eastland's Top of the East restaurant itself includes the charming sweep of the old port city below, Casco Bay, the pine-clad hills and rocky promontories of the seacoast, and, off to the west, Mount Washington and the White Mountains of New Hampshire.

Central Location

Location is a strong attribute, beginning with the hotel's central location on the walkable three-mile peninsula that is the backbone of Portland. The Eastland Park is 15 minutes from Freeport, the home of L.L. Bean, and myriad celebrated outlet stores. Also, within short drives up and down the coast and inland are numerous museums, recreation destinations, and sports and entertainment venues. And everywhere are the grand old public, commercial,

EASTLAND'S SPECIAL TOUCHES MAKE
GUESTS' STAYS MEMORABLE.

and industrial buildings of the past several centuries; historic mansions; New England-style cottages; country views; and seaside vistas, together with the ships, boats, docks, buoys, lighthouses, and endless visual delights that make Maine such a popular destination.

The Eastland is quite comfortably a participant in the community. Since it is in the heart of Portland's Arts District, the hotel works actively with art and music groups of the area, bringing low-cost and free entertainment programs to Congress Square for the delight of lunching downtown workers, locals, and tourists.

Holiday season programs at the Eastland typically offer storytelling, gingerbread-house decorating, and Santa visits for children, as well as special events for adults. The owner's philosophy is to be involved in the community at large—to be a centerpiece of downtown, as well as an active player in its activities.

Part of the Magna Hospitality Group

For professionals who stay at the hotel regularly, the hotel offers the Magna Hotels Preferred Members Club Program. Member benefits include preferred availability status on high-occupancy nights, a member coordinator to assist with special needs, a newsletter and special invitations, and a variety of gifts. Its range of rooms and rates allows the hotel to offer accommodations to a clientele encompassing sophisticated business travelers, as well as family vacationers.

The Eastland Park is owned by the Magna Hospitality Group. Magna was formed in 1998, and is an outgrowth of the Grand Heritage Hotels, owner and/or manager of 25 historic hotels in the United States, and with franchises and support for more than 80 hotels in Europe.

In addition to the Eastland Park Hotel, the Magna Hospitality Group owns the Hagerstown Ramada Inn

in Maryland; owns the Holiday Inn Plantation/Sawgrass and a Days Inn in Florida; and manages Le Grand Lodge in Mont-Tremblant, Quebec. Magna recently acquired the Hotel Lawrence in Dallas, formerly the Paramount Hotel.

The Magna Hospitality Group was formed by William F. Burruss, its president, after he sold Grand Heritage, which he also founded. The group has achieved notable success in purchasing and restoring once-great hotels that are in distress, then marketing them as quality destinations. The group's secret is to return the historic buildings to their prime condition and then provide modern amenities within them.

At the Eastland Park, the uniqueness is evident. The hotel's prime historic condition and its modern amenities are the visible part. The experience of the Eastland's staff, carefully planned and nurtured, provides the magnificence. ●

THE TOP OF THE EAST IS A MAGNET FOR
EVENING RELAXATION AND TABLE-SIDE
SERVICE.

BLUE ROCK INDUSTRIES CONDUCTS AN ACTIVE COMMERCE IN A NUMBER OF FIELDS RELATED TO ITS BEST-KNOWN INDUSTRY AS A MAJOR PAVING CONTRACTOR AND SUPPLIER OF NATURAL STONE, LOAM, AND SIMILAR PRODUCTS. TODAY AN INDUSTRY LEADER WITH FACILITIES THROUGHOUT MAINE, BLUE ROCK BEGAN IN 1920 WITH TWO HORSES, DUMP CARTS, WHEELBARROWS, HAND PICKS, A TWO-INCH WATER PUMP, AND A KEYSTONE SHOVEL. BY 1930, THE COMPANY WAS HANDLING THE

largest road-building contract ever let by the State of Maine (seven miles).

In the mid-1900s, Blue Rock was the state's largest airport builder, with projects including Portland International Jetport. In 1985, Blue Rock was the first to recycle pavement, and in 1997, it paved the new Casco Bay Bridge, the largest of its kind in North America.

To the public, the attractive face of Blue Rock Industries is its Stone Center in Westbrook. The company invites the public, designers, and construction professionals to browse through its indoor and outdoor displays, complete with a large selection of granite and marble slabs; floor tiles; and stone for patios, walkways, and landscaping. Blue Rock's products fill needs as diverse as sand for golf courses and huge boulders for major sewage drainage projects.

In the Stone Center's fabrication facility, stone slabs are customized into beautiful, multi-angled kitchen and bath countertops and other customer-requested products. Stone experts provide advice for projects, and free how-to demonstrations are conducted.

Superior Materials and Service

Blue Rock is a major hot mix supplier, as well as a highway and driveway contractor. Because of its superior quarrying capabilities and extensive aggregate supply, the company's hot mix product enjoys steady demand in Maine. Its large, technically advanced paving crews are efficient in meeting the varying needs of paving customers.

The company provides concrete for all areas of residential and commercial construction, including highways, sidewalks, driveways, foundations, parking structures, fuel tank enclosures, and insulated concrete housing.

Blue Rock's state-of-the-art specialty products for the construction industry include applications

such as geotextiles for weed control, silt fencing, soil and drainage stabilization, sealants, crack filler, and calcium chloride.

Environmental and Community Focus

The environmentally oriented end of Blue Rock's business takes tired, worn-out roads and reclaims the old pavement as a quality base ready for a new top layer. This process significantly reduces reflective cracking after repaving. Blue Rock has made a major investment in recycling technology and equipment to save resources and money for its customers.

Many large corporations in the area have their heavy vehicles taken care of at Blue Rock's 32,000-square-foot service and maintenance facility. Originally developed for Blue Rock's extensive fleet of heavy equipment, the facility handles servicing, body work, painting, and welding. The shop also provides snowplowing services for shopping centers, hospitals, cities, and towns.

Blue Rock Industries has established a strong reputation for excellence in eight product lines, as well as the strength to assure reliable quality and community participation well into the future. ●

BLUE ROCK INDUSTRIES' LARGE, TECHNICALLY ADVANCED PAVING CREWS ARE EFFICIENT IN MEETING THE VARYING NEEDS OF PAVING CUSTOMERS.

IN BLUE ROCK'S FABRICATION FACILITY, QUARRIED STONE SLABS ARE CUSTOMIZED INTO BEAUTIFUL, MULTI-ANGLED KITCHEN AND BATH COUNTERTOPS AND OTHER CUSTOMER-REQUESTED PRODUCTS.

SYSCO FOOD SERVICES OF NORTHERN NEW ENGLAND, INC., A TECHNOLOGY-DRIVEN COMPANY, IS A BROAD-LINE FOOD SERVICE DISTRIBUTOR. THE FIRM SERVES CONSUMER OUTLETS AND COMMERCIAL AND INSTITUTIONAL CLIENTS THAT ARE CONCENTRATED IN MAINE AND NEW HAMPSHIRE. WITH ITS TOP-OF-THE-LINE CERTIFIED ANGUS BEEF AND THOUSANDS OF OTHER QUALITY PRODUCTS, THE COMPANY IS THE LARGEST BROAD-LINE DISTRIBUTOR IN NORTHERN NEW ENGLAND.

SYSCO Northern New England is rapidly growing through the company's technical modernization; dedicated, superior corps of workers; and close attention to customer service. The company has passed $160 million in annual revenues on a track to reaching $325 million through the current decade.

As a branded company, SYSCO Northern New England emphasizes the specifications and quality of the national SYSCO line of food products. Sixty percent of the company's food products are branded. SYSCO Northern New England also distributes food items from other local, regional, and national companies, as well as produce and commercial food service products from tableware to cooking equipment. While the firm can avail itself of the tremendous buying power of the $23 billion Fortune 500 national company of which it is a part, SYSCO Northern New England is a fully autonomous regional organization.

Around-the-Clock Operation

SYSCO Northern New England's around-the-clock operation receives and distributes a tremendous amount and variety of products daily through its highly automated warehouse. An experienced workforce, trained to ensure efficient and accurate order fulfillment, handles the process in facilities that include various zones of temperature control, date-sensitive stock handling, and the latest automation and data management procedures throughout.

The high-level development of technology at SYSCO Northern New England, which is state of the art in the industry, is a key factor in the company's renowned customer service.

The regional company fully exemplifies SYSCO's focus on complete customer satisfaction.

Through the parent corporation's decades as a public company, SYSCO's operating companies have built the loyalty of customers one by one, city by city, and region by region as a result of their ability to provide quality products delivered on time, in excellent condition, and at reasonable prices. SYSCO has achieved its position as an industry leader in food service marketing and distribution by leveraging product innovation, information technology, new warehousing techniques, and transportation advances to continue building customer loyalty.

Extensive Customer Satisfaction Program

One of SYSCO's priorities is the raising of customer loyalty

THE SYSCO FOOD SERVICES OF NORTHERN NEW ENGLAND, INC. FLEET CONSISTS OF 67 TRACTORS AND 70 TRAILERS WITH MULTI-TEMPERATURE COMPARTMENTS.

to an even higher level by focusing on converting mildly satisfied customers into completely satisfied customers. To achieve its customer satisfaction objectives, SYSCO created a formalized process and action plan known as the C.A.R.E.S.(Customers Are Really Everything to SYSCO) initiative. Goals of the program include building customer retention and substantially increasing sales to each customer. Adding new customers is also important to SYSCO, which has a 10 percent share of the ever growing, $165 billion food service distribution market.

To launch C.A.R.E.S., SYSCO surveyed customers, analyzed performance information, and developed training materials, as well as measurement and reporting tools, based on input from SYSCO operating companies. The surveys defined what customers believe to be the most valued aspects of their relationship with SYSCO. New reports and techniques were designed to address those criteria.

The data in these reports monitor customer retention, market penetration, and the key elements of service performance. Especially meaningful to customers are a few basic services they consider high priority, such as receiving all the products on time, in undamaged condition, and accurately invoiced.

Product Innovation for Competitive Edge

Product innovation is another key customer satisfaction component, and SYSCO products give the company a competitive edge. Distinctive to SYSCO, these goods are produced in compliance with exacting specifications, and they provide consistent quality and exceptional yield—or servings per container—in comparison with competitors' offerings.

SYSCO Northern New England is a Certified Angus Beef distributor, one of 60 in the country for this very high-end product. Having originated as a division of Portland's Jordan's Meats, SYSCO Northern New England continues to buy extensively from the Jordan's line and to distribute Jordan's products in a business arrangement with the new owners. SYSCO Northern New England maintains similar agreements with numerous other regional producers such as Barber Foods, Oakhurst Dairy, Jasper Wyman, and various seafood companies.

As the American consumer's appetite for meals prepared away from home has grown, so has the family of SYSCO Brand products. From humble beginnings in the early 1970s, with products such as cut green beans, the cornerstone brand now accounts for more than 29,000 items. Anyone who has enjoyed a meal served at a restaurant, college cafeteria, resort hotel, or sports stadium has probably encountered the palate-pleasing tastes of SYSCO Brand products.

Leading Marketer and Distributor

SYSCO is a leading marketer and distributor of food and food service products in North America.

The SYSCO Brand family has grown to include brands designed for specific market segments, Brandables total menu concepts, specialty meat and product brands, and even SYSCO's own branded technology, which drives every facet of the organization. SYSCO has evolved from a broad-line company to its current status as a broad brand supplier with a depth of service unique within the industry.

SYSCO's wide array of food products—such as custom-cut meat, seafood, fruit, vegetables, and prepared foods, including desserts—are offered in four quality levels: Supreme, Imperial, Classic, and Reliance. Food service supplies run from soup kettles to soup spoons, dishwashers to dinnerware, cleaning solutions to carryout cartons.

While SYSCO Northern New England benefits from the resources of finance, product, and information provided by its industry-leading parent company, the firm is closely linked to the history, people, and commerce throughout Maine, as reflected in the statewide distribution from its facilities today.

Deep Roots in Maine

Jordan's Meats was founded in 1927 as a meat-processing company. Joseph F. Jordan came to the United States from Germany, at the age of 16, as an apprentice sausage maker. He and his wife, Emma, founded Jordan's. After Joseph's death in 1949, Emma carried on the company until their three sons returned from military service. Joseph C., H. Steven, and David F. Jordan all worked for the company. Joseph C., known as Chet, was chairman of the board and the company's affiliated divisions until his death in 1994.

Jordan's Meats' fledgling food service business came under the management of Richard Giles in 1974. Over the next 10 years, the division expanded in Maine and New Hampshire, growing in sales from $1 million to $50 million. At that point, the company began building its current Westbrook, Maine, facility, which has the capacity and technology to handle the $325 million in business volume predicted in the next few years. The new building allowed the eventual closing of facilities in Bangor and in Laconia, New Hampshire, and consolidation of the operations into Westbrook.

Over the next few years, Jordan's acquired several companies, including Twin City Fruit, Chishom Fruit, Horizon Foods, and Jimmy's Wholesale Foods. Sales continued to grow, and in 1990, Jordan's acquired the L. Hershburg Co. in Burlington, Vermont. Jordan's operated the Westbrook and Burlington plants until the 1998 SYSCO acquisition—by which time sales had grown to $140 million.

Maine SYSCO began in 1951 as a coffee distributor, Vicker's Foods, in Bangor. In 1969, company founder Adrian Vicker sold the firm to Richard Stone, who moved it to Newport, Maine, and changed the name to Bangor Wholesale Foods. Over the next several years, the sales and product lines were expanded. In 1975, John Amoroso purchased Bangor Wholesale Foods, whose business base was rapidly enlarged to encompass the area from Portland north to the Canadian border. A new facility was constructed in 1978.

SYSCO purchased Bangor Wholesale Foods in 1986 and operated it until the merger with the newly acquired Jordan's operation. Its annual sales had grown to $50 million by then.

Formed in May 1998 as a result of merging Maine SYSCO of Newport, Maine, with Jordan's Foods of Portland, the new SYSCO Food Services of Northern New England, Inc. became one of the largest broad-line distributors in northern New England. The facilities in Westbrook have been enlarged and renovated into a state-of-the-art operation to serve an ever expanding customer base, with an eye toward more than doubling its size, while maintaining SYSCO's unparalleled level of customer satisfaction. ●

SYSCO NORTHERN NEW ENGLAND'S DRY WAREHOUSE WAS CONSTRUCTED IN 1999.

THE NAME MERRILL HAS BEEN ASSOCIATED WITH THE EFFICIENT MOVEMENT OF GOODS IN NEW ENGLAND FOR MORE THAN 70 YEARS. ITS LONGEVITY AND INFLUENCE ARE A REFLECTION OF THE SOLID, TRADITIONAL NEW ENGLAND VALUES OF FRUGALITY, FOCUSED EFFORT, AND COMMITMENT TO EMPLOYEES AND COMMUNITY— ALL OF WHICH HAVE BEEN EMBRACED BY THE MERRILL FAMILY SINCE THE COMPANY WAS FOUNDED. ■ IN 1929, PAUL E. MERRILL BEGAN HIS CAREER WHILE STILL A HIGH SCHOOL STUDENT BY TRUCKING HAY TO

the Portland waterfront and returning with truckloads of supplies for the farmers in his rural community. This early connection with the harbor blossomed toward the end of his life into a groundbreaking commitment to renew ocean commerce in Portland.

SANDY AGRAFIOTIS

A Leading Terminal in the Northeast

From an initial investment in a used truck, Merrill grew his enterprise into a diversified mini-conglomerate including trucking, lumber, ready-mix, chemical manufacturing, warehousing, and insurance. In 1977, he made his initial commitment to Portland's then-dilapidated, but historic waterfront, at the time the site of a restaurant, a few small warehouses, and storage tanks. Merrill's contribution to the now-hailed waterfront revival was the development of a unique, privately owned general cargo marine terminal to fill a need he saw for a regional service to industry.

Completed in 1983, Merrill's Marine Terminal is now the leading dry-cargo and forest-products terminal between Philadelphia and St. John, New Brunswick. It annually handles nearly 600,000 metric tons, including wood pulp exported by New England paper manufacturers to ports around the world, newsprint imported for the major presses of the Northeast, recycled metals exported to the Far East, and industrial coal imported to fuel the power requirements of the paper industry.

The company employs 63 men and women full-time and relies upon dozens of part-time workers at the terminal and the 300,000 square feet of paper-grade, high-quality warehousing Merrill's Marine Terminal maintains off-site.

Community Leadership

Still a family-owned business, Merrill's Marine Terminal is actively involved in the social welfare of the Portland community and in the environmental protection of the Gulf of Maine estuary. As their legacy to the city, Paul E. and Virginia Merrill provided the lead gift of $1 million that led to the magnificent restoration of the historic Portland City Hall Auditorium as a world-class concert venue.

That legacy continues today. Merrill's Marine Terminal grows as an anchor for Portland's now-thriving working waterfront. The harbor's authentic commercial flavor and function have made it a model for balanced development among small port cities in North America, and an attraction for natives and visitors alike.

The heritage of Merrill's Marine Terminal goes back to the high school boy of 1929. Its future is as strong as Maine's forest-products industry and Portland's commitment to its seafaring port. ●

JON BONJOUR PHOTOGRAPHY

COMPLETED IN 1983, MERRILL'S MARINE TERMINAL IS THE LEADING DRY-CARGO AND FOREST-PRODUCTS TERMINAL BETWEEN PHILADELPHIA AND ST. JOHN, NEW BRUNSWICK. IT ANNUALLY HANDLES NEARLY 600,000 METRIC TONS, INCLUDING WOOD PULP EXPORTED BY NEW ENGLAND PAPER MANUFACTURERS TO PORTS AROUND THE WORLD, NEWSPRINT IMPORTED FOR THE MAJOR PRESSES OF THE NORTHEAST, RECYCLED METALS EXPORTED TO THE FAR EAST, AND INDUSTRIAL COAL IMPORTED TO FUEL THE POWER REQUIREMENTS OF THE PAPER INDUSTRY.

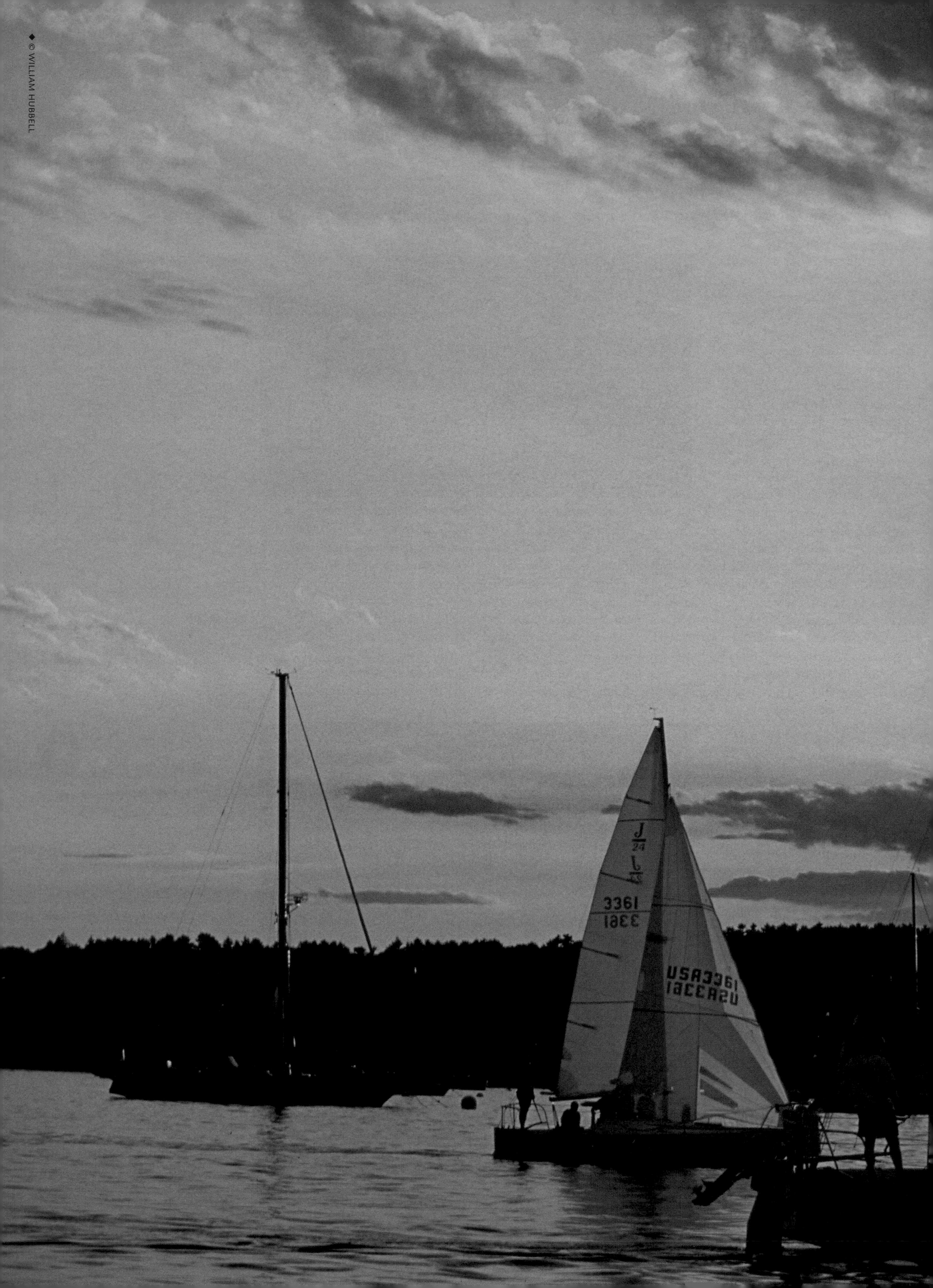
J/24
3361
USA3361

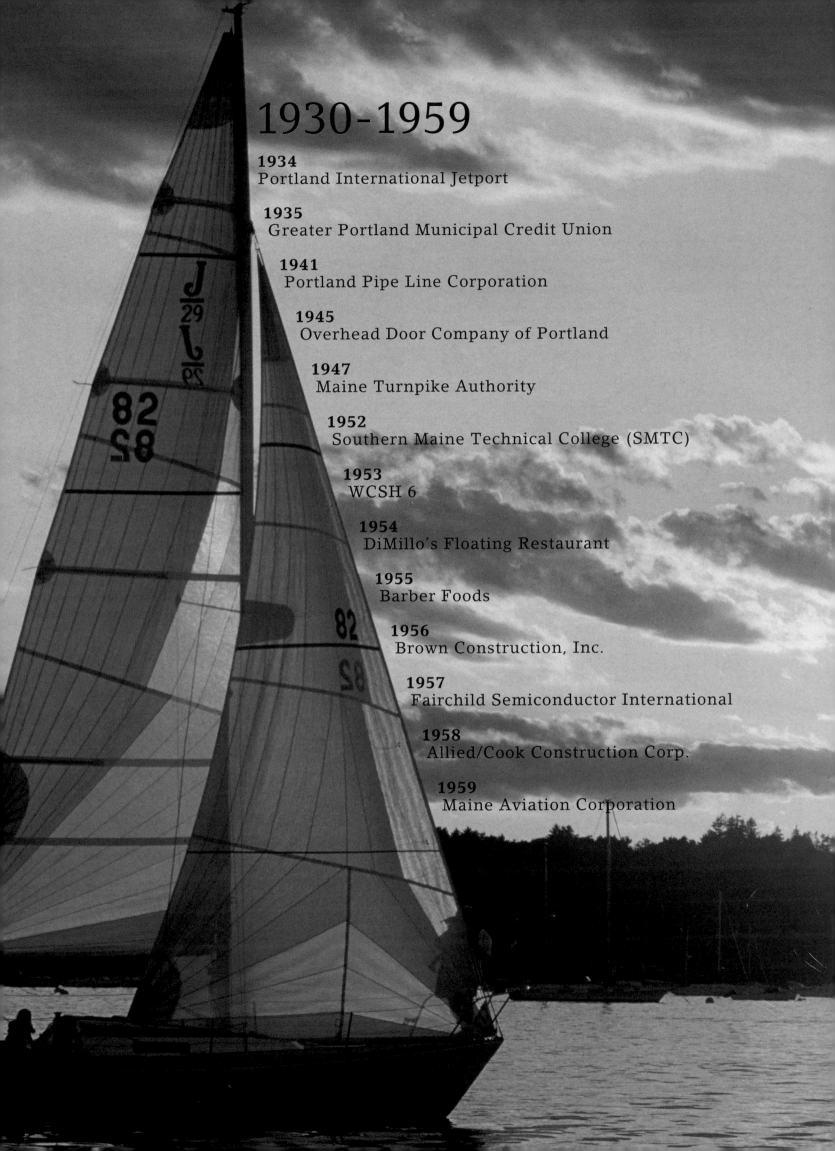

1930-1959

1934
Portland International Jetport

1935
Greater Portland Municipal Credit Union

1941
Portland Pipe Line Corporation

1945
Overhead Door Company of Portland

1947
Maine Turnpike Authority

1952
Southern Maine Technical College (SMTC)

1953
WCSH 6

1954
DiMillo's Floating Restaurant

1955
Barber Foods

1956
Brown Construction, Inc.

1957
Fairchild Semiconductor International

1958
Allied/Cook Construction Corp.

1959
Maine Aviation Corporation

L IKE MANY COMMUNITY AIRPORTS, PORTLAND INTERNATIONAL JETPORT HAD ITS BEGINNINGS AS A FLYING FAN'S PRIVATE FIELD. TODAY, THE FACILITY SERVES NEARLY 1.4 MILLION PASSENGERS A YEAR, FLYING ON THE MOST MODERN EQUIPMENT OF MOST OF THE MAJOR AIRLINES. ■ IN THE LATE 1920S, DR. CLIFFORD "KIP" STRANGE FIRST AGREED TO PROVIDE SPACE ON HIS EXTENSIVE PORTLAND LAND FOR HIS BROTHER-IN-LAW ALBERT JOHNSON'S CURTISS JENNY. JOHNSON HAD DECIDED HE WANTED TO LEARN TO FLY. BEFORE LONG,

Strange himself was hooked, and shortly thereafter there were a couple of grass runways on his land that attracted other flyers.

Meanwhile, Boston & Maine Airways inaugurated airline service at the Portland facility when it moved there from Scarborough, Maine, on December 17, 1934. A Portland Chamber of Commerce project had produced the Scarborough airport in 1931. Aero historian Leo Boyle notes that the beginnings of today's extensive Portland facility really took place when the City of Portland bought the airfield in 1936 and built a third runway.

Air shows were big during the 1930s, and Boyle recalls some colorful characters and events that also drew attention. Fixed-base operator Milton Smith, who founded Northeast Airways (now Northeast Airmotive), was a well-known aircraft dealer. His rival was Harold Troxel of Portland Flying Service. The two never cared much for each other, and used to engage in dogfights over the airport. Every once in a while the Federal Aviation Administration would get a call about their antics.

STROUDWATER FIELD, HAVING BEEN RE-NAMED PORTLAND MUNICIPAL JETPORT AFTER ITS PURCHASE BY THE CITY IN 1936, RECEIVED ITS THIRD RUNWAY IN THE LATE 1930S (TOP).

PORTLAND'S FIRST AIRLINE SERVICE WAS LOCATED AT STROUDWATER FIELD ON WESTBROOK STREET, NOW THE PORTLAND INTERNATIONAL JETPORT. A BOSTON & MAINE AIRWAYS STINSON SM6000B LOADS PASSENGERS ON THE FIRST DAY OF SERVICE (BOTTOM).

LEO BOYLE

The War Years and After

I n 1940, the depression-era Works Progress Administration built Portland's first real terminal, a brick structure that now is the general aviation terminal. During World War II, the airport was closed to most civilian traffic, but was visited by numerous lend-lease aircraft on their way to Canada.

When U.S. neutrality forbade cross-border flights, the Canada-bound

planes would fly from Portland to Houlton, Maine, and were then towed into Canada by horses or tractors. Among the interesting aircraft that came through were Curtiss Helldivers, which were put on a French aircraft carrier that was diverted to Martinique when France fell to the Nazis. The planes rotted away on a sunny hillside and were never flown in the war. The Portland airport was also the base for Civil Air Patrol planes that searched coastal waters for enemy submarines.

Following the war, Troxel renewed his rivalry with Smith when he founded the Port-au-Maine Airport in Scarborough. However, Troxel's airfield was in the flight path for the Portland facility, and eventually was sold for industrial development.

The Portland International Jetport began to take its existing form in the 1950s and 1960s. The present main runway was built in 1957 and lengthened in 1966. The basic layout of the airport as it now exists was completed with the opening of the current terminal building on December 8, 1968, when jet aircraft arrived. The terminal has been expanded at least twice since then.

For many years, Northeast Airlines was the commercial mainstay in Portland. It was a big event when

NORM HOULE

Northeast won a Florida route, beginning the spring vacation tradition. Northeast's DC6B piston-driven planes, called Sunliners, were succeeded by Vickers Viscount prop jets; then, in 1968, with the arrival of the jet age, DC9s became the dominant aircraft. The "yellow bird" jets sported the unusual color scheme of yellow and white.

The only other airline in Portland over those years was Bar Harbor Airlines. Northeast was bought in 1972 by Delta Airlines, which remains one of the major carriers at the jetport. The 1970s and 1980s saw the influx of other airlines, and the airport really began growing in 1983.

As the jetport has changed over the years, its connection to the past has continued to remain alive and well. In addition to setting in motion the events that gave way to today's modern jetport facility, the Strange family developed a long history with aviation. Daughter Beth became a pilot and later an airline flight attendant; she married a Northeast Airlines pilot. In later years, son Neal maintained a floatplane at his home in Raymond, Maine, and grandson Keith operated a seaplane base in Lincoln, Maine.

One other prominent thing that has not changed is the designation of Portland International Jetport as PWM. That harks back to the early days, when airline pilots would follow beacon lights from airport to airport. The last light before Portland was at Westbrook, 10 miles to the west, so the initials PWM were derived from Portland-Westbrook-Municipal.

The Future

Today, the extensive plans for improvements at Portland International Jetport are tied more to continuing modernization and new safety regulations than to an expectation of a surge in growth. With a consistent annual increase in passengers over the past few years and much higher volume of air cargo, business is closely tied to the economy. Because of this, a 10-year capital program will proceed to improve the airport's current facilities. The enhancements will be carefully designed to continue the airport's value as an asset to business travelers and the traveling public, as well as to the area's thriving economy in general—as witnessed by the opening of Maine Turnpike Exit 7a, which links the jetport to Maine's most important roadway.

Plans for the jetport's future include lengthening the primary runway by 400 feet; in-pavement runway lighting to improve low-visibility conditions; a new, 1,500-space parking garage; and expansion of the terminal and baggage claim facilities.

Airport managers and planners are very conscious of the jetport as part of the community and its growth. While the facility is positioned as a one-stop service to the world, and as Maine's strategic link to the global economy, the staff is proud that the jetport has been a part of the community over all of its years of service. Jeff Schultes, airport manager, points to the convenient proximity of gates, baggage, and parking to each other as much as he talks of the direct jet service to most of the hub airports in the eastern half of the United States. "As we have developed a modern airport, we have still preserved the small-town feel of Maine," Schultes says. "And we will maintain that feel." ●

M

ARIANN GOFF OF GREATER PORTLAND MUNICIPAL CREDIT UNION (GPM) STRUCTURES HER APPROACH TO FINANCIAL SERVICE TO THIS QUOTE: "MEMBERS CAN GET THE SAME DOLLAR AT THE CREDIT UNION THAT THEY CAN GET FROM THE BANK DOWN THE STREET—THE DIFFERENCE IS ALL IN THE HOW IT IS GIVEN." ■ AS PRESIDENT AND CEO, GOFF KNOWS THE MYRIAD WAYS THAT THE "HOW" OF GPM ENSURES ITS STATUS AS A RAPIDLY GROWING INSTITUTION WHOSE

CHARTERED IN 1935, GREATER PORTLAND MUNICIPAL CREDIT UNION IS A MEMBER-OWNED, NOT-FOR-PROFIT FINANCIAL COOPERATIVE THAT PROUDLY SERVES MUNICIPAL EMPLOYEES OF PORTLAND, SOUTH PORTLAND, CAPE ELIZABETH, AND SCARBOROUGH; EMPLOYEES OF SELECT EMPLOYEE GROUPS; STUDENTS OF THE SOUTH PORTLAND AND CAPE ELIZABETH SCHOOL DISTRICTS; AND FAMILY OF ELIGIBLE MEMBERS.

members love to tell why they enjoy the service of GPM. Primarily, GPM provides old-fashioned customer service, delivered in the most innovative financial products through the most current technology.

Chartered in 1935, GPM is a member-owned, not-for-profit financial cooperative that proudly serves municipal employees of Portland, South Portland, Cape Elizabeth, and Scarborough; employees of select employee groups; students of the South Portland and Cape Elizabeth school districts; and family of eligible members. Since 1995, the credit union has doubled in asset size and added a new branch without increasing staff. Goff attributes this growth and success to wise use of technology—implementing technological advances without losing member touch and focus.

Habit of Innovation

Living up to its mission to provide members exceptional service, personalized financial solutions, and value-priced products, GPM was one of the first credit unions in the state to offer members account access 24 hours a day, seven days a week through the convenience of debit cards, electronic home banking, and automated bill payment via personal computer.

GPM provides members convenient access to surcharge-free ATMs as a member of SURF—a statewide, credit union-owned network of ATMs. Through a strategic partnership with Dirigo Financial Group, GPM offers members access to nontraditional services such as mutual funds, life insurance, and financial planning.

Social Awareness

GPM is committed to being a good neighbor in the communities where members live and work.

In the last 10 years, the staff have generously raised and donated nearly $100,000 to local charities that provide food and shelter to the homeless. In addition, youth programs such as Special Olympics, Boys & Girls Clubs of Greater Portland, Junior Achievement, D.A.R.E., Day One, and Toys for Tots receive annual support from GPM.

GPM Credit Union was established to meet member needs of the time—encouraging saving through payroll deduction and providing low-cost credit for municipal and school department employees. Through the years, members' needs have changed, requiring more complex financial products and greater ease of access through sophisticated delivery systems. GPM met the changing needs and, through critical strategic partnering, continues to improve and enhance products and delivery. Meeting the needs of members was, is, and will continue to be the focus of GPM Credit Union. ●

BUILT IN 1941 AS PART OF THE NATIONAL DEFENSE EFFORT IN WORLD WAR II, PORTLAND PIPE LINE CORPORATION'S (PPL) PIPELINE HAS BECOME A KEY PART OF THE BUSTLING NETWORK OF COOPERATIVE ENERGY SUPPLIERS SHARED BY CANADA AND THE UNITED STATES. PPL ALSO IS AN IMPORTANT ELEMENT IN THE SOUTHERN MAINE ECONOMY, AS WELL AS A TOP AWARD WINNER FOR LEADERSHIP IN ENVIRONMENTAL PROTECTION. ■ AS THE WESTERN HEMISPHERE FELT THE

KIP BRUNDAGE

effects of World War II, reliable year-round delivery of crude oil to the Montreal refineries became vitally important to the economy. Portland Harbor, the nearest ice-free port, was chosen as the southern terminus of a new supply line, and the work was completed in five months of seven-day weeks and 11-hour workdays.

The pipeline—today consisting of one 18-inch line and one 24-inch line—runs 166 miles through Maine, New Hampshire, and Vermont, and then an additional 70 miles in Canada. Eight pump stations along the way keep the oil moving, as the pipeline rises from sea level at South Portland to a maximum elevation of 1,960 feet in northeastern Vermont. The original 12-inch pipeline laid in 1941 was replaced as the volume increased tenfold in the first 30 years. Today, PPL pumps in the range of 450,000 barrels a day.

Today, 250 big tankers a year bring in more than 170 million barrels of crude oil destined for pipeline transport to Montreal. That makes PPL the major generator of traffic and cargo in the harbor, and PPL constitutes decisive support for the infrastructure of the busy working harbor: the pilot and tugboat companies, the ship chandlers, and ships' agents that make for a seaport industry. Portland Harbor is one of the largest oil ports on the East Coast, and the facilities required for the oil transport industry service have various other uses as well.

Clean Environment

At the same time, PPL has twice won the U.S. Coast Guard's coveted William M. Benkert Award for excellence in marine environmental protection. While that means continuous attention to spill prevention and recovery preparation, another tangible demonstration is the presence of the flora and fauna that thrive in the area of the tanker off-loading facilities located near Spring Point in South Portland.

The Portland Pipe Line Corporation, which was swiftly built in desperate times, has grown and expanded into a healthy, major contributor to the economies of two regions, one in Canada and the other in northern New England, and continues to serve the communities and the environment of the Portland area and beyond. ●

PORTLAND PIPE LINE CORPORATION'S (PPL) PIPELINE HAS BECOME A KEY PART OF THE BUSTLING NETWORK OF COOPERATIVE ENERGY SUPPLIERS SHARED BY CANADA AND THE UNITED STATES.

KIP BRUNDAGE

Overhead Door Company of Portland has roots that reach back to 1921, to a barn in Detroit where the first overhead door was produced. In 2001, as one of more than 400 distributors nationwide, Overhead Door of Portland helped the Overhead Door Corporation celebrate its 80th birthday. ■ Founder C.G. Johnson began his company with a dedication to quality and a commitment to customer service. This legacy has endured and prospered through

eight decades, evolving into one of the most unique supplier/distributor relationships in the industry. More than 40 percent of distributorships are second- or third-generation companies.

In Portland, Maurice True's legacy followed much the same road—one paved with integrity, dedication, and diligence. Beginning in the home insulation industry in 1945, True transformed the company into a building specialties business. During the 1950s, he redirected the company into the garage door markets for home and industry.

A Distributor since 1972

The mission of Overhead Door Company of Portland has always been to provide value-added customer service through commitment to providing the highest-quality products, installation, and service. True started down this road of excellence in 1972, when he made one of the most important decisions of his life to become the exclusive authorized distributor for Overhead Door Corporation products in central and southern Maine and New Hampshire. With the help of sons Michael and James, True built an organization that began with four employees and two trucks into one operating from five locations in three states. The original workforce and vehicle fleet grew to today's total of some 60 employees and 35 trucks.

True realized that accomplishing his goals and achieving success required skilled, motivated employees. He passed on his passion for customer service through his own example, and developed skills through training. True promoted solutions and relationship selling techniques to grow his customer base. He encouraged employees to leverage the skills and resources of the company to increase product and service capabilities. True created a work environment of high ethics and a commitment to hard work that resulted in loyal, professional employees.

Today, the company's customers include many of the most successful contractors and businesses in Maine and New Hampshire. The company strives to provide the same level of service to all clients—from home owners to industry. Standard products include Thermacore insulated steel garage doors; OverDrive auto-

matic door openers; Jetroll high-performance, roll-up doors; and McGuire loading dock equipment. Unique product offerings, from custom carriage house garage doors for the home to sophisticated, computer-controlled automatic door systems for industry, are also available.

Partnership Produces Mutual Success

The Portland company's partnership with Dallas-based Overhead Door Corporation is the basis for their mutual success. Overhead Door's commitment to quality-engineered products and to providing world-class manufacturing solutions to meet customer delivery needs provides competitive advantages for its distribution network. The corporation's extensive research and development facility protects the quality and competitive cost of today's products, while providing innovative solutions to future customer needs. Together with the nationwide distribution system bearing the Overhead Door name, this teamwork is the primary factor in the company's success plan.

Home owners, businesses, and builders look for the red banner trademark that tells them they are dealing with the genuine and original Overhead Door. Customers know this company will not sacrifice quality and safety for price. ●

CLOCKWISE FROM TOP:
THE MISSION OF OVERHEAD DOOR COMPANY OF PORTLAND HAS ALWAYS BEEN TO PROVIDE VALUE-ADDED CUSTOMER SERVICE THROUGH COMMITMENT TO PROVIDING THE HIGHEST-QUALITY PRODUCTS, INSTALLATION, AND SERVICE.

OVERHEAD DOOR COMPANY PROVIDES A WIDE VARIETY OF QUALITY DOORS.

IN 2001, OVERHEAD DOOR CORPORATION CELEBRATED 80 YEARS OF SERVICE.

MAURICE TRUE, A DECORATED ARMY AIR CORPS OFFICER, RETURNED FROM WORLD WAR II IN 1945 TO FOUND A HOME INSULATION COMPANY THAT, IN 1972, BECAME A DISTRIBUTOR FOR OVERHEAD DOOR CORPORATION.

COMPLETED IN 1947, THE MAINE TURNPIKE WAS THE FIRST SUPERHIGHWAY BUILT IN NEW ENGLAND AND ONLY THE SECOND TOLL HIGHWAY BUILT IN THE UNITED STATES. WITH ITS BROAD LANES, SMOOTH SURFACE, AND PROMISE OF FAST, EFFICIENT TRAVEL, THE TURNPIKE REVOLUTIONIZED HOW MAINE RESIDENTS—AND THE COUNTRY—THOUGHT ABOUT AUTOMOBILE TRAVEL. ■ WHILE SUPERHIGHWAYS ARE NOW COMMONPLACE, THE MAINE TURNPIKE CONTINUES TO BE A LEADER IN SAFE AND EFFICIENT HIGHWAY TRAVEL.

Maine's Economic Lifeline ▶

The highway stretches 109 miles, from Kittery to Augusta. A critical link in a vast network of highways serving New England's largest state, the turnpike connects 10 of the state's 12 most populous urban centers, including Portland, the state's largest city. Nearly 70 million vehicles used the turnpike in 2000, and the highway continues to serve as Maine's economic lifeline.

The Maine Turnpike Authority was among the very first facilities in the Northeast to adopt a sophisticated electronic toll collection system. Today, nearly a third of the turnpike's users pay their tolls electronically without stopping at tollbooths. Maine Turnpike travelers are provided real-time information about road conditions, construction, and traffic delays on 1610 AM, the turnpike's highway advisory radio station. Traffic information is also relayed over a network of roadside electronic message boards.

A wealth of travel information, including emergency advisories, is available on the Maine Turnpike Authority's Web site, and thousands of turnpike users subscribe to the authority's e-mail traffic alert service. This communications system is constantly monitored and updated from the authority's central offices in Portland, so turnpike users can depend on getting accurate, timely information to help them plan their travel.

Thinking Ahead

During the spring of 2000, the Maine Turnpike Authority launched its Widening and Modernization program, a five-year, 30-mile, $135 million project. When the project is complete in late 2004, the turnpike will have a new, third travel lane from York to South Portland, as well as safety enhancements that will modernize the highway.

Working with cities, towns, and the Maine Department of Transportation, the Maine Turnpike Authority continues to design and build new interchanges that provide greater access to the turnpike, as well as much needed traffic relief to local roadways. The organization is also investing and promoting viable transportation alternatives like the Rideshare Program, serving southern and central Maine; the ZOOM Turnpike Express bus, which serves commuters from Biddeford and Portland; and the return of passenger rail service between Boston and Portland.

More than 50 years ago, the Maine Turnpike Authority took a bold step toward a promising economic future for Maine. As it enters the 21st century, the authority remains dedicated to providing innovative and outstanding service to Maine citizens and to welcoming millions of visitors every year. ●

CLOCKWISE FROM TOP:
MORE THAN 70 MILLION VEHICLES TRAVEL ON THE MAINE TURNPIKE EVERY YEAR.

THE MAINE TURNPIKE WAS ONE OF THE FIRST TOLL HIGHWAYS IN THE NORTHEAST TO ADOPT ELECTRONIC TOLL COLLECTION.

A TEAM OF TURNPIKE DISPATCHERS KEEPS TRAVELERS INFORMED OF TRAFFIC CONDITIONS 24 HOURS A DAY VIA THE INTERNET (WWW.MAINETURNPIKE.COM), TURNPIKE RADIO (1610 AM), AND ELECTRONIC MESSAGE BOARDS LOCATED ON THE HIGHWAY.

S OUTHERN MAINE TECHNICAL COLLEGE (SMTC) IS GROWING TO MEET THE NEEDS—BOTH ECONOMIC AND EDUCATIONAL—OF THE STATE OF MAINE. BY PREPARING QUALIFIED WORKERS DURING THESE TIMES OF FULL EMPLOYMENT, THE COLLEGE HAS BECOME INCREASINGLY RECOGNIZED AS THE SOLUTION TO THE LABOR NEEDS OF GREATER PORTLAND AND SOUTHERN MAINE. ■ WAYNE H. ROSS, PRESIDENT, EMPHASIZES THAT SMTC'S CONTINUED GROWTH LIES IN THE FACT THAT THE COLLEGE'S FOCUS IS

always on the student. "Students succeed when they are involved in meaningful relationships with business and industry," says Ross. "At SMTC, we make a commitment to providing a real-life professional connection whenever possible."

Based on enrollment rates, *Biz Magazine* has ranked SMTC among the 10 highest-rated colleges and universities in the state. SMTC also has one of the lowest tuition rates of all of the state's some 30 higher education institutions.

A History of Success

L ocated on Casco Bay, Southern Maine Technical College is the largest and oldest of Maine's technical colleges. The 80-acre campus was the former site of historic Fort Preble, and includes more than 40 buildings of architectural significance. Set on a peninsula jutting into Portland Harbor, the college offers students direct access to Maine's spectacular coastline, as well as close proximity to Portland's cultural and social offerings.

Founded in Augusta as a trade school for returning GIs in 1946, the college moved to south Portland in the early 1950s, after the army abandoned Fort Preble. Southern Maine Vocational Technical Institute became Southern Maine Technical College in the late 1980s, reflecting the school's growth away from strictly vocational training.

Community Partnerships

B ecause SMTC's focus is on preparing students to succeed in their communities, many of the college's certificate and degree programs are conducted in partnership with local commercial and noncommercial enterprises.

SMTC and the South Portland Housing Authority jointly operate the Betsy Ross House, a 123-unit, congregate care facility adjacent to the campus. The intent is that, once the facility is fully occupied, SMTC students will provide internships in the areas of food service, security, landscaping, and incidental maintenance. Students will also provide care to at-risk community members and, in return, gain valuable professional experience.

SMTC's Peter A. McKernan Hospitality Center is an eight-room inn and conference center boasting extraordinary views of the Portland skyline and Casco Bay. The center serves as a practicum site for students enrolled in the Hotel, Motel, Restaurant Management Degree Program. The center caters to businesses and educational groups, as well as weddings and anniversaries. It is managed and staffed by students under the professional guidance of faculty. Lodging at the center is competitively priced and available year-round. Lunch is served to the public on Mondays and Tuesdays by reservation. The companion Culinary Arts Program serves public lunches in the SMTC dining room Wednesday through Friday. Similar to the McKernan center, the program serves as a practicum site for students enrolled in the Culinary Arts Degree Program. The dining room, located on the top floor of the Culinary Arts Center, overlooks Casco Bay.

The campus's computerized learning classroom is available to work groups in need of training facilities. The Spring Point Media Center

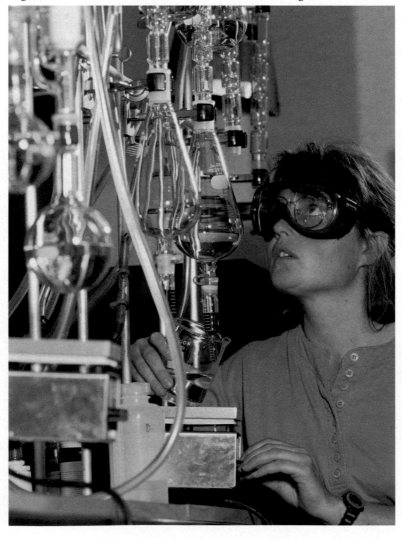

TECHNICAL DEGREE PROGRAMS ENABLE SOUTHERN MAINE TECHNICAL COLLEGE (SMTC) STUDENTS TO MEET MAINE'S GROWING NEED FOR A HIGHLY SKILLED LABOR FORCE.

offers—at cost—multimedia marketing services to area nonprofit organizations. The Early Childhood Development Program places interns at local businesses, public schools, and nonprofit organizations—greatly strengthening the area's growing demand for skilled child care workers.

The Portland Harbor Museum, Casco Bay Keeper, Maine Fire Training and Education program, Center for Environmental Enterprise, and Marine Animal Lifeline are all located on SMTC's campus, providing bridges between student experience and the Portland community. The college's Tech Prep program works to prepare high school age students in the field of technology.

The Students

Since 1990, SMTC has been in a growth spiral. "The job market has been so tight that some students finish their first semester here and employers are already offering them jobs," Ross says. "Our allied health programs have become so accomplished that local hospitals, such as Maine Medical Center, have been known to hire entire graduating classes."

SMTC attracts a high percentage of first-generation college students. Some 40 percent of SMTC's student population comes straight out of high school, but an astonishing 42 percent have had previous postsecondary education and are returning for training in new job skills.

The average SMTC student is 27 years old. Although the largest percent-

age of students comes from southern Maine, the school draws students from all over the state and beyond. The fastest-growing programs are in technology and computers, but construction, plumbing, and heating and air-conditioning continue to grow as well.

The College's Success

Ross says that Southern Maine Technical College's ability to react quickly to the needs of business and industry has been the key to its

success. "Unlike a four-year school, we can change gears within a few months," Ross explains. "If an outside employer has a training need, we can accommodate without having to go to our board of trustees for approval. If the needs continue, we take it to our board and make it a permanent part of our curriculum. Community colleges are the fastest-growing segment of postsecondary education. We just seem to keep outgrowing everything we do." ●

FROM THE DAYS OF PIONEERING TELEVISION COVERAGE OF THE MAINE LEGISLATURE TO LIVE COVERAGE OF NATURAL DISASTERS, THE WCSH 6 STAFF HAS EARNED A RICHNESS OF AWARDS. IN ADDITION TO RECOGNITION FROM THE MAINE ASSOCIATION OF BROADCASTERS, MAINE ASSOCIATED PRESS, NATIONAL RADIO TELEVISION NEWS DIRECTORS ASSOCIATION, AND OTHER PROFESSIONAL ORGANIZATIONS, THE AWARD THAT REALLY COUNTS COMES FROM THE VIEWERS WHO CONSISTENTLY CHOOSE NEWS CENTER 6.

News Center 6 broadcasts have led the Nielsen ratings in the area since 1986 in the early morning, at noon, and for the four afternoon-evening broadcasts from 5 to 11 p.m. WCSH 6 audience share points reach up to 69 percent.

WCSH 6 is proud of its long-standing leadership and dominance in the southern Maine market. Steve Thaxton, president and general manager, speaks with pride of the public acceptance of the station's statewide News Center and public affairs commitment. "The ultimate recognition for a news station is long-term viewership," Thaxton says. "Our team never takes that support for granted."

News, Service, Stability

Community service and the station's approach to news at WCSH 6 are so integrated that it is hard to separate them. An important element in WCSH 6's brand identity is the stable character of the local staff. The core on-air team, for example, has been together for more than a decade. Many staffers have served more than 20 years. Many staff members are stakeholders in local community activities, continuing a dedication to volunteerism that began with the original owners, the Rines-Thompson family.

WCSH 6 was launched in 1953 by William Rines, a member of the family that founded WCSH Radio, Maine's first commercial radio station, in 1925. When Rines' sister, Mary Rines Thompson, became chairman of the family-owned business, she guided the television station through many years of prominence as the top-ranked news source in the Portland market. Thompson's insistence on community involvement through volunteerism continues as a hallmark of WCSH 6 today.

When the Rines-Thompson family decided to transfer ownership of WCSH 6 in Portland and WLBZ 2 in Bangor, they spent a year seeking a new owner with the same community dedication, values, and staff loyalty the stations had promoted during their 73 years of broadcasting in Maine. Fred Thompson, then president and chairman of the board, said the family had found such an owner in the Gannett Company, the publisher of *USA Today*.

New Owner, Added Strength

WCSH 6's preeminence in news and public affairs has continued under the Gannett ownership. Gannett Broadcasting consists of 22 television stations covering 17.4 percent of the homes across the nation. The Gannett Company also publishes 99 daily newspapers and 200 nondaily publications in the United States, including *USA Today*, the nation's

CLOCKWISE FROM TOP: WCSH 6 IS CURRENTLY LOCATED AT ONE CONGRESS SQUARE.

(FROM LEFT) KEVIN MANNIX, SHARON ROSE, AND LEE NELSON MAKE UP NEWS CENTER'S NUMBER-ONE-RATED MORNING TEAM.

NOTED FOR HER COMMUNITY SERVICE EFFORTS, MARY RINES THOMPSON WAS THE PRESIDENT AND CHAIRMAN OF THE BOARD OF WCSH 6 FROM 1970 TO 1983.

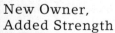

largest in circulation, and has media properties abroad. Gannett Broadcasting also has a strong Internet presence.

WCSH 6 brought much to its new relationship with Gannett, including a history of local community involvement, as well as the station's unusual status as one of the original affiliates with the NBC network. On display in the lobby is what is thought to be the only remaining set of the original NBC chimes in the country.

Gannett Broadcasting has also added to the strength of its Maine stations. Investments in equipment have made it possible for both WCSH 6 and WLBZ 2 to better serve their audiences and sponsors. The shared News Center concept allows the stations to uniquely serve the entire state and parts of Canada. Gannett ownership opened the doors to shared ideas and high-tech investments. "We share ideas," says Thaxton. "A good idea is originated and refined somewhere in the group, and then we consider it for our Maine viewers."

Public Outreach

WCSH 6 creates events to be shared with a participating public. Since 1965, the annual WCSH 6 Sidewalk Arts Festival has attracted more than 60,000 people to downtown Congress Street in August. More than 270 artists from the East Coast and Canada display their original art at the one-day festival, which is one of the largest such events on the East Coast. During the festival, Congress Street is closed to all traffic to accommodate the return of pedestrians to the city center.

In 1982, WCSH 6 created the Maine State Parade in Maine's second-largest city, Lewiston. The spring event draws tens of thousands of spectators to watch the marching of more than 100 groups, observe the competitive floats, and cheer on their favorite school bands, which compete for prizes and trophies.

In its long history of volunteer recognition, WCSH 6, in cooperation with United Way of Greater Portland

and Peoples Heritage Bank, sponsors 6 Who Care, a gala celebration to honor men and women from throughout the state of Maine who unselfishly make a difference in the lives of others. The community service of young people is recognized in a separate Teens Who Care awards program. Once a week during the school year, Bruce Glasier, WCSH 6 sports director, profiles outstanding student athletes on a varsity club segment. Over the years, many of Maine's youth have included that recognition on their college application forms.

The ongoing Many Hands program assists a staff-chosen volunteer organization from somewhere in Maine. Each month, that organization receives heavy on-air support, as the group's own members staff a bank of telephones to log in offers of funds and help. Many Hands taps into Maine's barn raising heritage. Some organizations have gained hundreds of new volunteers as a result of the program.

WCSH 6 is a unique local television station in a unique broadcast group that cherishes Maine tradition, reports the news, reflects the values of Maine people in Maine communities, and celebrates Maine's motto, "Maine, the way life should be." ●

CLOCKWISE FROM TOP:
THE NEWS CENTER 6 P.M. ANCHOR TEAM OF (FROM LEFT) CINDY WILLIAMS, PAT CALLAGHAN, BRUCE GLASIER, AND JOE CUPO HAS BEEN TOGETHER ON WCSH 6 FOR MORE THAN A DECADE.

THE ORIGINAL OPERATIONS ROOM AT WCSH RADIO WAS LOCATED ATOP THE CONGRESS SQUARE HOTEL.

ONE OF SEVERAL WCSH 6 COMMUNITY SERVICE EFFORTS, MANY HANDS HELPS FIND VOLUNTEERS FOR LOCAL NONPROFIT ORGANIZATIONS.

SINCE 1982, DiMillo's Floating Restaurant has been serving exceptional seafood, as well as American and Italian cuisine, to the citizens of Portland. Yet, DiMillo's place in Portland's history and culture goes far beyond simply being a top-quality restaurant. ■ The restaurant's founder, the late Tony DiMillo, is credited with sparking the resurgence of what was until the 1970s a decaying Old Port district. Against a lot of advice, DiMillo purchased an old car

ferry and renovated it into a restaurant that has become nationally famous. And yes, the restaurant really is afloat. At low tide, the hull rests on 12 feet of Portland Harbor water.

From Cars to Cuisine

DiMillo's first restaurant, Anthony's, opened on Fore Street in 1954. DiMillo trumpeted the freshness of the seafood with the slogan, "The clams you eat here today slept last night in Casco Bay." In 1960, the restaurant moved a few blocks to Center Street. Then, as DiMillo's on the Waterfront, it opened on Commercial Street in 1967. DiMillo's Lobster House quickly became one of Portland's most popular restaurants, as people came from all over the country for its renowned lobster dinners.

In 1978, DiMillo bought the dilapidated Long Wharf, which projected into the harbor at a point just across the street from the site of his existing restaurant. He built DiMillo's Marina,

THE LONG WHARF PROMENADE, WHICH RUNS ALONG THE WEST SIDE OF LONG WHARF, WAS DESIGNED BY THE DiMILLO FAMILY TO GIVE THE PUBLIC CONVENIENT ACCESS TO PORTLAND'S PICTURESQUE WATERFRONT.

THE DiMILLO FAMILY MAINTAINS A HANDS-ON APPROACH TO THE MANAGEMENT OF ITS RESTAURANT. PICTURED HERE ARE (SEATED, FROM LEFT) JEANETTE BREGGIA, ARLENE DiMILLO, JUSTINA IRES, (STANDING, FROM LEFT) GENE DiMILLO, JOHNNY DiMILLO, CHRIS DiMILLO, DAN DiMILLO, TONY DiMILLO JR., AND STEVE DiMILLO.

and soon developed a business that filled all 130 boat slips. DiMillo was one of the first entrepreneurs to develop one of the harbor piers into a consumer-oriented business that co-existed side by side with commercial fishing and the other marine-related industries that still used the waterfront.

In 1980, DiMillo purchased a deactivated car ferry, outfitted its interior as a quality place to enjoy a meal, and opened it as DiMillo's Floating Restaurant. The waterborne restaurant—sitting at Long Wharf among hundreds of boats—is one of the largest such businesses in the United States and the only one on the upper East Coast.

Originally commissioned as the *New York* in 1941, the boat ran as a car ferry in several East Coast areas and was a clubhouse and boat storage facility in Port Jefferson, New York, when DiMillo bought it. The boat is 206 feet long and 65 feet in the beam. It weighs 701 tons and still contains a deactivated, 1,500-horsepower steam engine.

The onetime ferry, its bare steel interior now warmly appointed in

wood paneling and brass rails, numerous authentic nautical artifacts, and photos from the vessel's past, opened as a restaurant in 1982. It seats 600 in the First Deck Dining Room, Port Side Lounge, Second Deck Dining Room, and three outside decks.

In 1994, a 225-ton, steel-and-concrete hull was welded over the 53-year-old original. The first hull was narrow—suitable for a ferry. The new one is broad, making it extraordinarily stable. Hurricane-force winds will cause the boat to heel no more than 1 percent. The addition of four feet of freeboard largely eliminated the slope when customers come aboard from the wharf at low tide.

As was not at all unusual with DiMillo, the hull project was something of a show. Three tugboats moved the restaurant down the waterfront to the Bath Iron Works dry dock, where the new hull awaited installation. The shell was dropped underwater, the restaurant vessel positioned above it, and the dry dock raised. After the welding, 450,000 pounds of concrete was poured between the hulls.

The restaurant was named by *Restaurant Hospitality* magazine as one of the top 100 revenue generators in the country, but that is not the whole story. Late in life, DiMillo developed Long Wharf into a public walkway and harbor-viewing platform, complete with a genuine segment of the Berlin Wall taken down when the Communist regime collapsed in East Germany in 1989.

A Family Dedicated to Portland

DiMillo's unremitting loyalty to Portland, and his faith in the city, existed from his boyhood on India Street. He bought Long Wharf around the time the city was acting to remove raw sewage from the harbor. DiMillo correctly predicted an influx of local people and tourists, together with businesses and the accompanying economic boom.

DiMillo died in 1999, but today at the restaurant there is always a DiMillo on board. The family members share the management, decision making, and supervision of DiMillo's. Tony's wife, Arlene DiMillo, is actively involved in the business. His sisters, Justina Ives and Jeanette Breggia, who worked with him from day one at Anthony's in 1954, still work there. DiMillo's six sons—Gene, Steven, Tony Jr., Dan, John, and Chris—are involved in the restaurant and in the associated marina and its store.

DiMillo was praised for his vision and courage, and his fellow citizens did not forget his contributions to Portland. The year before he died, DiMillo was the guest of honor at a surprise unveiling of a monument to

him on Commercial Street in front of DiMillo's Floating Restaurant.

Bluntness and a sense of humor were among DiMillo's trademarks. When an interviewer asked him in 1999 whether the public-access project

on the wharf had an undertone of enticing people into the restaurant, he replied, "Trust me. If you go out there and it's a pleasant day, like today, they're all brown baggers, which is fine." ●

SET IN THE SCENIC PORTLAND HARBOR, DiMILLO'S FLOATING RESTAURANT HAS BEEN A PORTLAND LANDMARK SINCE ITS FOUNDING IN 1982.

DiMILLO'S FLOATING RESTAURANT ALSO FEATURES A GIFT SHOP WHERE PATRONS CAN PICK UP THAT PERFECT GIFT.

SERVING AS A SPECIALTY FOOD PRODUCTS COMPANY—ONE WHICH IS EXTREMELY SUCCESSFUL IN A MARKETPLACE WHERE SOME OF ITS MANY COMPETITORS ARE 100 TIMES ITS SIZE—BARBER FOODS GOT ITS START IN PORTLAND IN 1955 BY FOUNDER AUGUSTUS (GUS) BARBER. BARBER INVENTED THE COMPANY'S LEAD SPECIALTY, A STUFFED CHICKEN ENTRÉE, AMONG OTHER NOW-STANDARD AMERICAN AND INTERNATIONAL FOOD ITEMS. ■ THE SUCCESS OF BARBER FOODS, REPRESENTED BY DOUBLE-DIGIT ANNUAL GROWTH, COMES FROM CONSTANT

innovation, the courage to take risks, a rigid insistence upon quality, and a significant investment in the company's people. Now, more than 500 food items are manufactured in a state-of-the-art plant staffed by more than 750 associates from 49 countries, speaking 52 distinct languages.

Yet, this is a family company now driven by the second generation of the Barber family. The Barber leadership of today builds upon Gus Barber's early success by introducing new products and enlarging the customer base, just as the elder Barber did for 30 years until he handed the company over to his son Stephen in 1985.

Focus, Innovation, Quality

Current President Stephen Barber says the secret to the modern Barber Foods is its organizational focus. "We design the business so we can be very effective in the areas we decide to enter. It's the specialist versus the generalist. We'll be the best at what we've picked in our ability to execute. We're not trying to be a very large firm," he says. David Barber, vice president of sales and marketing, emphasizes two essential elements in the company's success: product innovation and product development.

Julie Barber, sister of Stephen and David, serves as director of national accounts. Her description of Barber Foods' corporate culture intermingles

BARBER FOODS HAS BEEN FAMILY RUN SINCE ITS INCEPTION. MEMBERS OF THE BARBER FAMILY CURRENTLY INVOLVED IN THE BUSINESS INCLUDE (FROM TOP LEFT) DAVID, STEPHEN, KATHRYN, GUS, MARJORIE, AND JULIE.

STUFFED CHICKEN BREASTS ARE A BARBER FOODS SPECIALTY.

the concentration on quality with the concept of how people and human values permeate the organization. "Product quality is what brings our success," she says. "People prefer our great quality over the big companies with whom we compete. Our associates make it happen. Success doesn't preclude having a heart."

Julie recalls a most unexpected example of associates' commitment outside the process itself. A huge snowstorm, which caused the plant roof to cave in, hit the area while all the family members were away. Julie, the first of the Barbers to arrive at the scene the next day, found the place full of associates clearing the snow and wreckage, building temporary walls, and setting the plant up to operate again as quickly as possible. The employees were not called to come in

and clean up the wreckage. "The supervisor said they all just kept showing up," she says.

Roots of a Clever Company

The reason for that kind of loyalty and commitment is plain, as is the source of the company's marketplace agility. It is Gus Barber himself, born of Armenian parents who left Turkey, along with a group of other refugees, to escape persecution. The small colony of Armenian families stuck together, and young Gus Barber worked in a fellow Armenian's supermarket on Congress Street after returning from World War II. His entrepreneurial spirit sent him into business for himself in a few years, opening his own beef-and-chicken preparation operation with

ASSOCIATE DIVERSITY AND EDUCATION
ARE KEYS TO BARBER FOODS' SUCCESS.

nothing but a sharp knife, an old truck, and wife Marjorie, who did all the bookkeeping.

Gus Barber was inventive, putting together circumstance and a shrewd sense of people's needs in ways that produced a series of landmark product introductions. He was the first to market separate chicken parts rather than the entire bird, the first to sell boned chicken breasts, the first with sized portions. Then he invented the battered-breaded chicken nugget/finger. Then he dreamed up the stuffed chicken breast. In each instance, he took a need or desire expressed by a customer, or the waste byproduct of another process, or a bright idea, and came up with an instant bestseller.

"It's part of my heritage," Gus Barber says. "We wouldn't throw anything away. It also was a willingness to take chances when people warned it just wouldn't work."

Through it all, the company has maintained an obsession with quality. Barber Foods has never competed on the basis of price. Gus Barber refused to run that kind of business, because the things that mattered to him went in the other direction; providing what people want, and making it good. The growth of the company is the best proof of that philosophy.

Commitment: People, Diversity, Training

One important corollary of the company's emphasis on quality, and a major result of Gus' personal heritage, is the way employees are treated at Barber Foods. The company has been nationally recognized for its training and education programs and its commitment to diversity. Gus teaches citizenship in the programs, which also include English as a Second Language, computer skills, and mathematics.

In a more basic way, Barber Foods puts its decisions where its statements are. While its low turnover rate is often the envy of the industry, it can't find all the people it needs to fill associate positions. So the company, like every other heads-up organization, is looking to future automation. One standing expectation is that no one will lose a job as the process undergoes innovation. The commitment to associates, product quality, and Barber Foods' customers will always come first. ●

GUS BARBER ESTABLISHED A HERITAGE OF
NEW PRODUCT INNOVATION.

BROWN CONSTRUCTION, INC. HAS PROVIDED BUILDING AND RENOVATION SERVICES FOR INSTITUTIONAL, INDUSTRIAL, AND RETAIL CLIENTS SINCE 1935, AND THE COMPANY HAS BEEN ONE OF SOUTHERN MAINE'S LEADERS IN CONSTRUCTION INDUSTRY QUALITY AND INNOVATION FOR DECADES. ■ KNOWN AS A BUILDER OF QUALITY PROJECTS SUCH AS SCHOOLS, HOSPITALS, AND INDUSTRIAL FACILITIES, BROWN CONSTRUCTION'S VOLUME OF BUSINESS HAS DEVELOPED A LONG LIST OF SATISFIED CLIENTS

over its many years of service, with $10 million in annual revenue. Companies and institutions built in cooperation with Brown include Bath Iron Works, L.L. Bean, Poland Spring, General Electric, Data General, Wal-Mart, and Maine Medical Center.

In the late 1960s, Brown began erecting pre-engineered buildings by becoming an authorized builder for several leaders in the field. With the growth of its capabilities in that area, Brown Construction also established itself in the forefront of the design/build construction management method of operation.

Expertise in Design/Build

Brown's expertise in combining design and construction functions under its one-source management is a strong component of its market position. Brown can assure the client of reduced cost in both construction and ongoing operation of the new facility, while shortening the construction schedule and retaining the quality upon which Brown has built its reputation.

Although the company remains highly competitive in the conventional owner/architect/contractor relationship through competitive bidding, Brown feels that the design/build method benefits the owner most by ensuring quality at reduced cost and

time, while dealing with a single source of responsibility.

Brown has handled projects up to $13 million in value, ranging in square footage from 2,400 to 280,000. Exacting specifications are normal procedure for Brown, having built high-tech clean rooms for National Semiconductor of South Portland, as well as specialty manufacturing quarters for other clients that required air and temperature control and/or exotic piping and systems; freezers as part of buildings for Shaw's Supermarkets; and enormous manufacturing buildings for Bath Iron Works.

Brown was the first company in Maine to build a rack-supported structure on a super-flat slab, which it did in 1985. The company's work

has received numerous awards for quality and its safety record.

Succession of Employee Owners

Brown's reputation and record depend upon the company's practice of retaining longtime, experienced employees, and continuing to add newer associates with the latest skills in technology and materials.

Edward Brown began his construction company in 1935. The modern version of Brown Construction dates from 1956, when six employees bought the company and incorporated it. Since then, ownership has been handed down from one group of employees to another in a remarkable display of continuity and confidence. Current owners are President Gerard P. Maskalenko and Vice Presidents Paul Henick and Jeffrey D. Girardin.

The future, in the thinking of Brown's leaders and employees, will be one of innovation. New materials, new technologies, and new construction techniques mean a greater range of choices and scheduling challenges than ever before.

Brown Construction, Inc., having pursued its original philosophy of quality through a history of innovation, is ready to meet the needs of future customers and exceed their expectations of service. ●

KNOWN AS A BUILDER OF QUALITY PROJECTS SUCH AS SCHOOLS, HOSPITALS, AND INDUSTRIAL FACILITIES, BROWN CONSTRUCTION'S VOLUME OF BUSINESS HAS DEVELOPED A LONG LIST OF SATISFIED CLIENTS OVER ITS MANY YEARS OF SERVICE.

WHEN DONALD W. COOK STARTED ALLIED/COOK CONSTRUCTION CORP. IN 1958, THEN KNOWN AS ALLIED CONSTRUCTION CO. INC., HE WAS VIRTUALLY THE ONLY EMPLOYEE. HE BORROWED WORKING CAPITAL FROM HIS MOTHER AND WIFE, ALICE, AND OPERATED FROM HIS HOME. COOK WAS INVOLVED IN ALL ASPECTS OF THE BUSINESS—THE ESTIMATING, SELLING, AND PROJECT MANAGEMENT— ALTHOUGH HIS EXPERIENCE HAD BEEN LIMITED TO SUPERVISING THE CONSTRUCTION WORK ITSELF.

But Cook had one advantage in the marketplace: People enjoyed doing business with him. As son David, now president of the company, says, "People liked and trusted him. He did what he said he'd do."

More than four decades later, a much-larger and more complex company, building large business structures in a far different world, prides itself on having preserved that tradition of integrity. In fact, three project superintendents hired by Cook in the early 1960s—Al Greene, Joe Robey, and Gordon Robinson—are still with the company today.

Family Involvement

When Donald Cook died in 1977, he left the business to his wife and five children. David, 26 years old at the time, had been a full-time company employee for five years. He bought out the other stockholders in the mid-1990s, becoming sole owner of the company. For some years, David's brothers Donald Jr. and Richard also worked with the firm.

When the company name changed in 1998 to Allied/Cook Construction Corp., a reality that had existed for some 15 years was recognized: No longer simply a general contractor, Allied now was a construction management and design/build company. While outsourcing design work as needed, the firm concentrated on its specialty: the planning, management, and the successful delivery of building construction projects.

Another significant change came in the mid-1990s, with the culmination of a long effort, as David Cook puts it, "to get the right people and get the buildings we wanted to do." Marketing Vice President Tom Perry arrived at that time, and was a key figure in a business approach in which Allied/Cook does not just look at buildings or projects, but looks beyond to opportunities for long-term relationships.

Philosophy Continues

That approach continues the philosophy of Cook who, in 1958, set out to develop a clientele that supported the company through referrals and repeat business—the source of a large part of the current business.

As the third generation is moving into the company, David's son Daniel handles personnel and resource issues in the field. Another son, Matthew, is a student at the University of Denver earning advanced degrees in business, construction management, and real estate. His daughter Sarah provides technical support to project managers and estimators.

There are some 12 construction professionals in the office, along with a field staff, 12 superintendents, and some 40 skilled craftspeople, all of whom have helped Allied/Cook along the way. Signature buildings for the company include Blue Cross/ Blue Shield Anthem and the Guy Gannett Building, both west of the Maine Mall in South Portland; 100 Middle Street in downtown Portland; the Shops at Falmouth Village; and the Department of Human Services building on Marginal Way in Portland.

Today, nearly 100 percent of Allied/ Cook's business is done on a private negotiated basis, continuing the tradition of trust established by Donald Cook. "We've carried that trust culture through the company's development," David Cook says. "When you do what you say you'll do, people trust you. The business has changed a lot—it's much more complex today. But people don't change." ●

SOME OF ALLIED/COOK CONSTRUCTION CORP.'S MOST NOTABLE PROJECTS INCLUDE (FROM TOP) 100 MIDDLE STREET, THE PRINTING FACILITY FOR GUY GANNETT PUBLISHING CO., AND BLUE CROSS/BLUE SHIELD ANTHEM.

FAIRCHILD SEMICONDUCTOR INTERNATIONAL IS A COMMERCIALLY DYNAMIC GLOBAL CORPORATION HEADQUARTERED IN SOUTH PORTLAND, MAINE. THE COMPANY DESIGNS AND BUILDS THE WORLD'S LARGEST PORTFOLIO OF HIGH-PERFORMANCE BUILDING BLOCK SEMICONDUCTORS USED IN MULTIPLE END MARKETS. THESE PRODUCTS ARE THE INTEGRATED CIRCUITS USED IN REGULATING POWER IN CELL PHONES, SPEEDING DATA TRANSFER ON THE INTERNET, INCREASING THE PORTABILITY OF WIRELESS

FAIRCHILD'S PRODUCTS, SOME SMALL ENOUGH TO BE CARRIED OFF BY AN ANT, ENSURE INCREASED PORTABILITY OF A WIDE VARIETY OF TECHNOLOGIES, INCLUDING HAND-HELD GAMES, CELLULAR PHONES, AND MOBILE COMPUTERS.

A 40-FOOT BANNER, WHICH WAS USED ON THE FRONT OF THE NEW YORK STOCK EXCHANGE DURING FAIRCHILD'S LAUNCH ON WALL STREET IN AUGUST 1999, IS SHOWN ON THE COMPANY'S SOUTH PORTLAND MANUFACTURING PLANT ON WESTERN AVENUE.

applications, illuminating displays in all types of appliances, and helping to provide electrical power to just about every type of product that plugs into a wall socket.

Fairchild was launched as an independent company in 1997 as the industry's first management-led leveraged buyout. Since then, Fairchild has tripled revenues and successfully introduced thousands of new products into the semiconductor market. With more than 1,600 employees in South Portland and nearly 11,000 worldwide, the company offers exciting and diverse opportunities.

Kirk Pond, president, CEO, and chairman of the board of Fairchild, has been a key part of the focused transitions of recent years. Pond took the helm in 1997, when Fairchild was reborn. Several acquisitions and the strategic multi-market business model focusing on power solutions for more than 50,000 customers worldwide have made Fairchild the leading multi-market supplier of high-performance

components. The success of these strategies positioned the company to go public on the New York Stock Exchange in August 1999.

Grassroots History

With the original Fairchild Semiconductor recognized as the founder of California's Silicon Valley, Fairchild is built on a legacy of innovative excellence, with roots that reach into the beginning of the semiconductor industry. In 1957, Sherman Mills Fairchild, founder of Fairchild Camera and Instrument Corporation, sponsored a small group of young scientists in their development of a new process for the manufacture of transistors.

The goal of the Fairchild scientists—among them Robert Noyce and Gordon Moore, eventual founders of Intel Corporation—was to develop, mass produce, and market semiconductor components that would meet the most stringent specifications. They reached that goal in 1959, with

the introduction of the planar process. Planar technology became the fundamental method of producing transistors and integrated circuits, and is still in use today.

The company's early integrated circuits made history, helping the United States win the race to the moon and revolutionizing the computer industry. Now Fairchild is recognized for another distinctive characteristic: It is the world's first company focused exclusively on the design and manufacture of high-performance semiconductor products for multiple applications, serving the computing, Internet hardware, telecommunications, consumer, industrial, automotive and aerospace markets.

Diverse Business Units

Fairchild is comprised of the Interface & Logic Group in South Portland, Maine; the Discrete Power and Signal Technologies Group in San Jose, California; the Power Device business in Puchon, South

Korea; the Analog & Mixed Signal Group in West Jordan, Utah; and the Optoelectronics Group also in San Jose, California. These businesses create the products that light up dashboards, power cell phones and remote controls, process information on laptops, control CD and DVD players and power the technologies that shape how our world interacts.

Fairchild has assembly and test plants in Cebu, the Philippines; Kuala Lumpur and Penang, Malaysia; and Wuxi, China. The South Portland site has continuously manufactured semiconductors longer than any facility in the world.

A Legacy of Innovation

Through the years, Fairchild has captured worldwide attention for semiconductor innovation and manufacturing excellence. When the U.S. Postal Service issued a stamp to commemorate the introduction of the integrated circuit as part of its Celebrate the Century series, it used a diode-transistor logic chip that was developed by Fairchild Semiconductor in 1964. Fairchild hosted the worldwide unveiling of the stamp in 1999.

Fairchild continues to enable its customers to maintain a competitive edge in meeting and exceeding the needs of growing global markets now and in the future. The keys include the company's focus on new product development, high-quality manufacturing, and superior customer service, all supported by Fairchild's skilled workforce. Its strategy looks to make a prosperous future for the company whose roots gave life to the semiconductor industry. ●

FOR BUSINESS TRAVELERS IN THE PORTLAND AREA WHO ARE TIRED OF THE HASSLES AND RUNAROUND INVOLVED WITH FLYING A MAJOR AIRLINE TO MEETINGS—THE FIXED SCHEDULES, THE PLANE CHANGES, THE LARGE FARES—THERE IS AN ALTERNATIVE. MAINE AVIATION CORPORATION CAN SAFELY AND EFFICIENTLY TRANSPORT TRAVELERS TO AIRPORTS ONLY MINUTES FROM ANY MEETING SITE, AND THEN RETURN THEM THAT SAME DAY—ELIMINATING TIME AND MONEY SPENT ON UNDESIRABLE OVERNIGHTS, LONG TICKET

lines, parking hassles, flight delays, and even lost luggage.

Maine Aviation was founded by brothers Joe and Tom Caruso, who, just out of the military after World War II, took the advice of their Uncle Sully and started flying scenic flights in a seaplane from the Hinckley boat dock in Southwest Harbor in 1947. By their third year, the brothers had leased the Bar Harbor Airport, finding a permanent home for their aviation business. Then, in 1959, Joe Caruso moved his family to Portland, where he established Maine Aviation Corporation.

There never was any question about the future of Allyn "Al" Caruso, Joe's son: He literally grew up on the flight ramp at the Bar Harbor Airport, and during his high school years fueled and washed planes at the Portland airport. Al Caruso flew for Bar Harbor Airways and, at age 19, became an airline captain.

Today, Al Caruso is joined in operating Maine Aviation by his wife, Alysan, general manager, and their younger son, Travis, who is director of maintenance. Al and Alysan's

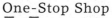

MAINE AVIATION CORPORATION IS PROUD TO BE NEW ENGLAND'S OLDEST CESSNA AIRCRAFT DEALER (TOP).

MAINE AVIATION'S SALES TEAM PROVIDES PROFESSIONAL ADVICE AND SUPPORT ON EVERY ASPECT OF THE SALES TRANSACTION, WHETHER IT IS A SINGLE-ENGINE AIRCRAFT OR A LARGE CORPORATE JET (BOTTOM).

older son, Tom, was the company's chief pilot for several years, and now flies for Continental Airlines.

For three generations, Maine Aviation and the Caruso family have been providing aviation services to the private, corporate, commercial, and general aviation community. Maine Aviation's Cessna Pilot Center has been teaching people to fly for more than 40 years. "Maine Aviation's success is a result of our dedication

to total customer satisfaction as our number one business objective," says Al Caruso. "Our broad range of services and capabilities permit us to offer a full complement of professional support—from aircraft management to charter, maintenance, aircraft sales, flight training, and shared ownership programs. Our company takes great pride in our excellent reputation for exceptional standards of safety, reliability, and professionalism."

One-Stop Shop

Maine Aviation operates a fleet of charter aircraft based in several locations to serve a broad range of charter needs. The company's on-demand aircraft charter offers a variety of aircraft, from large luxury jets to light jets and turboprops for the shorter trips. Maine Aviation's experienced dispatchers and professional customer service personnel are available 24 hours a day, seven days a week, to meet clients' most demanding travel requests. These employees are able to respond quickly with the right solution for any travel itinerary. "Only one phone call for all travel needs—from ground transportation, catering, and hotel arrangements to comfortable, direct charter flights—is just part of our exceptional service," Alysan

Caruso says. "We aim to be our clients' travel solution."

Maine Aviation is proud to be New England's oldest authorized Cessna Aircraft Dealer and one of the top Cessna single-engine aircraft dealers in the country. Al Caruso says, "Each year, an increasing number of our sales are from repeat or referral customers—a testimony to the quality of our sales assistance and postsale attention. Our numbers speak for themselves."

Aircraft Ownership Made Easy

Maine Aviation makes aircraft ownership easy. An experienced sales staff helps evaluate the buyer's needs and makes recommendations—whether for a single-engine aircraft or a corporate jet—based on firsthand experience. Throughout the entire process, Maine Aviation provides professional advice and support on every aspect of the transaction, from price negotiations and contract details to prepurchase inspections, test flights, and postdelivery modifications. Guided by Maine Aviation's knowledge and market experience, the buyer always purchases the best aircraft at the best price.

Maine Aviation's maintenance facility is a licensed FAA repair station. Whether it is an inspection, general maintenance, airframe or power-plant repairs, or a major overhaul, experienced, factory-trained technicians are committed to responding promptly to maintenance needs. Routine and prepurchase inspections are available on all general aviation aircraft from single-engine aircraft to large corporate jets. "Our avionics department provides complete in-house capabilities and the latest avionics equipment

specifically tailored to the individual needs of our customers," says Travis Caruso. "We inspect, install, troubleshoot, service, and repair nearly every type of equipment. Our avionics center is staffed with highly trained and experienced technicians supported by state-of-the-art test equipment."

Aircraft ownership can make substantial demands on company time and personnel. Maine Aviation's management professionals can manage a client's aircraft while the client retains full control. Maine Aviation offers management programs that are customized to suit any requirements. Dedicated, professional flight crews; service scheduling; sales consulting; accounting services; and quality main-

tenance are all part of the company's management program. Aircraft owners benefit from the firm's discounts with fuel programs, insurance premiums, and other operating expenses. Maine Aviation can offset fixed costs by chartering the aircraft when the owner is not using it.

A Diverse, Strong Company

Maine Aviation is uniquely situated with its five divisions of aviation-related operations, enabling the company to provide valuable products and services to the aviation industry. Al Caruso credits the company's diversity as the reason for its strength: "It has always been very instrumental in keeping us strong." Maine Aviation has also created a Web presence at www.maineaviation.com to give customers easy access to the company's range of services.

Overall, the Carusos attribute their success to teamwork. At Maine Aviation Corporation, teamwork and dedication are encouraged and rewarded. "In our core mission to the aviation community, we provide the highest quality of aviation services to our customers in a safe, reliable, and professional manner, and, in turn, build lasting value for our customers, employees, and owners," says Al Caruso. ●

MANY BUSINESSES HAVE DISCOVERED THE BENEFITS OF CORPORATE TRAVEL WITH MAINE AVIATION'S PRIVATE CHARTER FLEET.

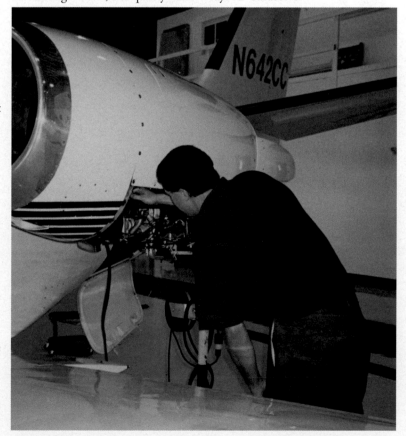

MAINE AVIATION IS STAFFED AT EVERY LEVEL BY HIGHLY TRAINED AVIATION PROFESSIONALS WHO ARE COMMITTED TO SAFETY AND THE HIGHEST STANDARDS OF SERVICE.

1960-1979

1962
PricewaterhouseCoopers LLP

1965
Drummond Woodsum & MacMahon

1967
WMTW Broadcast Group, LLC

1969
Pape Chevrolet

1970
Scotia Prince Cruises Limited

1972
Preti Flaherty Beliveau Pachios & Haley, LLC

1974
Berry, Dunn, McNeil & Parker

1976
Troiano Waste Services, Inc.

1977
Albin, Randall & Bennett

1978
Intelligent Controls, Inc.

THE APRIL 2000 RELOCATION OF NEWS 8 WMTW INTO ITS STUNNING NEW FACILITY OVERLOOKING A HIGH-PROFILE SQUARE IN DOWNTOWN PORTLAND WAS THE MOST PUBLIC OF A HALF-DOZEN MAJOR NEWS STRATEGIES, MOVING WMTW BROADCAST GROUP, LLC INTO A FUTURE DESIGNED AND CONSTRUCTED BY THE COMPANY ITSELF. ■ THE FUTURE OF ABC 8 WMTW INCLUDES THE INTEGRATION OF NEWS 8 WMTW, NEWS TALK WMTW RADIO, AND WMTW.COM INTO A SINGLE

entity known as Maine's News Source, a multiplatform news and information system delivering information on time, both on-line and on the air. Maine's News Source is tailored to the news consumer, and follows the model of delivering the news when, how, and where news consumers want their information.

Maine's News Source is the future of news, combining the power of television with the speed of radio and the immediacy of the Internet. News 8 WMTW is uniquely positioned for that future. As a longtime local company consistently honored for quality and service, the now-surging WMTW Broadcast Group considers community service as an equal and integrated goal with the continual enhancement of WMTW's on-air product.

WMTW BROADCAST GROUP, LLC IS LOCATED ON PORTLAND'S MONUMENT SQUARE (TOP).

NEWS 8 WMTW'S JOHN DOUGHERTY IS A NATIVE MAINER AND PORTLAND'S MOST EXPERIENCED NEWS ANCHOR (BOTTOM).

Family Business

With its dynamic present and vigorous future, WMTW Broadcast Group also has deep roots in a distinguished past. In 2002,

ABC 8 WMTW is set to celebrate its 35th year of family ownership. Owned by the Harron family, it is an autonomous Maine company, based in Portland, and not a local outlet of a national concern.

More important, in an age when family companies are passing from the scene, WMTW Broadcast Group is investing heavily in the Portland

community. The company's engagement with the southern Maine marketplace is an aggressive and imaginative set of initiatives in improving and expanding the product to the benefit of the community.

An engineering investment that will have a very significant effect is the company's transfer of its television broadcasting tower from its long-term location in New Hampshire to a competitive location in Maine. ABC 8 WMTW can now deliver the area's strongest signal, and therefore has the potential to reach the greatest number of households, a significant service to both viewers and advertisers.

Major Radio Initiative

In May 2000, WMTW Broadcast Group purchased five radio stations: WLAM-AM, WTHT-FM, WMEK-FM, and the simulcast stations 870-AM and 106.7-FM News Talk WMTW.

As part of the News Source strategy, some of that radio capacity has been reconfigured into a 24-hour News Talk station, with an emphasis on news and newsmagazine programming. Content and talent will be supplemented by a cooperative agreement with the *Portland Press Herald/Maine Sunday Telegram*, MaineToday.com, the *Central Maine*

1960-1979

1962
PricewaterhouseCoopers LLP

1965
Drummond Woodsum & MacMahon

1967
WMTW Broadcast Group, LLC

1969
Pape Chevrolet

1970
Scotia Prince Cruises Limited

1972
Preti Flaherty Beliveau Pachios & Haley, LLC

1974
Berry, Dunn, McNeil & Parker

1976
Troiano Waste Services, Inc.

1977
Albin, Randall & Bennett

1978
Intelligent Controls, Inc.

A ROUND THE WORLD, THE NAME PRICEWATERHOUSECOOPERS LLP IS SYNONYMOUS WITH HIGH-QUALITY PROFESSIONAL SERVICES. MAJOR COMPANIES IN NEARLY EVERY INDUSTRY RELY ON PRICEWATERHOUSECOOPERS FOR AUDIT, ACCOUNTING, AND TAX ADVICE; MANAGEMENT, INFORMATION TECHNOLOGY, AND HUMAN RESOURCE CONSULTING; FINANCIAL ADVISORY SERVICES, INCLUDING MERGERS AND ACQUISITIONS, BUSINESS RECOVERY, PROJECT FINANCE, AND LITIGATION SUPPORT;

business process outsourcing services; and legal services through a global network of affiliated law firms.

Portland is no exception. Since first establishing a Portland office in 1962, the practice has grown to more than 50 audit, tax, and business advisory professionals, most of whom are native Mainers. Today, PricewaterhouseCoopers is the only Big Five professional services firm with an office in the state. As a firm and as individuals, PricewaterhouseCoopers is committed to exceeding client expectations, improving the economic and business climate in the state, and giving back to the community. The firm is actively involved in numerous organizations that support business growth, and has a strong commitment to local communities in its volunteer and contribution support.

PricewaterhouseCoopers was formed by the 1998 merger of two of the largest accounting firms: Price Waterhouse LLP and Coopers & Lybrand LLP. Both of these firms contribute a rich, 100-year history to the development of the accounting profession. The present-day firm is the world's largest professional services organization, with more than 160,000 partners and staff members in some 160 countries and territories around the globe, helping clients solve complex business problems and measurably enhance their ability to build value, manage risk, and improve performance in an Internet-enabled world.

To best serve its clients, the firm operates three distinct industry practices: Global Financial Services, which encompasses banking, capital markets, insurance, investment companies, and other industry sectors; Consumer, Industrial Products and Services, which spans manufacturers, distributors, retailers, health care, government, education, utilities, and professional services; and Technology, Info-Com and Entertainment, which delivers a broad spectrum of services to software, Internet, computer and peripheral manufacturing, networking and communications, life sciences, venture capital, and media and communications companies.

While the firm is well known as a professional services provider to leading global corporations,

PricewaterhouseCoopers also places a strong emphasis on serving closely held, growth-oriented businesses; emerging businesses; and companies considering going public.

Middle Market Advisory Services

Because growth-oriented, middle market companies face complex challenges—from financing to protecting intellectual capital to building a staff—PricewaterhouseCoopers developed a separate business unit devoted exclusively to serving the unique needs of entrepreneurially managed businesses. The Portland office's Middle Market Advisory Services practice is comprised of audit, tax, and business advisory professionals providing clients with creative, strategic business solutions to help them stay abreast of today's emerging and fast-changing business environment, and to develop and implement solutions to take advantage of tomorrow's opportunities.

Wide Range of Services

The Portland office offers a wide range of services for many of the largest and most well known businesses in the state, many of Maine's nationally recognized not-for-profit institutions, and scores of emerging public and private companies. The firm's service offerings are organized into lines of service, each staffed with highly qualified, experienced professionals and leaders in the profession. Assurance and Business Advisory Services provides high-quality, cost-effective solutions to organizations' financial control, regulatory reporting, shareholder value, and technology issues.

Tax and Legal Services offers corporate and individual tax consulting to assist clients in formulating effective tax strategies, implementing innovative tax planning, and effectively managing compliance. The firm also

CORE TO THE PRICEWATERHOUSECOOPERS LLP CLIENT SERVICE APPROACH IS OPEN AND ONGOING DIALOGUE WITH CLIENTS. DAN HUTCHINS (LEFT), MANAGING PARTNER OF PRICEWATERHOUSECOOPERS' PORTLAND OFFICE, CONSULTS WITH A RETAIL CLIENT.

SONDRA SNEED

PRICEWATERHOUSECOOPERS' UNITED WAY VOLUNTEER CHRIS BOND GIVES BRENDA EUNG A BOOST OF CONFIDENCE BEFORE SHE LOBBIES MAINE'S LEGISLATURE FOR FUNDING TO BUILD A NEW TEEN CENTER.

offers a variety of consulting services in the areas of strategic change management, process improvement, and technology solutions; human resources consulting in the areas of compensation, actuarial benefits and insurance, outsourcing, and organizational effectiveness and development; and financial, economic, and strategic advice to companies facing business opportunities or other issues.

While its range of services is diverse, the firm's areas of expertise are all united by a common goal: to help clients operate their businesses more effectively, efficiently, and profitably.

Community Involvement

PricewaterhouseCoopers, as an organization and through the personal commitment of its people, has made a positive impact on community service in Maine. The firm is a significant supporter of United Way of Greater Portland. Members of the PricewaterhouseCoopers office hold cabinet-level positions with United Way of Greater Portland, and the firm's Portland office is proud to have been honored as having the highest employee campaign participation rate among the professional services firms participating in the organization's campaign. Firmwide, PricewaterhouseCoopers places a heavy emphasis on supporting charitable organizations focused on the nation's youth. Locally, the company's employees carry out this dedication through their volunteer

efforts with organizations such as the Boy Scouts of America, Boys and Girls Club, Junior Achievement, Susan Curtis Foundation, Big Brothers and Big Sisters, and Portland Mentoring Alliance.

The firm's local leadership is equally committed to supporting the advancement of Maine's business climate through its participation in local civic and economic development groups. In the mid-1990s, PricewaterhouseCoopers' Portland office leadership chaired the Governors Productivity Realization Task Force, leading the effort to make government more effective and reduce its cost of operations. The firm has also taken a

leadership role with other local civic groups, such as the Maine International Trade Center, Maine Chamber of Commerce, and Portland Chamber of Commerce.

The history, reputation, expertise, and service for which PricewaterhouseCoopers LLP has become known make the firm the first choice of many of Portland's businesses. Through its endeavors—both community and professional—the company remains focused on quality and leadership. So whatever the business challenge might be, PricewaterhouseCoopers has the experience, knowledge, and professionals to provide a top-notch solution. ●

USING LEADING-EDGE TECHNOLOGY, PRICEWATERHOUSECOOPERS' PROFESSIONALS WORK TO DEVELOP STRATEGIC SOLUTIONS FOR THEIR CLIENTS.

A S ONE OF NORTHERN NEW ENGLAND'S MOST PROMINENT LAW FIRMS, DRUMMOND WOODSUM & MACMAHON EMBODIES THE CHARACTER AND UNIQUENESS OF ITS COASTAL HOME—A PLACE WHERE CUTTING-EDGE GROWTH AND SUCCESS ARE BUILT UPON TIME-TESTED VALUES OF COMMITMENT AND COMMUNITY. TODAY, THE FIRM'S UNIQUE MIX OF GLOBAL PERSPECTIVE AND LOCAL, REAL-WORLD PRAGMATISM—COMBINED WITH A CONSTANT DEDICATION TO CLIENT SERVICE—

has set Drummond Woodsum apart from other law firms.

A Tradition of Leadership

From its historic offices overlooking Portland's Old Port district and waterfront, Drummond Woodsum has been a witness to remarkable business and community growth—and has played a key part in such expansion, both locally and beyond, serving as legal counsel to many of New England's most prestigious enterprises. Drummond Woodsum clients include Fortune 500 companies, multinational cor-

porations, and leaders in education, communications, biotechnology, and manufacturing.

Like the national and international clients it serves, the impact and leadership of Drummond Woodsum extend far beyond the borders of Maine's communities. Robert E. Hirshon, a member of the firm and a Portland native, leads the American Bar Association (ABA) as its president, beginning in 2001. Leadership also extends to local legislatures and even the halls of Congress, where political leaders such as Tom Allen, a member of Congress from Maine's First District

and a former member of the firm, have represented Maine and the nation. The recognized leadership of Drummond Woodsum attorneys encompasses the halls of academia as well—including Yale University, where Ed Woodsum, a founding member of the firm, served as a member of the Yale Corporation and as athletic director of the university.

Talent, Innovation, and Commitment to Service

Locally, within the Drummond Woodsum offices, a diverse group of attorneys, public policy specialists, paralegals, and staff work to serve clients with integrated, comprehensive legal counsel and services. Chosen for their demonstrated depth of legal expertise and an ability to achieve big-picture perspective in managing critical issues, Drummond Woodsum attorneys are known as bright, experienced, and savvy—

CLOCKWISE FROM LEFT:
DRUMMOND WOODSUM & MACMAHON ATTORNEYS HUGH MACMAHON AND AMY TCHAO MEET ON CAMPUS WITH WILLIAM D. ADAMS, PRESIDENT OF COLBY COLLEGE, ONE OF THE NATION'S OLDEST INDEPENDENT COLLEGES OF LIBERAL ARTS (FOUNDED 1813). THE FIRM PROVIDES LEGAL COUNSEL TO A BROAD GROUP OF PRESTIGIOUS PUBLIC AND PRIVATE EDUCATIONAL INSTITUTIONS.

AMERICAN BAR ASSOCIATION (ABA) PRESIDENT AND FIRM ATTORNEY BOB HIRSHON (LEFT), PREPARING FOR A TRIP TO THE CZECH REPUBLIC TO PRESENT AN ABA HUMANITARIAN AWARD TO CZECH PRESIDENT VÁCLAV HAVEL, CONFERS IN PORTLAND WITH CONGRESSMAN TOM ALLEN, A FORMER MEMBER OF THE FIRM.

CULINARY DELIGHTS ABOUND IN PORTLAND—ESPECIALLY AT STONEWALL KITCHEN, MAKER AND MARKETER OF GOURMET PRODUCTS FOR FOOD LOVERS AROUND THE GLOBE. DRUMMOND WOODSUM ATTORNEYS LIKE RICK SHINAY—SHOWN HERE WITH STONEWALL'S DENISE SKILLINGS—HAVE COUNSELED THE MAINE-BASED COMPANY THROUGH ITS GROWTH AS A WORLD-RENOWNED RETAILER.

NANCE S. TRUEWORTHY

JIM DANIELS

NANCE S. TRUEWORTHY

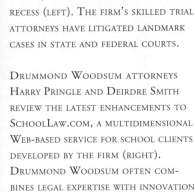

MELISSA HEWEY, A KEY MEMBER OF THE DRUMMOND WOODSUM TRIAL SERVICES GROUP, TAKES A BREAK DURING A TRIAL RECESS (LEFT). THE FIRM'S SKILLED TRIAL ATTORNEYS HAVE LITIGATED LANDMARK CASES IN STATE AND FEDERAL COURTS.

DRUMMOND WOODSUM ATTORNEYS HARRY PRINGLE AND DEIRDRE SMITH REVIEW THE LATEST ENHANCEMENTS TO SCHOOLLAW.COM, A MULTIDIMENSIONAL WEB-BASED SERVICE FOR SCHOOL CLIENTS DEVELOPED BY THE FIRM (RIGHT). DRUMMOND WOODSUM OFTEN COMBINES LEGAL EXPERTISE WITH INNOVATION TO CREATE UNIQUE SERVICES TO ADDRESS CLIENT NEEDS.

driven by both temperament and training to see beyond the surface of issues and problems to deliver superior, real-world results, whether in the courtroom or in the boardroom.

To better serve clients, attorneys are organized into focused practice groups, an innovative firm structure that makes deep, specialized expertise available to clients while also allowing an efficient, cross-disciplinary approach to complex issues. The firm's Business Services Group provides a complete range of legal services for corporate and commercial clients, including specialized counsel in taxation, mergers and acquisitions, immigration matters, intellectual property law, and securities. In litigation, clients can rely on seasoned trial attorneys and highly experienced trial teams from the Trial Services Group. The firm also provides a full range of mediation services, backed by decades of trial experience. The Indian Services Group, which includes major tribes in Maine and the United States among its clients, and the Public Sector Group—providing school, municipal, labor, disability rights, and environmental law counsel—round out the specialized Drummond Woodsum practice groups.

Underlying the bricks and mortar of its offices and the skilled lawyers within them is the foundation of the Drummond Woodsum law practice: a deep commitment to responsive, personalized client service. In the face of an otherwise rapidly changing world, this guiding principle has been constant throughout the decades since the firm's founding in 1965. As both a tangible part of daily practice—expressed in explicit client service

standards—and the distinguishing hallmark of the firm, the Drummond Woodsum client service commitment today sets the firm and its people apart. This constant focus on serving clients better, for example, has led to client service innovations like SchoolLaw.com, a unique Web site that not only allows school clients to receive legal services more efficiently, but also helps solve critical recruitment and staffing problems faced by schools.

Public Service and Community Values

The Drummond Woodsum commitment to client service, with its strong focus on responding to and meeting needs, also gives rise to a focus on the needs of the community and the human dimensions of law. The result has been an ongoing tradition of Drummond Woodsum pro bono service to assure that those of lesser means are not foreclosed from access to the law or professional

representation. The Drummond Woodsum pro bono tradition was recognized by the Maine Bar Foundation with its first Pro Bono Publico Award, now proudly displayed in the lobby of the Drummond Woodsum offices. Drummond Woodsum's long-standing commitment to public service and community is reflected in other ways as well, from its generous support of community performance arts to the simple pictures, painted by Portland schoolchildren, that line the entry hall to the law offices.

Today, against the urban backdrop of Portland—a vibrant center of community, opportunity, and commerce—the attorneys of Drummond Woodsum stand as trusted advisers to businesses, public and private institutions, and individuals, both in Maine and around the world. As unique as Portland itself, Drummond Woodsum & MacMahon leads the legal community with uncommon expertise, perspective, and service. ●

AS KEY LEGAL ADVISERS ON ALL ASPECTS OF BUSINESS DEVELOPMENT—FROM FINANCING TO BUSINESS STRUCTURING TO COMPLEX ENVIRONMENTAL PERMITTING—DRUMMOND WOODSUM ATTORNEYS ARE INSTRUMENTAL IN THE ECONOMIC GROWTH AND SUCCESS OF THEIR CLIENTS. SHOWN HERE ARE FIRM MEMBERS RON WARD (LEFT) AND BILL PLOUFFE, ON-SITE AT CONSTRUCTION OF A NEW MAINE ENERGY CENTER BY CALPINE CORPORATION, THE NATION'S LEADING INDEPENDENT POWER PRODUCER.

THE April 2000 relocation of News 8 WMTW into its stunning new facility overlooking a high-profile square in downtown Portland was the most public of a half-dozen major news strategies, moving WMTW Broadcast Group, LLC into a future designed and constructed by the company itself. ■ The future of ABC 8 WMTW includes the integration of News 8 WMTW, News Talk WMTW radio, and WMTW.com into a single

entity known as Maine's News Source, a multiplatform news and information system delivering information on time, both on-line and on the air. Maine's News Source is tailored to the news consumer, and follows the model of delivering the news when, how, and where news consumers want their information.

Maine's News Source is the future of news, combining the power of television with the speed of radio and the immediacy of the Internet. News 8 WMTW is uniquely positioned for that future. As a longtime local company consistently honored for quality and service, the now-surging WMTW Broadcast Group considers community service as an equal and integrated goal with the continual enhancement of WMTW's on-air product.

Family Business

With its dynamic present and vigorous future, WMTW Broadcast Group also has deep roots in a distinguished past. In 2002,

ABC 8 WMTW is set to celebrate its 35th year of family ownership. Owned by the Harron family, it is an autonomous Maine company, based in Portland, and not a local outlet of a national concern.

More important, in an age when family companies are passing from the scene, WMTW Broadcast Group is investing heavily in the Portland

community. The company's engagement with the southern Maine marketplace is an aggressive and imaginative set of initiatives in improving and expanding the product to the benefit of the community.

An engineering investment that will have a very significant effect is the company's transfer of its television broadcasting tower from its long-term location in New Hampshire to a competitive location in Maine. ABC 8 WMTW can now deliver the area's strongest signal, and therefore has the potential to reach the greatest number of households, a significant service to both viewers and advertisers.

Major Radio Initiative

In May 2000, WMTW Broadcast Group purchased five radio stations: WLAM-AM, WTHT-FM, WMEK-FM, and the simulcast stations 870-AM and 106.7-FM News Talk WMTW.

As part of the News Source strategy, some of that radio capacity has been reconfigured into a 24-hour News Talk station, with an emphasis on news and newsmagazine programming. Content and talent will be supplemented by a cooperative agreement with the *Portland Press Herald/Maine Sunday Telegram*, MaineToday.com, the *Central Maine*

WMTW Broadcast Group, LLC is located on Portland's Monument Square (top).

News 8 WMTW's John Dougherty is a native Mainer and Portland's most experienced news anchor (bottom).

Morning Sentinel in Waterville, and the *Kennebec Journal* in Augusta.

The news content is a composite of news talk radio, the Associated Press, ABC Network Radio, and News 8 WMTW, along with reports and on-camera reporters from the other media partners.

The engineering and content projects have their impact on programming, with the result that the News 8 WMTW news product will be showcased in longer morning and noontime periods. The entire News Source package also is available on the Internet at wmtw.com.

Solid Foundation

The enhancements of ABC 8 WMTW are built on a solid foundation, and moving to the state-of-the-art facility in downtown Portland capped the transformation. The 17,000-square-foot complex has the radio stations broadcasting live from street-level show windows facing Monument Square on the busiest part of Congress Street; the cutting-edge television newsroom and studio on the mezzanine; and the signature time-and-temperature sign on top of the building, boldly visible for miles.

WMTW Broadcast Group is Maine's most-honored broadcast news organization, with awards that include the Dupont-Columbia Silver Baton for investigative reporting; several New England Emmy awards; several New England Edward R. Murrow awards from the Radio and Television News Directors Association; Maine's Associated Press Station of the Year, 1996 through 1998; and dozens of awards from the Associated Press and the Maine Association of Broadcasters, including best newscast, best election coverage, best sports play-by-play, and best videography.

ABC 8 WMTW is the only television station in Maine to produce and telecast local and professional sporting events throughout the year. ABC 8 WMTW is the exclusive home of all of these locally produced sports franchises, such as Portland Pirates hockey, Portland Sea Dogs baseball, and NFL Sports Rap Live with Norm Karkos and Steve DeOssie. The station also exclusively carries New England Patriots preseason football, the *Patriots All-Access Show*, and *Monday Night Football*.

Long Public Service History

WMTW Broadcast Group is a good citizen of Portland and Maine with a long history of community involvement. Besides volunteering and fund-raising for the United Way Annual Campaign, WMTW Broadcast Group has donated more than $600,000 annually of pro bono production services, airtime, and Web site support.

Each year, WMTW Broadcast Group partners with more than 20 local and regional organizations, providing media support for more than 30 events, cultural and educational programs, and public awareness campaigns. WMTW has joined the *Portland Press Herald/Maine Sunday Telegram* as the local sponsor of the Jefferson Awards, a nationally based program to honor outstanding community service.

The Bob Elliot/ABC 8 WMTW Journalism Scholarship honors the spirit of one of Maine's most-beloved storytellers. The scholarship awards $1,500 each May to a graduating high school senior within the viewing area who plans to major in journalism or a related field.

As a vigorous and innovative Portland business in the field of public service, WMTW Broadcast Group, LLC looks to the future it is creating as one full of promise not only for itself, but also for the community of which it is an inseparable part. ●

As a leading dealership in the South Portland area, Pape Chevrolet wins a lot of awards. While awards are important to the company, it is the customer satisfaction numbers that generate the most pride. ■ "You don't stay in this business as long as we've been in it if you're not focused on your customer," says Fred Pape III, president of the Pape dealerships in South Portland. "And things come pretty easily if you just stay that way." While most customers perceive

price as an important concern, customer satisfaction actually involves a much broader set of expectations that Pape Chevrolet carefully accounts for in providing full service.

Pape Chevrolet consistently is among the highest performers for the brand in New England, and was among very few dealers in the nation to win the Chevrolet Genuine Leader Award in 2000. The four factors on which the award is based are sales volume, sales satisfaction, service satisfaction, and overall profitability.

The companion Mitsubishi franchise has been recognized as top in the country in customer rating among 550 dealerships. In contributing to the rating, customers respond to a 30-question survey that covers a complete rundown on service and sales satisfaction beginning with the initial contact in the relationship.

Opening to Excel

Pape Chevrolet opened at Cash Corner in South Portland in 1969, when General Motors (GM) asked Frederick W. Pape Jr., the

current president's father, if he would be interested in taking over a vacant dealership. Fred Pape Jr. had been working with his brother, William, in the latter's Chevrolet business in Huntington, New York.

Fred Pape Jr. came to Maine to take a look, and never left. Pape Chevrolet moved to its present location on Westbrook Street in 1972. Land had become available, and the original building was not particularly suitable. At the time, there was no Interstate 295, and no Maine Mall. The highway, the mall, and the Pape building all came into being at the same time.

Since that time, numerous automobile dealerships have come and gone, but not this one. In reflecting on what it takes to be successful, the current president adds two important additional factors to the idea that customer focus must come first: "You have to be incredibly consistent, and without employee loyalty it is a very difficult business to do."

Pape's consistency shows in both internal and external marketing. There is not, as Fred Pape III says, a crazy carnival atmosphere in which employee incentives are changing all the time, along with incentives to customers. The secret is a fair and

PAPE CHEVROLET HAS BEEN LOCATED ON WESTBROOK STREET SINCE 1972 (TOP).

THE COMPANY IS CURRENTLY RUN BY FRED PAPE III AND FRED PAPE JR. (BOTTOM).

solid way of doing business, which pleases customers and removes employee anxiety. Every sales and service employee is empowered to satisfy the customer, everyone knows they will be backed up if they give the customer what that customer wants.

Employees Specialize in Service

Pape Chevrolet certainly got the employee loyalty part right. It has virtually no turnover among key employees. Its managers have been with the company a minimum of 15 years, and some for more than 25 years. One technician has been on the job since the Papes arrived in 1969.

And these are quality employees. Ben Welch is the number one GM salesperson in the country, which is a notable accomplishment. GM, the largest corporation in the United States, is consistently first in sales volume among Fortune 500 companies. Welch had been with Pape for 18 years by the turn of the century.

The results are there to be seen. No longer a small company, the Pape organization posts annual sales exceeding $60 million. It has fully developed departments for parts, service, body work, finance and insurance, the new car dealerships, and used car sales.

The company's growth has been very substantial, rising from $25 million in 1994 to $60 million in 2000. In terms of automobiles sold, the numbers went from 1,000 vehicles in 1991 to 3,000 in 1998, and the

dollars per sale also rose. Yet, Fred Pape III points out, the average buyer's out-of-pocket expense for buying a vehicle is proportionately less today than it has ever been.

Prominent in Community Service

In keeping with the way the Papes operate the business, the company has always been very involved in the outside community and the industry itself. The senior Pape has been a director and a longtime supporter of the Cerebral Palsy Center, a trustee of Maine Medical Center, campaign chairman for United Way of Greater Portland, and chairman of the board of the Greater Portland Chambers of Commerce. He received the Henri A. Benoit Award of the Greater Portland Chambers for outstanding leadership

in the private sector, and the Spurwink Foundation Humanitarian Award.

Fred Pape III is on the boards of Maine's Children's Cancer Center and the Cerebral Palsy Center. The corporation serves on the General Motors Advisory Board. Fred Pape Jr. has long been involved in countless community organizations and events.

For the future, the Pape organization intends to continue expansion of its Chevrolet, Mitsubishi, and used-car businesses. As Fred Pape III says, "As long as you're focused on the customers, they'll keep coming back. I truly believe, if you like people and are interested in satisfying a need, this is a fun business."

With a commitment to quality service and an employee team that is second to none, it is clear that Pape Chevrolet will continue to be successful well into the future. ●

THE PAPE ORGANIZATION ALSO MANAGES AN EXTENSIVE USED-CAR LOT AND A MITSUBISHI DEALERSHIP.

A T EACH TURNAROUND OF THE M/S *Scotia Prince* ON ITS VOYAGE FROM PORTLAND'S INTERNATIONAL MARINE TERMINAL TO YARMOUTH, NOVA SCOTIA, 700 CRUISE PASSENGERS AND SOME 200 VEHICLES DISEMBARK. WAITING FOR THE 11 HOUR RETURN JOURNEY ARE NEW PASSENGERS WITH MORE CARS AND RECREATIONAL VEHICLES. IN THE SPRING AND FALL, HUNDREDS WILL MAKE A ROUND TRIP CRUISE EVERY DAY—A LUXURIOUS MINI-VACATION. EACH DAY THE *Scotia Prince* TAKES ON FUEL,

food and beverage, and gift shop supplies; a thousand berths are made-up; and 330 cabins are cleaned. All of this hard work—and its positive economic impact on the community—is the responsibility of Scotia Prince Cruises Limited.

More impressive is how this service came about. Henk A. Pols, president, was recruited from Holland American Cruise Lines in 1972. "In the late 1960s, Portland was not in very good condition economically, and the Waterfront and the Old Port District were among the most stagnant parts of the city," says Pols. "There was no Civic Center, no hockey team, neither ballpark nor baseball team, no art museum, few fine hotels and restaurants, no Old Port commercial development, and no marine terminal. Then everything changed."

THE *SCOTIA PRINCE* PASSES PORTLAND HEADLIGHT ON ITS OVERNIGHT VOYAGE TO NOVA SCOTIA (TOP).

PASSENGERS ENJOY INVIGORATING OCEAN BREEZES FROM THE SHIP'S WIDE DECKS (BOTTOM).

Beginning of Portland's Renaissance

L ed by City Manager John Menario, the city started redeveloping its transportation infrastructure, including the Franklin and Spring Street arterials, the High Street—State Street one-way system, and an aggressive program of constructing parking garages. As that process produced results, the city looked for ways to expedite private investment and increase the use of the inner city and the waterfront.

Clark Neily, city director of economic development, was the catalyst for the coalition of city and chamber of commerce leaders who went after a potential Maine-Nova Scotia maritime service. At that time, Baron Stig Leuhusen of Sweden was looking at various sites along the New England coast for the U.S. terminus of a new service to Nova Scotia.

As a result, the Baron invested almost $10 million in a ship built specifically for the purpose of transporting people and vehicles between Portland and Yarmouth. Portland had to find and acquire a site then design, finance, and construct a terminal. Additionally, the Portland business community was asked to pledge $1 million to guarantee that the new service could cover its operating expenses. The guarantee was put in place but never utilized since the ferry service was a success from the beginning,

even though it operated only from May to October. The city, through its lease agreements for the terminal, has fully recovered its investment.

The *Prince of Fundy*, the first ship, set out on its maiden voyage in June 1970. A second ship, the *Bolero*, was added in 1973. In 1976, faced with skyrocketing fuel costs during the oil embargo, the company decided to reposition itself in the marketplace and replaced the two ships with a single larger vessel, the *Caribe*—a cruise ship with facilities for vehicles. The *Scotia Prince* became the line's vessel in 1987 and she has been lengthened and refurbished to enhance her present role as a cruise ship with full facilities, but without any diminution in her capacity to allow 200 or so families to bring their vehicles.

A Heavy Economic Contribution

P ols likes to point out that the revitalization of the Old Port and the city at large began with that first success. He also notes that the cruise line's ongoing contribution to the economy is considerable. A ship the size of the *Scotia Prince* consumes approximately $10,000 in fuel daily during the summer season, adding up to $1.5 million a year spent in Portland. A similar amount is spent on high-quality consumables from champagne, lobsters, and roast beef to more than 100,000 hamburgers

RUSSELL FRENCH

and hot dogs; 70,000 pounds of beef, pork and ham; and 80,000 gallons of beverages. Other expenditures include $1 million in passenger support services, an average of $4 million dollars spent on maintenance and support for the ship's annual running and dry-dock costs, an onboard payroll of more than $3 million, and $2 million for marketing.

In an average year, some 165,000 passengers, 32,000 passenger vehicles, and 600 motor coaches pass through the terminal. "When you see a motor coach in the downtown area during the summer, the chances are good that it's here because of the *Scotia Prince*," Pols says. "Most of the visitors spend at least one night in Portland, have dinner, and gas up their cars before boarding. The disposable income of the *Prince*'s passengers and their local spending both tend to be higher than those of the typical summer cruise day visitors from the itinerant cruise line services."

Pols notes that in addition to the onboard crew, the company employs a large number of Portland area residents on-shore with local year-round payroll and associated spending on professional and other services exceeding $3 million. In 1980, the Greater Portland Chambers of Commerce commissioned an economic impact study of the service. Based on the conclusions of more than $18 million direct and indirect benefits in 1980, the passage of time/inflation and the additional tonnage employed, it seems probable that the benefits in 2000 will have exceeded $50 million.

A Future of Possibilities

The future of *Scotia Prince* appears solid, although the competitive marketplace is changing. The Portland Waterfront itself is in for some major development. The departure of the Bath Iron Works dry

dock may make room for a new cruise and ferry ship terminal. The original owners sold *Scotia Prince* in 2000 to a family owned business headed by Professor Matthew Hudson. He is chairman of Scottish Transport Group and says, "The sale was based on the impending rebirth of the Portland waterfront and conceived with great care to protect the historical nature and commitments of the cruise line."

Once the waterfront and international marine facilities have been redeveloped, the *Scotia Prince* itself may well be a candidate for replacement or rebuilding, and Pols talks of conducting an orderly transition in management as he looks to retirement. Under the new ownership he sees great possibilities in expanding the ship's itinerary to warmer waters throughout the winter months. ●

THE *SCOTIA PRINCE* FEATURES FIVE-STAR DINING, LAS VEGAS-STYLE CASINO EXCITEMENT, FLOOR SHOWS, AND OUTSTANDING SERVICE.

NANCE C. TRUEWORTHY

PRETI FLAHERTY BELIVEAU PACHIOS & HALEY, LLC ANSWERS THE CALL OF A DIVERSE BUSINESS COMMUNITY WITH A SOPHISTICATED PRACTICE, INTERNATIONAL REACH, DEDICATED SERVICE, AND MULTISTATE EXPERIENCE. ONE OF MAINE'S LARGEST LAW FIRMS, PRETI FLAHERTY IS KNOWN FOR HIGH-POWERED LEGAL TALENT, INCLUDING FORMER SENATE MAJORITY LEADER GEORGE J. MITCHELL, AND EXCEPTIONAL CREDENTIALS WORKING WITH STATE AND LOCAL GOVERNMENTS.

Preti Flaherty has helped many of the region's most successful companies grow and thrive. Newcomers to the state, as well as long-established local businesses, call on the firm's corporate and regulatory experience and litigation know-how to help them navigate Maine's sometimes rocky legal landscape. Preti Flaherty's clients include firms in telecommunications, publishing, health care, manufacturing, energy, and many other industries.

To best serve its clients, Preti Flaherty works in a variety of legal fields. These include business law, employment, energy and utilities, environmental, estate planning, franchising, health care, insurance, intellectual property, labor, legislative, regulatory and governmental services, litigation, media, and technology.

PRETI FLAHERTY BELIVEAU PACHIOS & HALEY, LLC IS ONE OF MAINE'S LARGEST LAW FIRMS, WITH OFFICES IN AUGUSTA (LEFT), PORTLAND (RIGHT), BATH, AND CONCORD, NEW HAMPSHIRE.

But perhaps the best way to get to know Preti Flaherty is through recent examples of its work.

Rent-A-Husband: Fixing Up the Fixer-Uppers

Rent-A-Husband, along with its founder, Kaile Warren, is a homegrown success story. This Portland-based franchisor and operator of handyman-service businesses has operations throughout the United States. Warren is now the national home improvement correspondent for CBS' *The Saturday Early Show,* and has been featured on numerous other television shows, including *Oprah Winfrey* and *The Today Show.*

In Preti Flaherty's first 12 months as part of the Rent-A-Husband family, the firm helped the company recruit an experienced management team,

raise several million dollars in venture capital, refocus its franchising and intellectual property strategies, reorganize its existing financial obligations and corporate structure, negotiate deals with multiple franchisees, and develop new operations in more than five states and two countries. Today, Rent-A-Husband is a more focused and robust company with a solid foundation for growth in the future.

Bath Iron Works: Show of Strength

Maine-based Bath Iron Works (BIW) is one of the United States' preeminent shipyards and one of the state's largest employers. Over the years, Preti Flaherty has helped BIW resolve commercial disputes and litigation, obtain

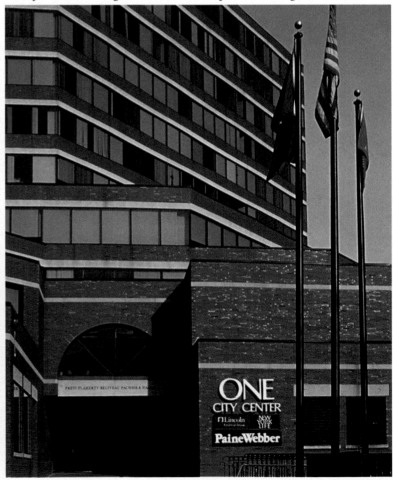

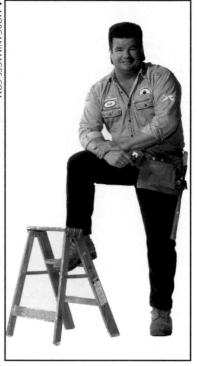

PRETI FLAHERTY WORKS WITH SOME OF MAINE'S MOST NOTABLE COMPANIES, INCLUDING MAINE BIOMEDICAL RESEARCH COALITION AND RENT-A-HUSBAND (RIGHT).

regulatory clearances, support labor negotiations, and handle employment matters involving its more than 7,000 employees.

In the late 1990s, Preti Flaherty was instrumental in resolving litigation that enabled BIW to build one of the most modern shipbuilding facilities in the world, keeping it at the forefront of surface combatant design and construction. The firm also works with BIW's parent company, General Dynamics Corporation, in litigation matters.

Maine Biomedical Research Coalition: Financing the Future

When the Maine Biomedical Research Coalition, a coalition of five of Maine's top scientific research facilities, needed new legislation to help fund biomedical research, it asked for Preti Flaherty's help. The firm drafted and lobbied for passage of state legislation creating the Biomedical Research Fund and helped the coalition secure $10 million in funding from the Maine legislature.

Since the fund was created, coalition members have received commitments for $47 million in outside grants. The first year saw $17 million in state and outside grant money pumped into the local economy. Within five years, the

$10 million invested by the state is expected to yield $54 million in outside grant spending and more than $100 million in spin-off benefits, including new facilities, enhanced research teams, and 225 well-paying jobs, as well as the chance to improve the quality of life for people around the world.

Kingspan Group plc: Building from the Ground Up

Kingspan Group plc saw its future in the United States, but needed help finding its way through unfamiliar territory. The Irish company is a leading manufacturer of raised-access flooring used by 60 percent of European and Asian computer and telecommunications companies to make it easier to add capacity and reconfigure office layouts. In a transaction worth $120 million in cash and equity, Preti Flaherty helped Kingspan acquire the leading U.S. raised-access flooring company, guiding the multistate transaction from letter of intent to closing in just over 60 days.

Herbs, Etc.: A New Age of Trademark Protection

Santa Fe-based Herbs, Etc. helps a nation rest easier with its best-selling herbal remedy, Deep Sleep.

But the company got a rude awakening when it found that a larger company had registered and was using the same Deep Sleep mark for a competing product. With limited assets and its number one product on the line, Herbs, Etc. needed a fast resolution. Preti Flaherty filed suit for infringement in June, and showed conclusively during discovery that the competitor had adopted the Deep Sleep name with full knowledge of Herbs, Etc.'s prior rights. The case settled in December, with the competitor assigning its trademark rights to Herbs, Etc. and paying attorneys' fees.

In addition to groundbreaking work with its clients, Preti Flaherty attorneys frequently contribute articles and columns to a number of local and national professional publications, as well as teaching and participating in legal and business conferences. On the international scene, a Preti Flaherty lawyer represents the International Trademark Association in negotiation of the proposed Hague Convention on Jurisdiction and Enforcement of Foreign Judgments, attending in that capacity the recent diplomatic conference on the Convention in The Hague and preliminary meetings in Geneva, Ottawa, and Edinburgh.

Preti Flaherty Beliveau Pachios & Haley, LLC is proud to be a part of the Portland tapestry, and to work with the dynamic companies who make up the community. ●

B ERRY, DUNN, McNEIL & PARKER (BDMP) PUT DOWN STRONG MAINE ROOTS IN 1974 AS A PROGRESSIVE, ENTREPRENEURIAL FIRM OF CERTIFIED PUBLIC ACCOUNTANTS AND BUSINESS CONSULTANTS. BDMP HAS SINCE GROWN INTO ONE OF THE LARGEST INDEPENDENT CERTIFIED PUBLIC ACCOUNTING AND MANAGEMENT CONSULTING FIRMS IN NEW ENGLAND, AND IS AMONG THE TOP 50 IN THE UNITED STATES. BDMP PROVIDES A WIDE RANGE OF AUDIT AND ACCOUNTING, TAX, INFORMATION TECHNOLOGY, ESTATE AND FINANCIAL

planning, and management consulting services to a variety of industries, individuals, estates, and trusts, with offices in Augusta, Portland, and Bangor, Maine; and in Lebanon and Manchester, New Hampshire. The firm's primary objective is to help clients create, enhance, and preserve value by providing professional services that consistently meet or exceed clients' expectations. BDMP's experience across a variety of industries and its depth of technical knowledge allow the firm to provide unique solutions to the challenges clients face in today's complex business environment.

The Founders

B DMP is a different kind of firm because its founders set out to make it so. Veterans of other large local firms, Burch Dunn, Bob Berry, and Mike McNeil understood the enduring qualities represented by their experience, but wanted true adaptability and the entrepreneurial energy of a new firm. Rather than affiliate with a national accounting firm, the trio chose to establish a firm that was client and community focused—a firm that had its roots in Maine and provided national-caliber expertise to its clients. Building a firm that stressed employee satisfaction and emphasized balance between work and personal life was equally important to the founders. Each founder was firmly committed to the community where he worked and made community service an integral part of his life. The successful integration of Chester M. Kearney and Company's Bangor office with the firm added Larry Parker to the masthead and established BDMP's

presence there. Parker's client orientation and values mirrored those of the original founders, and enhanced BDMP's ability to serve clients throughout Maine. Both McNeil and Parker are still active in the firm, and they play prominent roles in the Portland and Bangor communities. Dunn's extraordinary community commitment was recognized posthumously when one of the region's most innovative elementary schools was named in his honor.

Commitment to Clients

P ersonalized service and in-depth understanding of client needs remain the hallmarks of Berry, Dunn, McNeil & Parker. BDMP's relationship-based approach is that of a trusted advisor, excelling at customer service. BDMP works in a proactive

BERRY, DUNN, McNEIL & PARKER'S (BDMP) FOUNDING PARTNERS INCLUDE (FROM LEFT) BOB BERRY, MIKE McNEIL, LARRY PARKER, AND BURCH DUNN.

▼ STEVE MAINES

BURCHARD A. DUNN'S EXTRA-
ORDINARY COMMUNITY COMMITMENT
WAS RECOGNIZED POSTHUMOUSLY WHEN
ONE OF THE REGION'S MOST INNOVATIVE
ELEMENTARY SCHOOLS WAS NAMED IN
HIS HONOR.

manner with clients, maintaining an open dialogue to ensure that pertinent information is available for decision making. Through industry newsletters, client updates, and other communication, BDMP keeps clients up to date on relevant industry issues, legislation, and best practices.

A cornerstone of BDMP's success is the quality and rich experience base the staff brings to each of the firm's industry group practices. BDMP has made it a priority to develop a staff comprised of highly skilled, personable individuals who specialize in a particular industry or area, making them experts in the specific regulatory, financial, and business issues facing clients. To provide maximum value for each client, BDMP provides its customers with the full support of experts throughout the firm, including information technology consultants, tax advisers, estate and financial planners, and employee benefits plan consultants. Special areas of industry expertise include manufacturing, hospitality, health care, utilities and telecommunications, forest products, construction, financial services, real estate, and not-for-profit organizations.

To ensure that their expertise and technical resources keep up with the changing landscapes of the industries that they serve, BDMP professionals maintain active membership and serve as leaders in a variety of professional organizations, as well as local and national trade groups—including active membership in the SEC and the Private Companies sections of the American Institute of Certified Public Accountants. BDMP's leaders and staff members meet regularly with like-minded colleagues across the United States and internationally to share ideas and best practices, as well as to develop collaborative agreements that provide significant resources to clients. BDMP is able to serve clients with multiple geographic locations through an affiliate network of independent accounting and consulting firms worldwide, which share expertise and personnel as necessary to meet the needs of their respective clients.

Commitment to Employees and the Community

More than a quarter of a century since its founding, BDMP remains true to its roots. The firm continues to honor the founding values of community service by providing financial, professional, and human resources to a wide range of charitable and civic organizations in each of its communities. Employees of BDMP are encouraged to pursue opportunities in the community, and many routinely devote time to a wide variety of community service organizations and activities.

Berry, Dunn, McNeil & Parker is committed to providing a rewarding and challenging environment for personal and professional growth. The firm takes pride in its ability to help its employees maintain a healthy balance between professional, personal, and civic activities. BDMP provides the flexibility and tools to meet the needs of a diverse population of employees and, as a result, continues to attract and motivate highly skilled, dedicated people—the key to success. ●

BERRY, DUNN, McNEIL & PARKER

A COMMITMENT TO CLIENT SERVICE IS THE MISSION FOR ALL MEMBERS OF THE FIRM.

BDMP'S PORTLAND HEADQUARTERS IS LOCATED ON MIDDLE STREET IN THE HISTORIC OLD PORT DISTRICT.

T ROIANO WASTE SERVICES, INC. IS A FAMILY BUSINESS, AND HAS BEEN SINCE ITS START IN PORTLAND IN 1976. FOR FILOMENA AND MICHAEL TROIANO AND THEIR SONS, "FAMILY BUSINESS" IS NOT JUST A SLOGAN—THE OWNERS WORK BOTH ON THE TRUCKS AND IN THE OFFICE. TO THE TROIANOS, BEING A LONGTIME FAMILY BUSINESS MEANS RESPONSIVENESS AND DECISIVENESS, AS WELL AS RELIABILITY. "THAT'S OUR NAME ON THAT TRUCK GOING DOWN THE ROAD."

TO TROIANO WASTE SERVICES, INC., BEING A LONGTIME FAMILY BUSINESS MEANS RESPONSIVENESS AND DECISIVENESS, AS WELL AS RELIABILITY.

The company is the largest privately owned waste disposal service in northern New England, handling commercial accounts in an area centered on Portland, bounded by Lewiston and the Bath and Brunswick areas to the north, and including the Portsmouth-Dover section of New Hampshire to the south.

Troiano has handled some large jobs, including the *Julie N* oil spill in Portland Harbor in September 1996, for which the company hauled oil-soaked material 24 hours a day for 10 straight days. Troiano supported such major renovation projects as the Merrill Auditorium, the Lafayette Hotel, and Portland's federal courthouse. For the National Semiconductor construction project, Troiano provided 25 roll-off containers, and had a truck at the site 10 to 12 hours a day, six days a week. The firm's portable toilet service has worked with the huge Op Sail celebration, which attracted some 440,000 people, and the Beach-to-Beacon Road Race.

At any one time, Troiano has some 1,500 rear-load containers in service, as well as some 400 large, open-top containers. The company services 100 stationary trash compactors, half of which it owns. Troiano operates

four tractor-trailers, six 100-cubic-yard trailers, nine roll-off trucks, eight rear-load packers, and four portable toilet trucks. The firm also has several statewide clients, and services the large-volume, fast-turn-around business of the cruise ships in Portland Harbor.

One Truck and a Newborn Baby

T roiano is a local business that started essentially from nothing. Michael Troiano went to work in the hauling business in 1971 at the age of 17. Then, one day in 1976, he came home to tell his wife, Filomena, that he had bought a truck and gone into business for himself. That first

truck and the accompanying trash route cost $4,000. Troiano bought the little business from a hauler he had met at the Portland dump, when the man was planning to retire after 35 years in the business. Twenty-seven days later, the Troianos' son Michael Paul was born. As a toddler, Michael Paul was fascinated with trucks, and he would ride the routes with his father and mother. Michael Paul would later go to work for the company at age 16, and he continues to work on the trucks today. A second son, Thomas, helps with the company finances, as well as running a share of the business.

In the company's early years, today's extensive modern technology was long in the future. Troiano routinely carried 55-gallon drums on his back up six flights of stairs in Congress Street buildings, then hauled the full drums down. The hours weren't especially easy, either. During the extensive renovation work in the Old Port, Troiano would work the routes all day, then haul demolition debris all night at $25 a load.

For the first eight years, Michael drove the truck and Filomena handled the paperwork. That, too has changed. Today, the company's workforce totals some 40 people. Troiano built the business by knocking on doors, which he still does, and buying up routes from small haulers. The family name has been associated with a

TROIANO IS THE LARGEST PRIVATELY OWNED WASTE DISPOSAL SERVICE IN NORTHERN NEW ENGLAND.

The warmth extends to the firm's customers. Each Christmas, when the Troianos host a party to express appreciation to their clients, the event draws some 300 people. Ignoring the open house intent, people who come from miles away may stay for hours to chat.

That sort of relationship, much prized by Troiano Waste Services, Inc.'s owners, as well as by the company's customers, sometimes carries a price. When Troiano goes out to work a truck route these days, the run can take hours longer than normal because of the number of friendly chats that must take place along the way. ●

MICHAEL PAUL AND THOMAS TROIANO TODAY HELP THEIR FATHER GROW THE FAMILY BUSINESS.

solid work ethic, which contributed further to the growth of the business as clients recommended the company to newcomers. Key developments in recent years have included addition of the portable toilet business in 1998, and the opening of a transfer station for recycling demolition debris in 2000.

A Popular Logo

To the general public, Troiano is perhaps best known for its corporate logo, a colorful vulture that has become extremely popular, especially with children. Michael Troiano and an artist picked the design from a book years ago, when searching for a distinctive symbol to represent to the company.

Unexpectedly, the company began to find its containers and toilets all over the territory were being damaged, as people cut out the bird logo to take home and display. A large company flag was stolen within days of its initial hoisting. Today, the Troianos give away decals to reduce the unintentional vandalism,

and put the symbol on hats and T-shirts for people all over the country.

The informality of the firm's logo is a sign of something much deeper: the informal nature of the company as a whole. Troiano's employees experience a personal loyalty that is not like working in a factory, but rather is like being part of a family. The company's employees can talk directly to Michael or Filomena Troiano at any time.

A TROIANO TRUCK DUMPS CONSTRUCTION AND DEMOLITION DEBRIS AT THE COMPANY'S TRANSFER AND RECYCLING FACILITY.

FOUNDED BY ALAN LUKAS IN 1978, INTELLIGENT CONTROLS, INC. (INCON) SPECIALIZES IN ELECTRONIC MEASUREMENT SYSTEMS AND SOFTWARE FOR THE PETROLEUM AND POWER UTILITY INDUSTRIES, AND IN GENERAL LEVEL MEASUREMENT, MONITORING, AND PREDICTIVE MAINTENANCE APPLICATIONS. ■ INITIALLY AN ELECTRONIC ENGINEERING CONSULTING FIRM, INCON NOW DESIGNS, MANUFACTURES, AND SELLS PRODUCTS—INCLUDING RELATED APPLICATIONS AND COMMUNICATIONS

software—in two major categories: retail petroleum, for users including service stations, convenience stores, and private fuel depots; and power utilities, for monitoring the performance of transformers and circuit breakers in electric utility substations.

The intelligent instruments enable users to detect leaks, measure liquid levels, and perform general and predictive maintenance monitoring and protection of equipment as an early indicator of wear and potential failure. INCON is a people-driven company that uses its technical competence to put intelligence in devices that help its customers improve performance.

From a Saco Start-Up to the American Stock Exchange

Lukas returned home to Saco, Maine, after earning his engineering degree at the Massachu-

setts Institute of Technology, then working a few years in Boston and in Biddeford. In 1978, when the entrepreneurial bug bit, he founded INCON, where his brother Paul joined him a year later.

For the first 10 years, INCON's work consisted principally of consulting, and of designing embedded software—microprocessor products—for clients' measurement products and functions. In the late 1980s, the company decided to expand into the manufacturing sector of the business and began to produce hardware devices, the first of which were used on transformers in the utility industry. With INCON's growth came an infusion of venture capital and the hiring of additional people.

Another key move was going public in 1993 with a listing on the American Stock Exchange following

in 1995 (trading symbol: ITC). The company's gross annual revenue rose above $3 million, and its employment increased to 35 people.

A Major Challenge Met

In the mid-1990s, rapid growth threw INCON into management challenges in manufacturing, client service, and quality control. The company needed a major growth strategy, and launched this new strategy in late 1997 and early 1998. The board of directors brought in a new major investor and took steps to broaden the company's market, product research, and internal product development.

President and CEO Roger E. Brooks came aboard at that time. Brooks had spent 12 years helping build a Massachusetts manufacturing firm from $11 million in annual

AUTOMATED TESTING IS AN INTEGRAL PART OF THE ISO 9001 QUALITY CERTIFICATION PROCESS.

current applications by freeing them from landlines, but also to make possible new uses that were simply out of the question before, because of cost and other considerations.

INCON's business approach will continue to be that of searching out suitable niche markets and devoting the company's technical expertise and creative people to becoming strong in those markets. INCON intends to be perceived as a technical innovator, and will be positioned for growth. If and when chosen niches turn out to be significant breakthrough areas, INCON, as a niche player, will then be in a position to become a major force in the larger market.

Brooks considers the people aspect a large benefit for INCON. While the company takes pride in its technical reputation, supported by ISO 9001 certification, Brooks notes that the quality reputation driving its success is built by manufacturing personnel—the company's largest group; and sales, marketing, and administration employees, in addition to those in R&D and technical service.

Brooks believes Maine is steadily becoming better known as a base for technology companies and as an excellent place for those companies' employees to live. The more successful the state's technically strong companies become, the more they serve as a magnet for quality workers. ●

THE AWARD-WINNING SYSTEM SENTINEL MONITORING AND POLLING SOFTWARE IS INTELLIGENT CONTROLS, INC.'s (INCON) FLAGSHIP PRODUCT.

sales to more than $90 million. He had been looking to join a new company with growth ambitions and potential. He found it at INCON. Alan Lukas, while retaining the title of board chairman, concentrated on technical leadership as vice president for product development.

The early and mid-1990s were marked by INCON's successful development and marketing of instruments to help petroleum companies meet a December 31, 1998 EPA deadline requiring owners to equip fuel tanks with sensitive monitoring devices.

At the dawn of the millennium, INCON stood at 75 employees, with annual revenues of roughly $13 million. The petroleum market was no longer a source of growth, and the large potential power utility remote monitoring market was just beginning to develop. Future success called for the innovation that is a hallmark of the company.

Equipped for Innovation

INCON is at heart an electronics/software company, most of whose competitors were sensor-instrumentation companies that have tried, in Brooks' words, "to put smarts into their devices." INCON began with embedded software, added Windows client-server products, and now looks to a future structured around wireless and Internet applications.

Traditionally above average in its research and development investment, INCON expects the new technologies not only to change

SMART CIRCUITS ARE THE HEART OF INCON'S PRODUCT CAPABILITY.

A LBIN, RANDALL & BENNETT, FOUNDED IN PORTLAND IN 1977, IS A FULL-SERVICE ACCOUNTING AND CONSULTING FIRM WHOSE EMPHASIS ON QUALITY INCLUDES A HIGH LEVEL OF CUSTOMIZATION. THE COMPANY'S APPROACH TO CLIENT SERVICE, WHICH FEATURES PERSONAL RELATIONSHIPS, IS A STANDARD FUNCTION RATHER THAN SIMPLY A SLOGAN. THE FIRM HAS SIGNIFICANT ACCOUNTING AND MULTISTATE TAXATION EXPERIENCE, AND IS QUALIFIED TO HANDLE THE COMPLEX ISSUES AND TRANSACTIONS COMMON TO LARGE BUSINESSES.

While Albin, Randall & Bennett is a member of the Securities & Exchange Commission Practice Section of the American Institute of Certified Public Accountants, and therefore qualified to work with publicly traded companies, the firm concentrates on privately held businesses and entrepreneurs. A specialty is working with key figures in opening, acquiring, or selling a business. Its five partners—each a certified public accountant (CPA) and a member of the American Institute of Certified Public Accountants—head an overall staff of 20 professionals, most of them also CPAs. The company's offices are in Portland and Lewiston, Maine. The company also has a presence on the Internet at www.arbcpa.com.

THE ALBIN, RANDALL & BENNETT MANAGEMENT TEAM DRAWS ON ITS WEALTH OF EXPERIENCE TO BEST SERVE THE FIRM'S CLIENTS (TOP).

RONALD S. BENNETT SERVES AS MANAGING PRINCIPAL OF ALBIN, RANDALL & BENNETT. CHERI L. WALKER IS AN AUDIT PRINCIPAL WITH THE FIRM (BOTTOM).

Partners: Complementary Strengths

R onald S. Bennett, the company's managing principal, is responsible for responding to and consulting with other members of the firm's engagement team in a wide variety of accounting and tax matters. Bennett holds an MBA from the Amos Tuck School of Business Administration at Dartmouth.

Cheri L. Walker is an audit principal with the firm, and serves as the engagement principal for many of its auto dealership and credit union clients. Walker has extensive experience in these industries and has been an active participant and presenter at conferences and meetings.

Daniel P. Doiron holds client responsibilities for both accounting and taxation matters for most of the firm's major clients. In achieving his CPA designation, Doiron was the State of Maine Gold Medalist in the May 1987 CPA examination. He is also a certified valuation analyst, and has written numerous articles and taught seminars on a variety of issues.

William L. Randall has been in public accounting for more than 30 years, and has handled client responsibilities for most of Albin, Randall & Bennett's major clients. Randall is available to participate in any aspect of the firm's professional services. He is active at the national level in restructuring professional standards, and speaks at national conferences and meetings.

David V. Jean is a principal in the firm's Lewiston office, and has extensive experience in the manufacturing and construction industries. Jean also provides computer and management consulting services to the firm's commercial clients.

Full Range of Service to Business

A lbin, Randall & Bennett works extensively in assisting clients in representation before the Internal Revenue Service, as well as in estate and tax planning. The firm's professionals perform audits, reviews, and compilations of financial statements. Its in-house international expertise is complemented by its active membership in Summit International Associates, Inc., a worldwide association of accounting and consulting firms. Albin, Randall & Bennett's areas of concentration include manufacturing and distribution companies, auto dealerships, not-for-profit organizations of all sizes, credit unions, construction contractors, and high-wealth individuals. The firm's experience and extensive resources, applied to client concerns at a high level of professionalism and customization, make it a major resource for the companies it serves.

Albin, Randall & Bennett's steady growth over the years, built on client retention, is a powerful endorsement of the firm's success in meeting that commitment. ●

GAIL OSGOOD

THE MAINE LOBSTERMAN
BY VICTOR KAHILL

FOR THE WORLD'S FAIR A.D. 1939
PLACED IN THIS PUBLIC SQUARE BY
THE PORTLAND CITY COUNCIL A.D. 1977

1980-1989

1981
UBS PaineWebber Inc.

1982
OEST Associates, Inc.

1982
Orthopaedic Associates of Portland

1983
Lebel & Harriman, LLP

1983
Portland Tugboat and Ship Docking Co., Inc.

1983
Wright Express LLC

1984
IDEXX Laboratories, Inc.

1985
Granger Northern, Inc.

1987
National Semiconductor

1987
Portland Regency Hotel

1988
Casco Bay Weekly

1988
The Nelson Group, Ltd.

1989
Moon Moss

UBS PaineWebber Inc. is a leading financial services institution with a worldwide reach. The superb capabilities of the current UBS PaineWebber are set on the foundation that was laid in 1879 by Charles Cabot Jackson and Laurence Curtis, who opened a brokerage office in Boston, as well as by William A. Paine and Wallace C. Webber, whose firm opened a year later on the same street.

The Portland office of UBS PaineWebber opened in 1981 with the acquisition of the local firm Barker Deering Associates. The PaineWebber organization joined forces with the local Kidder Peabody office when the companies' parent organizations merged in 1995. And in 2000, UBS Warburg acquired PaineWebber, which became UBS PaineWebber Inc.

Integrated Core Businesses

UBS PaineWebber, a member of the UBS Financial Services group, provides investment advice and wealth management services to an affluent client base, including individuals, institutions, state and local governments, and public agencies. UBS PaineWebber, with its parent company UBS Warburg, combines state-of-the-art business and investment acumen with an unrivaled reputation for outstanding research and client service.

UBS Warburg is a leader in equities, corporate finance, merger and acquisition advisory and financing, financial structuring, fixed-income issuance and trading, foreign exchange, derivatives, and risk management. UBS Warburg also provides private equity financing through UBS Capital.

UBS PaineWebber clients, working together with their financial advisers, enjoy access to some of the most innovative and sophisticated investments and services available. UBS PaineWebber is distinguished by its characteristics of innovation, personal attention, friendliness, strength, reach, flexibility, and security.

Essential Character

The essential character of the present-day UBS PaineWebber as a financial services organization extends to community service, both by the business and by many of its staff people as individuals. UBS PaineWebber is a national sponsor of the Juvenile Diabetes Foundation, with the local branch supporting fund-raising events for a number of years.

The Portland branch of UBS PaineWebber is a major contributor to the United Way of Greater Portland, and has sponsored the annual Children's Museum Auction. The branch has contributed regularly to the Portland Partnership, a collaboration between Portland Public Schools and businesses, and has supported the capital campaigns of both the Maine Medical Center and the Portland Public Library.

UBS PaineWebber Inc.'s employees are active as board, committee, and participating members of many organizations in Portland. While the company's employees take part in the leading financial services globally and locally, those same employees are also responsible participants in promoting the betterment of the lives of their fellow citizens. ●

THE PORTLAND OFFICE OF UBS PAINEWEBBER INC. OPENED IN 1981.

IN A LOCATION CONVENIENT TO PORTLAND'S MAJOR HOSPITALS, ORTHOPAEDIC ASSOCIATES OF PORTLAND OFFERS 17 SPECIALISTS WHO PROVIDE A RANGE OF ORTHOPEDIC TREATMENT AND SUPPORT SERVICES. THE RESULT IS AN INTEGRATED APPROACH TO THE HIGHEST-QUALITY ORTHOPEDIC CARE, WITH THE PATIENT BENEFITING FROM PHYSICIANS WHO SUBSPECIALIZE IN PARTICULAR ASPECTS OF ORTHOPEDICS AND WHO HAVE RECEIVED INTENSE TRAINING AND HANDS-ON EXPERIENCE IN THEIR FIELDS. AS PART OF THE

group's commitment to patient satisfaction and convenience, the practice provides at its Portland location virtually all treatment short of those requiring a hospital stay: diagnostic services such as MRI and X-ray; clinical examination; an on-site day surgery center; casting services; and fabrication of orthotics.

Commitment to Quality

Founded in 1982, Orthopaedic Associates of Portland is comprised of 17 physicians and seven physician assistants who are supported by a staff numbering approximately 100. The group's Sewall Street location in Portland is within blocks of Maine Medical Center and Mercy Hospital. The practice subsidizes and supports significant continuing medical education and training for its support staff, in addition to providing fellowship training to other physicians.

Many of the physicians at Orthopaedic Associates, who subspecialize in particular aspects of orthopedics, received their training at renowned medical centers. Their expertise allows them to utilize detailed medical knowledge to quickly diagnose and effectively treat orthopedic medical problems.

As part of its commitment to quality, the organization has established within itself integrated orthopedic specialty care centers in which physicians focus on their particular areas of expertise. Specifically, Orthopaedic Associates of Portland is organized into the Sports Medicine Center, Orthopaedic Trauma Center, Joint Replacement Center, Hand Center, Spine Center, Orthopaedic Surgery Center, and MRI Center. Independent, on-site physical therapy services are also available through the HealthSouth Physical Therapy Center. In addition to its Sewall Street location, satellite offices are maintained in Yarmouth and Windham.

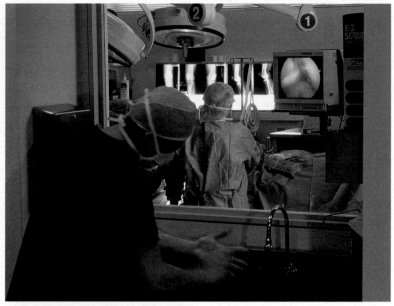

Quality Medical Experience

Orthopaedic Associates of Portland recognizes that a quality medical experience also requires excellent administrative and billing support. From the patient's first call to the office through the completion of care, a well-trained staff helps to set up appointment times, address clinical and nonclinical concerns, assist in clarifying billing and insurance issues, and provide general support services.

Orthopaedic Associates of Portland's logo is inspired by Leonardo da Vinci's famous drawing of the human body in *Divina Proportione*. The triadic nature of the artwork corresponds to the three points of Orthopaedic Associates' practice: clinical, surgical, and rehabilitative. The group's philosophy subscribes to da Vinci's words: "Those will be closest to perfection whose parts . . . are made so as to best operate in keeping with that which nature has ordained." ●

IN A LOCATION CONVENIENT TO PORTLAND'S MAJOR HOSPITALS, ORTHOPAEDIC ASSOCIATES OF PORTLAND OFFERS 17 SPECIALISTS WHO PROVIDE A RANGE OF ORTHOPEDIC TREATMENT AND SUPPORT SERVICES.

O EST ASSOCIATES, INC. OF SOUTH PORTLAND, A FULLY INTEGRATED ENGINEERING, ARCHITECTURAL, AND SURVEYING FIRM, PROVIDES SERVICES IN SITE AND BUILDING DEVELOPMENT. THE COMPANY, WITH A HISTORY OF PIONEERING WORK IN THE ENVIRONMENT AND START-TO-FINISH PARTNER RELATIONSHIPS WITH CLIENTS, MAINTAINS THE FULL RANGE OF SPECIALTIES AND DISCIPLINES REQUIRED, INCLUDING ENGINEERS, ARCHITECTS, LAND SURVEYORS, AND CONSTRUCTION MANAGERS. SINCE ITS FOUNDING IN 1982, THE FIRM

has served municipal, state, and federal agencies; land developers; and industrial clients. Founder Harvey J. Oest is now president of a company with some 40 employees.

While its primary business focus is within Maine, OEST has completed projects throughout the United States, including Department of Defense (DOD) work in Florida and Alaska. The firm's strengths include creation of well-thought-out, original designs to serve special client needs. OEST's design of a facility for the DOD to house KC-135 tanker aircraft–an octagonal building that maximized the use of space–has been repeated at sites across the country.

Technical Excellence, Human Considerations

OEST's combination of technical excellence and human considerations has been called into service for numerous projects, including the Sable Oaks development in South Portland, where the company created a unique, new office environ-

OEST ASSOCIATES, INC. HAS COMPLETED A VARIETY OF PORTLAND-AREA IMPROVEMENT PROJECTS, INCLUDING THE REVITALIZATION OF THE CAPE ELIZABETH DOWNTOWN AREA (BOTTOM) AND THE REMODELING OF THE PORTLAND INTERNATIONAL JETPORT (TOP).

ment that specifically included pleasant, people-friendly surroundings.

OEST's valuable role as a partner has been well demonstrated in its work with municipalities. The Sable Oaks project was the first Tax Increment Financing District in the area, and OEST has been in the forefront of developing implementation of such innovations for communities. Working as a full member of a project's development team and privy to its marketing strategy, OEST can provide valuable service in foreseeing problems and possibilities. OEST has been involved in numerous projects, including the Portland International Jetport, the Town of Cape Elizabeth, and the Maine Mall, that have contributed to the Maine community— both in quality and in economic terms. One of the company's most popular successes was the Christmas Tree Shops in South Portland. Previous projects had failed at the site, which was substantially impacted by environmental and geotechnical constraints. OEST worked with the state's Department of Environmental Protection and the Army Corps of Engineers to bring in an environmentally sound and economically successful project.

Start-to-Finish Services

OEST is structured to provide complete building design services—from initial pre-acquisition studies through conceptual design, final design, permit acquisition, and construction. The company offers comprehensive services in civil engineering; roadway design; utility and infrastructure design; environmental engineering; site design, including landscape architecture; and permitting.

The firm's structural engineers have worked throughout the United States for industrial, commercial, military, public, and private clients. OEST's staff has diverse and extensive experience in the design, inspection, evaluation, and analysis of new and existing facilities.

OEST has worked at more than 50 airports throughout the Northeast, providing such services as the planning, environmental, financial, and design elements of airport development projects. The company is affiliated with the American Association of Airport Executives. Also, its transportation work includes rail, most notably track upgrade engineering for the New England Passenger Rail Project.

Experience plus Broad Perspective

OEST's architectural staff has extensive experience in industrial, commercial, office, and health care facilities. This group works in new design and the restoration and rehabilitation of older structures. The firm's building services segment provides mechanical and electrical engineering designs and landscape architectural services.

OEST's surveying staff members work throughout Maine, New Hampshire, and Massachusetts. They have extensive experience on standard boundary, topographic, route, right-of-way, hydrographic, and property surveys. The group's projects have included roadway and pavement design, site layout and utility design, permitting, and facility expansions. OEST's crews are trained and experienced in operational requirements for projects located in deep-woods terrain and environmentally sensitive areas.

The company's construction management division offers clients the ability to apply a contractor's perspective to their projects during the design process, and provides the necessary trades to build the facilities. By applying constructability reviews at the design stage, OEST has the unique in-house capability to provide accurate cost estimating, value engineering, network analysis, and scheduling.

Technology Support across the Board

Aware that technology is an essential component of its core businesses, OEST always strives to own and effectively utilize its state-of-the-art equipment. Utilizing its extensive system of computer hardware and software, as well as its technical expertise, the company offers its clients a wide range of computer services during and after a project. OEST has Internet accessibility for rapid exchange of electronic information, and field data is collected electronically through global positioning system (GPS) units and electronic data collectors. The firm's computations are done through survey software, and its plans are produced by computer-aided design software. Additionally, each employee is provided with a computerized workstation to enhance the company's overall communications, internally and with its clients.

OEST's president has a long history of involvement with community service personally, as well as in the company's professional work. Oest's volunteer work has included serving as the president of the South Portland-Cape Elizabeth Chamber of Commerce, the director of the Greater Portland Chambers of Commerce, the chairman of the Chamber's Community Affairs Committee, and a member of the Economic Development Council of Maine.

OEST Associates, Inc. sees itself as a resource to the community, as well as to its clients, with a commitment to the long-term health of the environment and the economy. That sense of community has been demonstrated in projects that combine professional and volunteer work, such as facility renovation for the Center for Environmental Enterprise—an environmental technology incubator. That kind of commitment is only natural for a community-based organization committed to pioneering partnerships. ●

A NUMBER OF LOCAL BUSINESSES HAVE BENEFITED FROM OEST'S SERVICES, INCLUDING FAIRCHILD SEMICONDUCTOR, CATERPILLAR, AND THE MAINE MALL.

OEST HAS ALSO COMPLETED PROJECTS FOR CHRISTMAS TREE SHOPS, THE BASS SHOE WORLD HEADQUARTERS, AND AMERISUITES HOTEL.

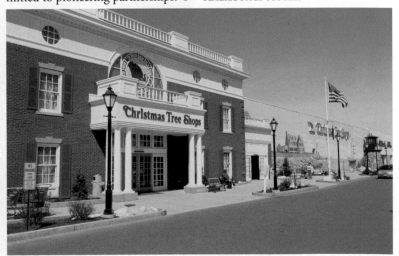

LEBEL & HARRIMAN, LLP IS A TRUSTED, CONFIDENTIAL ADVISER HELPING PEOPLE AND BUSINESSES BECOME AND REMAIN FINANCIALLY INDEPENDENT. THE FIRM, FOUNDED IN 1983, CONCENTRATES ON PROVIDING HIGH-VALUE, INNOVATIVE SERVICES TO FAMILY COMPANIES AROUND THE NATION, AND TO SMALL CLIENTS AND NONPROFITS OFTEN OVERLOOKED BY MAJOR CONSULTING FIRMS. ■ LED BY PRINCIPALS MICHAEL A. LEBEL AND PHILIP E. HARRIMAN,

the company offers two distinct practices: preservation of assets—advisory services dealing with matters such as estate planning and asset management for closely held companies; and accumulation of assets—retirement planning, mergers and acquisitions, and related subjects.

The firm's services can include design and implementation of customized employee benefits, such as a 401(k) program developed for one of the largest payroll companies in America. That company's average client—with just 15 employees—lacks the size to afford its own modern personnel services. The Lebel & Harriman product, which accumulated the payroll company's clients into a pool, gained for these clients the automated economies of scale.

Dedication to the Customer

Lebel & Harriman designs its services to provide up-to-date expertise to some of Maine's largest employers, as well as to companies adjusting to the growing pains of a thriving new business.

The firm's special areas of service are family businesses that need to work out succession planning, and small businesses going through transitions such as a change in ownership. Lebel & Harriman is proud of its ability—through its understanding of those processes—to preserve not only the family values involved, but also the business that means so much to its members.

Lebel & Harriman sees its customers as end users, such as the employee deciding whether to put money into a retirement program, or the small-business owner facing the burden of explaining to employees the intricacies of a transfer to a new money manager. The firm takes the role of allaying uncertainty on a person-to-person basis, lifting burdens from both employees and employers. The service is taken into the break room, as well as into the boardroom.

In keeping with its view of its role, Lebel & Harriman devotes itself to building an internal working environment in which employees are valued and their suggestions are heard and acted upon. This environment, in

turn, creates a sensitive climate for clients, as the firm handles their personal and financial affairs.

Community Involvement

Lebel & Harriman's people-oriented point of view, which the firm also applies to the wider community, has led to extensive work with nonprofit organizations, where the firm has provided employee services that rank with those of the business world. Harriman served eight years in the Maine State Senate, sponsoring such legislation as a bill creating the Maine International Trade Center, established to encourage synergies that lead to a better life.

Both principals of Lebel & Harriman are locals through and through, brought up in Maine and raising their families in the Portland area. They believe Maine is a place people want to settle in, raise a family, and operate a business. Their love for the region permeates the philosophy of Lebel & Harriman, LLP. Giving back to the community has and will continue to be the guiding force behind the firm's practice. ●

LED BY PRINCIPALS MICHAEL A. LEBEL AND PHILIP E. HARRIMAN, LEBEL & HARRIMAN, LLP OFFERS TWO DISTINCT PRACTICES: PRESERVATION OF ASSETS— ADVISORY SERVICES DEALING WITH MATTERS SUCH AS ESTATE PLANNING AND ASSET MANAGEMENT FOR CLOSELY HELD COMPANIES; AND ACCUMULATION OF ASSETS— RETIREMENT PLANNING, MERGERS AND ACQUISITIONS, AND RELATED SUBJECTS.

WHEN MASSIVE OCEANGOING VESSELS MUST BE SKILLFULLY MANEUVERED IN THE TIGHT CONFINES OF PORTLAND HARBOR, THE TUGS OF PORTLAND TUGBOAT AND SHIP DOCKING CO., INC. NUDGE AND GUIDE THEM TO SAFETY. THE PORT OF PORTLAND UNOBTRUSIVELY PROVIDES A MAJOR ECONOMIC INFRASTRUCTURE TO THE ECONOMY OF NORTHERN NEW ENGLAND AND NEIGHBORING CANADA, AND PORTLAND TUGBOAT IS RIGHT THERE IN THE THICK OF IT.

Long Years of Experience

The Portland Tugboat and Ship Docking Co. is backed by a wealth of professional experience. Massachusetts-native Arthur Fournier went to sea when he was 15 years old, sailing with Sheridan Transportation of New York, which operated 60 seagoing coal barges and six seagoing tugboats. Fournier got into the tugboat business at age 19 by purchasing a sunken tugboat for $1, and then equipping it with a GM 6-71 diesel engine from a wrecked Greyhound bus. The *St. Theresa* then went to work for Daniel J. Boylan, owner of Boston Sand and Gravel, towing sand barges in the Charles River. "Having the privilege of working with Mr. Boylan was like spending four years at Harvard Business School," says Fournier.

After years of working ships and barges in Boston Harbor, New York Harbor, and other New England ports, Fournier bought a tugboat company in Belfast, Maine—moving it to Searsport, Maine, in 1977 to serve the oil terminals and paper mills of down east Maine. Also in 1977, Fournier put two tugboats to work at Bath Iron Works (BIW) on the guided-missile frigate (FFG) shipbuilding program. Shortly after his arrival at BIW, Fournier was assigned as a docking pilot for the ship movements within the yard, and reported directly to Royce Young, senior vice president of production. Fournier moved the ships on nights and weekends, and introduced a system of moving the ships along the production line with tugs. "The BIW motto was 'Below budget and ahead of schedule,'" says Fournier. "It was a privilege to be part of the Bath Iron Works team and to share in its work ethic during the highly successful FFG building program."

In 1982, Fournier assigned a tugboat to BIW's new Portland Harbor dry-dock operation, and started Portland Tugboat and Ship Docking Co. At the same time, he became a docking pilot for Portland Harbor.

The circumstances have changed drastically over the years. Fournier saw the Oil Pollution Act of 1990 "hit this industry like a bolt of lightning." As a result of the *Exxon Valdez* oil spill disaster in Alaska, regulation tightened up. For any tanker docking operation, the owners and terminals now dictate tugboat size and horsepower requirements, allowable sea state, visibility, wind, and escorts.

"We no longer have to make those decisions," Fournier says. "It took the weight of the world off my shoulders. Earlier, you were judged as a pilot by how thick a fog that you could dock a ship. That is now ancient history."

Big Ships and Various Cargo

Tankers are the life's blood of Portland Tugboat, calling at the South Portland terminals of Gulf, Motiva, Sprague, Portland Pipe Line, and ExxonMobil. Their cargoes are crude oil, gasoline, home heating oil, fuel oil, jet fuel, kerosene, and road salt. Bulk carriers are another Portland Tugboat customer, and are headed for Merrill's Marine Terminal in Portland for general cargo such as pulp and paper products, coal, salt, and scrap.

THE COMPANY THAT BECAME PORTLAND TUGBOAT AND SHIP DOCKING CO., INC. WAS FOUNDED BY ARTHUR FOURNIER WITH THE $1 PURCHASE OF A SUNKEN TUGBOAT, WHICH WAS THEN FITTED WITH A GM 6-71 DIESEL ENGINE FROM A WRECKED GREYHOUND BUS.

There also are cruise ships and cargo vessels at the International Ferry Terminal, and special jobs at the BIW dry dock. When the dry dock was purchased in 1982, Portland Tugboat brought it up from Virginia. When it was hauled away in 2001, the familiar red-and-black tugboats with the yellow stacks were busily conducting the loading of the nine dry-dock sections, as well as assisting the 710-foot *Blue Marlin*, the world's largest submersible lift ship.

In 1987, Fournier beat out the established Boston competition for the prized opportunity to conduct the annual turning of the USS *Constitution* by making an offer the navy could not refuse: handling the job for one cent instead of the $1 traditionally bid. He considered it a "patriotic privilege" to be entrusted with the care, custody, and control of America's most venerable and oldest-commissioned warship. The tug *Captain Bill* was chosen to make the five-mile trip from Constitution Wharf to Castle

Island and back, all the while hosting 120 friends and customers on board. "It was a spectacular event never to be forgotten by those who attended," says Fournier.

Family Owned, Family Operated

The present-day Portland Tugboat and Ship Docking Co. is a family-owned business, with nine employees, five of them captains. Fournier and three of his sons run seven tugboats to handle the 24-hour-a-day/seven-day-a-week workload. Brian is a licensed captain and president of the company; Douglas is 18 years old and holds a 100-ton captain's license; and Patrick is 17 years old and holds a U.S. Coast Guard-issued six-pack license.

The youngest son, Patrick, started his own company—Towboat U.S., using two light, high-speed towboats for emergency service to summer pleasure boaters—while still a high school student. The Fourniers live in

South Portland, just minutes from the boats.

The Boats

In Portland, the Fourniers operate the tug *Pete*, a 7,000-horsepower, 149-foot tug—one of the largest and most powerful tugboats north of New Orleans. *Pete* is used on escorts and in the docking of crude oil carriers, and is equipped with a fire-and-foam system that has a capacity of 5,360 gallons of water a minute at 260 pounds per square inch.

Looking to the future, the company refitted the ex-navy tugboat *Wathena* with independently rotating propellers, so the 5,100-horsepower tugboat can turn at full power without moving an inch forward or astern. The Fourniers were ready for bigger ships and tighter quarters before the need arrived.

Two other, larger tugboats, *Fournier Boys* and *Fournier Girls*, both more than 100 feet long and with more than 4,000 horsepower, are approved for escort service by the Portland Pipe Line Corporation and its shippers. The company's other boats are *Stamford*, *Captain Bill*, and *Captain Sweet*, all stationed in Portland.

As Portland Harbor enters an exciting new era with the departure of the BIW dry dock, the shipping business faces more opportunities to expand, as well as many decisions that will affect Portland Tugboat and Ship Docking Co., Inc. "Regardless, we'll be there, leading the charge as part of the Portland team," says Fournier. "Whatever the future may hold for Portland Harbor, we'll be right here." ●

PORTLAND TUGBOAT WAS HIGHLY EXPERIENCED IN MOVING VESSELS THROUGH THE OLD MILLION DOLLAR BRIDGE.

TODAY, PORTLAND TUGBOAT MOVES EVEN LARGER SHIPS THROUGH THE CASCO BAY BRIDGE.

WHEN WRIGHT EXPRESS LLC WAS FOUNDED IN PORTLAND IN 1983, THE FOUNDERS COULD NOT HAVE FORESEEN TODAY'S LEVEL OF SUCCESS. THEIR IDEA WAS TO SERVE COMMERCIAL FLEETS BY CAPTURING AND REPORTING FUEL TRANSACTION DATA. NOW, WITH MORE THAN 3 MILLION COMMERCIAL CHARGE ACCOUNTS, WRIGHT EXPRESS IS THE NUMBER ONE COMMERCIAL FLEET CHARGE CARD PROVIDER IN THE UNITED STATES, AND OWNS ITS OWN COMMERCIAL BANK IN SALT LAKE CITY.

The company revolutionized the fleet card industry when it introduced information management tools delivered through a charge card program specially designed for businesses with company vehicles. Wright Express offers a variety of corporate commercial fleet charge card programs with reporting and maintenance capabilities to meet companies' needs.

A Bright Idea Plus Technology

The initial idea to work with both fuel providers and fleets was given impetus by the development and popularization of electronic data capture of credit card transactions. These devices could collect, transport, and organize transaction information. Compiled into easy to read reports, this timely information simplified fleet management, provided security, and helped control costs. Fleet man-

WRIGHT EXPRESS LLC IS THE NUMBER ONE FLEET CHARGE CARD PROVIDER IN THE UNITED STATES.

agers and business owners no longer had to study and justify stacks of individual drivers' receipts. A single report told them who bought what, where, and when, and how much it cost. This ability to provide detailed tracking, cost control, and performance information was brand new.

Technology drives Wright Express and makes new functionality possible. The company anticipates and keeps pace with technological developments, creating new products and features as technology changes. Today, Wright Express offers a variety of customized reports, Internet-based online account access and a state-of-the-art data warehouse that enables fleet managers to study and compare historical data from their desktops, as well as maintain their card and driver database.

To execute the company's mission and stay at the top of its market, Wright Express annually involves employees at all levels—and even its customers and partners—in an intensive strategic planning process. Such broad involvement in idea generation and formulation of business practices and products is a key ingredient in the company's success.

A Host of Innovative Products

The Wright Express mission is to be the defining force in innovation and customer service in its industry. With this focus, the company has made its Universal Fleet Card the leading fleet card program in the United States. The Wright Express fleet card is accepted at more than 160,000 fuel and service locations nationwide and provides the highest level of electronic transaction data capture in the fleet card industry. More than 150,000 commercial and government fleets use this card to make effective, cost-saving management decisions based on timely analyses of purchase data.

Wright Express also partners with petroleum marketers in private label card programs that carry the partners' brand names. Many of the major oil companies and many regional and smaller providers depend on Wright Express to administer and grow their commercial fuel card programs. Vehicle leasing companies and professional associations partner with Wright Express in jointly branded card programs. All the major vehicle leasing companies in the United

States and many smaller leasing companies partner with Wright Express on cobrand cards. Wright Express works closely with partners and fleet managers to develop card features, options, and reports that meet the clients' needs.

The Benefits of Wright Express

From the customer's viewpoint, Wright Express fleet cards offer a number of benefits, starting with better, timely, and more comprehensive data. Because the card is accepted at five out of six fueling sites and many vehicle service sites across the country, it is convenient for drivers to use. Transaction details are captured electronically for 99.5 percent of all purchases made with the Wright Express card.

Fleet managers can access this fueling data right from their desktops via a product called WEX*Online®*. Electronic data purchasing and fuel information output can be downloaded into the customer's system via a variety of file formats, such as Lotus, Excel, DBF, or ASCII. Fleet managers can then analyze or report on the data at their convenience. They also can maintain and change their accounts, adding or removing drivers and vehicles as necessary.

The card's tight electronic controls deliver transaction security. Drivers must enter their ID number and their vehicle's odometer reading before a transaction can begin. This helps prevent unauthorized purchases and reduce discrepancies and incon-

sistencies. It also provides vehicle performance data.

Overall, the Wright Express program helps fleet managers establish and enforce effective fueling policies. With the fleet charge card, fleet costs can be reduced by as much as 15 to 20 percent.

High-Performance Culture

The way employees work together is the essence of the Wright Express corporate culture—casual, but high performance. At the core of the company's growth are the people: independent thinkers and team players with an entrepreneurial spirit. Wright Express looks for people with a passion for excellence. The company values and practices regular and open communication to promote the sharing of information

and exchange of ideas. The achievements of employees are recognized and rewarded on a regular basis.

The Wright Express headquarters has its own pleasant high-energy personality: people are friendly and support each other. They celebrate holidays and have made Halloween a major company event. Wright Express people are encouraged to work actively in their communities, carrying the company's progressive internal practices and expertise to the outside world.

Wright Express lends its corporate support to the many nonprofit agencies with which its employees are active. Among the beneficiaries are the American Cancer Society, United Way, and the MS Society; cultural organizations such as the Portland Concert Association and the Maine State Music Theater; many programs for children, including Youth Alternatives, the Children's Museum of Maine, Junior Achievement, PROP, and the Center for Grieving Children; as well as hospitals, schools, and colleges. Wright Express supports the Maine Computers in the Schools program and established the Governor's Computer Science Scholarship to the University of Southern Maine.

The continuing growth of Wright Express LLC is based on the quality of its products, its strong commitment to customer service excellence, and, above all, on its people. Armed with these values and with a clear strategic vision, the company looks forward to continued growth and success for decades to come. ●

ANYONE WHO OWNS A PET; DRINKS MILK; EATS CHICKEN, PORK, OR BEEF; OR APPRECIATES CLEAN DRINKING WATER, MAY BE TOUCHED BY IDEXX PRODUCTS. BASED IN WESTBROOK, MAINE, IDEXX LABORATORIES, INC. IS A GLOBAL MARKET LEADER IN THE DEVELOPMENT AND COMMERCIALIZATION OF INNOVATIVE, TECHNOLOGY-BASED DIAGNOSTIC PRODUCTS AND SERVICES FOR VETERINARY, FOOD, AND ENVIRONMENTAL APPLICATIONS. IDEXX'S LABORATORIES, SALES OFFICES, AND PRODUCT DISTRIBUTION CENTERS SPAN THE

globe, with 36 locations that are supported by more than 2,500 employees.

More than 50,000 veterinary clinics worldwide rely on IDEXX products and services to help pets live longer, healthier, happier lives. Says IDEXX Founder, President, and CEO David Shaw, "Our largest business is focused on animal health, and our mission in this market is to provide veterinarians with the diagnostic products and services, information technology, and pharmaceuticals needed to practice the best medicine possible for the animals under their care."

IDEXX is the leading player in the veterinary diagnostics market worldwide and is the largest supplier of practice management software and Internet services to veterinarians. Recently, the company also expanded into the $8 billion veterinary pharmaceuticals market with a strong line of new and innovative products for applications in dogs, cats, horses, and commercial animals.

IDEXX also offers a network of products and services designed to

IDEXX'S MISSION IS TO BE "A GREAT COMPANY BY CREATING EXCEPTIONAL LONG-TERM VALUE FOR OUR EMPLOYEES, CUSTOMERS, AND STOCKHOLDERS THROUGH WORLDWIDE LEADERSHIP IN OUR BUSINESSES." THESE BUSINESSES INCLUDE VETERINARY PRACTICE MANAGEMENT SOFTWARE, REFERENCE LABORATORY SERVICES, AND SPECIALIST CONSULTING.

improve the safety of drinking water, milk, and meat products for human consumption. IDEXX's water-testing products lead the way in detecting bacterial contaminants in drinking water, wastewater, pharmaceutical, cosmetic, and other markets. From the dairy farm to milk-processing plants and government regulatory

agencies, IDEXX is also the market leader in the detection of drug residues in milk. In addition, the company provides poultry, cattle, and swine producers with diagnostic kits and computerized health monitoring systems.

Strong Roots in Animal Health

In the early 1980s, as a major technological revolution was brewing in the biological sciences, IDEXX began to harness the power of this new technology to benefit health and quality managers in the company's target markets. In 1985, working in a small building on the Portland waterfront, the company launched its initial line of veterinary diagnostic products with a staff of just a dozen people.

By 1994, IDEXX was publicly held and was generating more than $100 million in revenues. It had built an international reputation as the undisputed leader in the veterinary business, and it was beginning to expand into the food- and water-testing business. The company also began to focus more aggressively on international markets, and has now opened offices in Mexico, Japan, Taiwan, Australia, New

IDEXX PROVIDES MORE THAN 50,000 VETERINARY CLINICS WORLDWIDE WITH DIAGNOSTICS PRODUCTS AND SERVICES CAPABLE OF DELIVERING FAST, ACCURATE INFORMATION ON THE HEALTH STATUS OF COMPANION ANIMALS.

Zealand, England, France, Germany, Italy, The Netherlands, Sweden, Israel, Spain, Brazil, and Argentina.

Several years ago, IDEXX capitalized on its knowledge of veterinary markets and new technology by expanding into the market for computer software used to manage veterinary hospitals. The company is now the leading provider of these systems worldwide and has launched a business-to-business Internet venture to provide veterinarians with the benefits of Internet connectivity. The company's pharmaceutical operations are based in North Carolina—and, in that location, as well as in Maine, it is developing new animal drugs in categories ranging from parasite and wound care to antibiotics and allergy treatment.

Future Success from a Maine Base

Of IDEXX's 2,500-plus talented and dedicated employees, more than 700 work at the company's Westbrook headquarters. Seventy-five percent of the company's sales are within the United States, with virtually unlimited potential for growth. IDEXX became a publicly traded company in 1991 and is traded on the Nasdaq stock exchange under the symbol IDXX.

IDEXX is committed to continued innovation and growth in the future.

It invests heavily in research and development, constantly upgrading existing products and introducing new product and technology platforms that offer superior capabilities and performance for its customers. It is a company of firsts, having been the first to offer fast, point-of-care testing for veterinarians; the first to offer veterinary telemedicine via the Internet; and the first to offer computerized radiography in the veterinary industry.

IDEXX has been very successful in using some of the most exciting technologies of today to build strong businesses in very attractive markets. In a world with increasingly powerful technologies and a growing market demand for technology-based products, the future looks very promising for IDEXX—in Maine and around the world. ●

FROM THE DAIRY FARM TO MILK PROCESSING PLANTS AND GOVERNMENT REGULATORY AGENCIES, IDEXX IS THE MARKET LEADER IN THE DETECTION OF DRUG RESIDUES IN MILK (LEFT).

IDEXX'S WATER TESTING PRODUCTS LEAD THE WAY IN DETECTING BACTERIAL CONTAMINANTS IN DRINKING WATER, WASTEWATER, PHARMACEUTICAL, COSMETIC AND OTHER MARKETS (RIGHT).

IDEXX PROVIDES POULTRY, CATTLE, AND SWINE PRODUCERS WITH DIAGNOSTIC KITS AND COMPUTERIZED HEALTH MONITORING SYSTEMS.

GRANGER NORTHERN, INC. PROVIDES GENERAL CONTRACTING AND CONSTRUCTION MANAGEMENT SERVICES TO THE NORTHERN NEW ENGLAND MARKET—PRIMARILY MAINE, BUT ALSO NEW HAMPSHIRE AND VERMONT. BY 2000, UNDER THE LEADERSHIP OF THOMAS FREDERICK, PRESIDENT, THE COMPANY HAD GROWN TO BECOME ONE OF THE REGION'S LARGEST BUILDING CONTRACTORS. ■ GRANGER NORTHERN'S SLOGAN— RESTORING THE PAST. BUILDING THE FUTURE—CAPTURES THE FIRM'S RANGE OF CONSTRUCTION PROJECTS.

The company has acquired the experience and internal competence to handle the kind of detailed work involved in larger structures. Downtown Portland boasts many examples of Granger Northern's work, and the firm's structures can be spotted throughout Maine, New Hampshire, and Vermont, frequently as large schools or other public buildings.

Since its inception, Granger Northern has constructed or renovated projects valued at more than $500 million. Granger has extensive experience working with both private and public clients. It has worked as general contractor, construction manager, design builder, consultant, and trade contractor. The bulk of the company's construction experience is in education (K-12, colleges, and universities), health care (hospitals, medical office buildings, and assisted living), historic restorations (performing arts facilities, state offices, and

GRANGER NORTHERN, INC. HAS PROVIDED ITS SERVICES TO A NUMBER OF NOTABLE LOCAL PROJECTS, INCLUDING PIPER SHORES LUXURY RETIREMENT COMMUNITY (TOP) AND THE MAINE STATE HOUSE LEGISLATIVE CHAMBERS (BOTTOM).

hotels), office buildings, research laboratories, hotels, and retail stores.

One of the more striking of the Granger Northern projects was the renovation of the Merrill Auditorium in Portland City Hall. Working with 150-year-old stonework, Granger Northern rebuilt the walls to bear much heavier loads before completing the interior work. The $30 million historic restoration and telecommunications systems upgrade of the state house in Augusta was the work of Granger Northern, plus the $13 million renovation of the adjoining executive office building. Another big job was Piper Shores Luxury Retirement Community in Scarborough, Maine, a $25 million, 270,000-square-foot facility constructed on 130 acres with 800 feet of Atlantic Ocean frontage. Other large projects have included nearly 1 million square feet of K-12 public schools in Maine.

One of the Region's Largest

Granger Northern has built several of the more noticeable structures in the area, such as the multimodal transit center in Rutland, Vermont; the original building and a later addition to the luxury Harraseeket Inn at Freeport; and the U.S. Court House in Portland.

Granger Northern has the financial strength and ability to bond projects as large as $75 million and an aggregate bonding capacity in excess of $175 million. This bonding limit represents a third-party evaluation of Granger Northern's ability to capably perform work, and assures Granger Northern's clients that the company is respected and well run.

Granger Northern offers a full range of preconstruction services, including conceptual estimating and budget review, value engineering, scheduling, and constructability analysis. The company maintains a labor force of some 70 tradespeople for the parts of projects performed with the firm's own forces. Granger Northern's workforce provides the flexibility to tailor services to meet the specific needs of customers at the most competitive price. The office staff of 11 professionals and 12 field supervisors assures the expertise and specialization that owners and architects demand.

Value and Results

Granger Northern's business operation stresses value and results. Granger Northern can provide current, relevant budget information, obtained as a result of the company's weekly bidding activity in the Maine market. The company is committed to providing the highest-caliber construction services at the most competitive price.

The preconstruction/estimating staff at Granger Northern understands what it takes to complete a building without incorporating large budget contingencies or excessive schedule float. The real-world information Granger Northern provides enables

owners to make better-informed decisions regarding budget and the building program. The company's project personnel have proved their ability to manage projects with tight budgets and aggressive schedules.

Major Differences

From an annual volume of $20 million to $25 million in its first few years, Granger Northern has grown steadily as the company has taken on more difficult work and eventually found its niche. "We love difficult jobs, and we are rewarded with $70 million to $75 million a year in business and 100 dedicated employees," says Frederick.

Granger Northern's competence in construction management and design/build practices comprise one of the major differences between the firm and other companies. With effective scheduling, Granger Northern can start pouring concrete before the drawings are complete. The company

tries to do a substantial part of the work itself, like an old-style general contractor, which gives the firm greater control over project cost and schedule. Granger Northern pours its own foundations, erects its own steel, and does all of its own carpentry.

Granger Northern is almost entirely made up of Mainers, and many of them have been working at the company for years. "They've learned how to do those tough jobs," explains Frederick. There are Professional Registered Engineers on staff, and others have received engineering education. At the same time, the company makes extensive use of Internet connections, cell phones, and e-mail.

With a focus on quality and a determination to accept only the best work, Granger Northern, Inc. continues to restore the buildings that contribute to a city's sense of self and to build the structures that help to shape its future. ●

GRANGER NORTHERN'S PROJECTS HAVE ALSO INCLUDED THE MAINE MEDICAL CENTER RESEARCH INSTITUTE (TOP LEFT), ELLSWORTH HIGH SCHOOL (TOP RIGHT), AND THE MERRILL AUDITORIUM IN PORTLAND CITY HALL (BOTTOM).

Nﾠ ATIONAL SEMICONDUCTOR'S SOUTH PORTLAND FACILITY MANUFACTURES INTEGRATED CIRCUITS—TINY TECHNOLOGY AT THE HEART OF THE HIGH-TECH INDUSTRY. WITH MICROCHIPS DRIVING VIRTUALLY ALL ELECTRONIC PRODUCTS, THE SEMICONDUCTOR INDUSTRY IS INTEGRAL TO THE NATION'S ECONOMY, WHILE NATIONAL SEMICONDUCTOR IS AN INTEGRAL COMMUNITY PARTNER. ■ NATIONAL'S STATE-OF-THE-ART SOUTH PORTLAND FABRICATION FACILITY PRODUCES

eight-inch silicon wafers, each made up of tiny die (integrated circuits, or "chips"). Each die is a miniature cityscape, made of circuitry as small as 1/500th the thickness of a human hair. Products made here are found in many of the world's wireless telephones, information appliances, scanners, digital video disk (DVD) products, flat panel displays, digital cameras, and computer networks.

National, founded in 1959, established a presence in Maine in 1987 with the purchase of Fairchild Semiconductor (since spun off, enabling each company to concentrate on its core competencies). National's current flagship manufacturing facility was started in 1995, and began producing wafers in 1997. National plans to maintain its place on the cutting edge, bringing the next several generations of semiconductor technology to Maine.

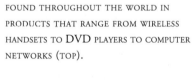

NATIONAL SEMICONDUCTOR CHIPS ARE FOUND THROUGHOUT THE WORLD IN PRODUCTS THAT RANGE FROM WIRELESS HANDSETS TO DVD PLAYERS TO COMPUTER NETWORKS (TOP).

NATIONAL SEMICONDUCTOR'S NEWEST MANUFACTURING FACILITY BEGAN PRODUCTION IN 1997, CONTINUING A MAINE PRESENCE THAT BEGAN IN 1987 (BOTTOM).

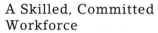

A Skilled, Committed Workforce

Nﾠ ational's South Portland operation is about 700 strong: manufacturing operators produce products around the clock, with

scores of engineers to support the equipment, process, and products, and an infrastructure of finance, facilities, human resources, and procurement. Also at the South Portland site are an advanced design center, a process development group, and the Enhanced Solutions product group. With a higher-than-local-average wage (80 percent of the positions require skilled labor), National's payroll has more

than doubled since 1998, and more than a quarter of the employees have been with the company for 10 years or more.

Health, Safety, and the Environment a Top Priority

Aﾠ t National, the health and safety of its employees and protection of the environment are essential components in business decisions. The facility was built and is operated with employee safety in mind.

Integral to the site's safety plan are the employees who comprise the firm's Emergency Response Team (ERT). This highly skilled team responds to any type of potential incidents, with the primary focus of protecting people's safety. The ERT works and trains in cooperation with South Portland's fire and rescue department, and is committed to making National Semiconductor the safest place in Maine to work.

Protecting the environment goes hand in hand with protecting employees. National Semiconductor is proud of its performance in pollution reduction and environmental initiatives; the

Another pillar in National Semiconductor's support of education is the company's Internet Training Initiative, which provides teachers with access to free Internet training and encourages Internet use in the classroom. More than 2,000 Maine teachers have received this training, and more than $450,000 has been granted to Maine teachers and their schools as part of the Internet Innovator Awards program. In the first three years of the awards program's existence, Maine has seen 11 schools win—some more than once.

Contributions to the Community

National believes businesses need to contribute to the development of the communities in which they are located and their employees live, as well as to the organizations that are important to the company's employees. The firm matches employee contributions of up to $500 to eligible charitable organizations through its Community Care program. In a unique program, employees' gifts of time can also be matched; they may apply for Dollars for Doers grants for the organizations at which they volunteer.

The employee matches and grants are a portion of the firm's larger philanthropic effort, the National Semiconductor Foundation. The goal of the foundation is to partner with educational institutions and non-profit organizations to make a significant impact in communities where National has a major presence. The State of Maine received the first grant from the foundation, for a program whose purpose is to provide every school leader in Maine with access to professional development opportunities to prepare them for technology leadership roles in their schools. ●

NATIONAL SEMICONDUCTOR'S SOUTH PORTLAND SITE PROCESSES EIGHT-INCH SILICON WAFERS. EACH CAN HAVE THOUSANDS OF DIE, WHICH ARE THEN ASSEMBLED INTO THE MORE FAMILIAR LOOKING CHIP.

company has reduced its use of hazardous substances, as well as its output of hazardous waste and toxic release.

Education a Key Focus

National believes that a well-trained workforce is essential for both the success of companies and the strength of communities, and has partnered with the public and private sectors to develop a skilled, educated workforce.

National works with the faculty in the University of Maine's engineering department on course offerings, and hires 12 to 15 co-op students each year, believing these programs are critical to the company's future success in Maine. The firm is also a founding member of the University of Maine's Microelectronics Scholarship Consortium.

National enjoys another strong partnership with Maine's Technical College System. National was one of the first companies to take a lead role in developing a specific curriculum to train students to work in the semiconductor industry. This program of study resulted in the current associate's degree in microelectronics offered at Southern Maine Technical College.

National also attempts to positively impact public education at the kindergarten-through-grade-12 level, primarily in the areas of science, math, and technology. National's employees are supported in their involvement in local classrooms, and the company matches employees' donations to public or private schools. National hosts the Maine Science and Technology Foundation science challenge for fifth graders; sponsors the Maine State Science and Technology Fair, and provides volunteers and judges for exhibits; and contributes to a science camp for girls.

NATIONAL SEMICONDUCTOR'S CLEANROOM IS LOCATED IN THE COMPANY'S STATE-OF-THE-ART MANUFACTURING FACILITY IN SOUTH PORTLAND, MAINE.

THE PORTLAND REGENCY HOTEL IS HOUSED IN A ONETIME MILITARY ARMORY WITH A COLORFUL PAST. SITUATED ON MILK STREET IN THE HISTORIC OLD PORT DISTRICT, THE HOTEL WELCOMES GUESTS WITH A BRICK-AND-STONE, CIRCULAR DRIVEWAY AND FOUNTAIN AT ITS FRONT ENTRANCE. INSIDE, GUESTS FIND LUXURY APPOINTMENTS AND A STAFF THAT IS READY TO ATTEND TO ANY NEED. THE 95-ROOM PORTLAND REGENCY IS LOCALLY OWNED, AND IS A MEMBER OF THE HISTORIC HOTELS OF AMERICA.

The Old Port district that surrounds the Regency is itself a tourist destination, and within walking distance there also are countless specialty shops, galleries, and restaurants. Scenic Casco Bay is a few blocks away, with its working waterfront. As the ferryboat line is on a nearby wharf, visitors can ride out to see the islands, the lighthouses, and the picturesque seaside cityscape, while touring the harbor and nearby waters.

Just up the street from the Regency, visitors can find the Portland Museum of Art; the Merrill auditorium, which is the venue for the Portland Symphony Orchestra; the Henry Wadsworth Longfellow home;

and numerous other historic and cultural attractions. Business locations are just minutes away in the compact metropolitan area.

A History of Change

The Portland Regency Hotel's building was erected by the city in 1895 at the request of citizens who wanted a drill facility. Since then, it has been used for public baths, a wartime dormitory for seamen on shore leave, a recreation center, a civic auditorium, and headquarters for units of the Maine National Guard.

The old place was the center of civic disagreement at various times throughout its history. The building

nearly came down in 1962, when it was declared surplus property by the National Guard and was taken over by the City of Portland again. The site was eyed as a fine spot for waterfront parking. This plan was opposed by the many veterans who had trained in the armory, and by city councilmen who thought the demolition and parking project would cost too much.

After more than a year of controversy, the building, called the State of Maine Armory or the Milk Street Armory, was sold to State Paper Co., which used it as a warehouse. The city retained repurchase rights, and the old building continued to attract interest periodically. In the late 1970s, and again in the early 1980s, interest was expressed in converting the building into a center for the performing and visual arts.

An Elegant Hotel

The building was eventually purchased for conversion into a hotel and, as always, was the center of intense public interest. Investor Eric Cianchette constructed a building on Presumpscot Street for the State Paper Co. to move to, and the new owners initiated renovation that transformed the building's interior at a total cost of $9.5 million. The Portland newspapers reported voluminously on the project, including a story about brothers who quarried marble in Greece and installed it in the Regency. The interior furnishings were custom built, except for some antique furniture.

The Portland Regency opened in 1987 as part of the revival of the Old Port. The restoration of the decaying district and its rise to immense popularity with local residents, as well as tourists, has been an exciting phenomenon, and the Regency has been in the center of it.

In converting the building to hotel use, the exterior was preserved, except for the addition of skylight windows

THE HISTORIC PORTLAND REGENCY HOTEL IS LOCATED IN THE HEART OF THE OLD PORT DISTRICT.

on the upper floors. Many of the original architectural elements create unique features in some of the spacious, traditionally appointed rooms. Highly detailed brick fireplaces, turreted corners, and windows of many shapes and sizes bring a special ambience to the guest's experience.

In 1990, in recognition of its preservation of a historically significant building, as well as of its superior service, the Portland Regency was invited by the National Trust for Historic Preservation to become a distinguished member of Historic Hotels of America. In 1998, the Regency's sister property, the Black Point Inn on Prouts Neck, also received the designation.

Modern Amenities

In essence, the Regency's character encompasses history, uniqueness, appointments, and service. As a modern luxury hotel, the Portland Regency has a wide variety of amenities. Carefully chosen employees, who attend to service with a smile, enjoy the environment so much that the hotel boasts a very low turnover rate.

The Portland Regency houses one of the city's most complete fitness facilities, the Regency Health Club. The club is open to the public, offering 30 classes a week; use of the facility is complimentary to hotel guests. The health club features aerobic classes, a wide range of equipment, an over-

sized Jacuzzi, a steam room, a sauna, massage therapy, and a tanning salon. Personalized training sessions are available as well.

While the Regency's roomy guest accommodations emphasize timeless elegance, there also are laptop rentals available; wireless, high-speed Internet access; in-room honor bars; and other appliances, services, and amenities. The hotel's conference and meeting facilities can accommodate groups from five to 150, and are equipped

with audiovisual and Internet equipment. The Armory Restaurant serves American cuisine for breakfast, lunch, and dinner; cocktails and lighter fare are featured in the Armory Lounge.

While it has endured many changes over time, the Portland Regency Hotel has remained a vital and visible testament to the city's history. Guests and city residents alike can appreciate its unique contribution to the city, and will continue to do so for years to come. ●

C*asco Bay Weekly* IS AN UNUSUAL ALTERNATIVE NEWSPAPER IN THAT IT HAS TAKEN ON THE ROLE OF A COMMUNITY PAPER, AND IS HEAVILY LOCAL IN CONTENT. WHILE THE OTHER LOCAL PAPERS ARE SEEN AS MORE REGIONAL IN SCOPE OR MORE SYNDICATED IN PRESENTATION, *Casco Bay Weekly* REMAINS INTENSELY FOCUSED ON WHAT'S GOING ON IN THE CENTER CITY. SUBJECT MATTER IS CENTERED AROUND PUBLIC AFFAIRS, PUBLIC PLACES, POP CULTURE, AND, TRUE TO TRADITION, THE WORK OF

columnists who conduct a thoroughly irreverent examination of the actions and behavior of people both official and otherwise.

The paper launched in 1988, expressing this concept: "The idea of a representative democracy assumes that the representatives are in close touch with those they represent. But we can't sit still and expect them to come to us. Our process has become too big for that. We have to go to them. The *Casco Bay Weekly* is our contribution to that process. We want it to become an instrument of community understanding. What do you want it to be?"

THE *CASCO BAY WEEKLY* STAFF MAKES A LAST MINUTE DECISION ON TUESDAY, ITS USUAL DEADLINE (TOP).

THE STAFF OF THE *CASCO BAY WEEKLY* GATHERS IN FRONT OF THE CONGRESS STREET STOREFRONT THAT SERVES AS ITS HOME BASE (BOTTOM).

Noble Sentiment, Tongue-in-Cheek Approach

The noble sentiment was sincere, but so was the tongue-in-cheek nature of then-Editor Monte Paulsen's cover story in that first issue, entitled "Political Power: How to Get Yours." That character is intact and thriving in the new century. Publisher Lael Morgan is proud of *Casco Bay Weekly*'s stance: "We're an edgy paper. We raise a lot of hell, but at the same time, we are very serious about carrying opinions not our own. We are a community paper as well as an alternative paper."

Morgan notes that the *Casco Bay Weekly* readers of years ago have grown, with Portland, into the suburbs. Yet the paper remains interested in the heart and soul of Portland, Maine. To Morgan, the suburban transplants still view the center city as their town, and therefore have stuck with the paper despite changes in their situation.

Dedicated Readership

In fact, as those readers have matured in age and economic station, they haven't changed their newspaper reading habits, and the "young turks" of ensuing generations have joined their ranks. Surveys show that two-thirds of the readers earn more than $35,000 per year, and nearly that proportion are in the 26-50 age bracket. Two-thirds are single. In its promotion, the *Casco Bay Weekly* repeats a 1998 *Wall Street Journal* quote: "Alternative papers are attracting that segment of the population that daily newspapers are struggling to get—active, urban singles." The *Casco Bay Weekly* is proof of that.

So the *Casco Bay Weekly* breezily publishes well into its second decade, in the pink and in the black. And, while it has proved to be a financial success, its alternative nature has never taken a back seat. ●

INCORPORATED IN PORTLAND IN 1988, THE NELSON GROUP, LTD. IS A PROFESSIONAL CONSULTING ORGANIZATION PROVIDING HUMAN RESOURCES AND ORGANIZATION DEVELOPMENT CONSULTING TO SERVICE, TECHNOLOGY, RETAIL, AND MANUFACTURING COMPANIES. THE TRADITIONS AND APPROACHES OF APPLIED AND INDUSTRIAL/ORGANIZATIONAL PSYCHOLOGY ARE DRAWN UPON HEAVILY, WITHOUT LOSING SIGHT OF THE NEED TO APPLY THEM MEANINGFULLY IN AN EVER-CHANGING BUSINESS ENVIRONMENT WHOSE REALITIES ARE GROWTH,

profit, and results. To meet its commitments around the world, The Nelson Group maintains relationships with dozens of other consulting groups in an atmosphere of mutual respect and professionalism.

PAUL LUISE

The Blend at Work

The Nelson Group works with both large and small business all around the globe, including a recent project involving the largest supplier of computing systems in the world. The client pursued computing and information-technology opportunities that propelled its sales force into a whirlwind of complexity far outside the conventional limits. The company turned to The Nelson Group for a worldwide sales assessment, feedback, and development initiative. In keeping with its accustomed manner, the client wanted the results on-line and at Internet speed.

The Nelson Group, in partnership with the senior management team and through the use of a customized assessment process, first helped develop and communicate the sales competencies required to fulfill business strategies, thus establishing the targets for success. Next was an unusual on-line sales assessment made available through the company's internal Web site that gives sales professionals feedback on their sales behaviors and motivators as they relate to corporate and strategic competencies as well as the requirements of their specific sales role.

The program also allows the sales manager to assess employees and provides a comprehensive training and development resources guide, an action planning process linked directly to the company's performance management system, and intranet coaching tools.

Another successful project was a career management/retention strategy system for a global software engineering company. Collaborating with the client, The Nelson Group managed to retain existing talent while attracting new people. A third was a people-based change-management process for a communications company unable to make a merger work after 18 months.

The Human Perspective

For a Fortune 50 company that had just undergone a vital and controversial reorganization, there was a special challenge: communicate the new company principles and provide

a relevant, educational session in three hours for 1,200 leaders speaking 10 different languages. To solve this daunting problem, The Nelson Group created a "leadership game." The result: To this day, people still use the game's cards and chips to reflect upon and prioritize the behaviors and principles in their work.

Regardless of the client, be it a small start-up or a global giant, The Nelson Group exhibits its trademark characteristics: It is fast, agile, and fully in possession of the human perspective. ●

MEMBERS OF THE NELSON GROUP, LTD. GATHER ON THE ROOFTOP OF THE COMPANY'S HISTORIC OLD PORT LOCATION (TOP).

THE HUMAN PERSPECTIVE IS CENTRAL TO THE NELSON GROUP'S ASSESSMENT-DRIVEN SOLUTIONS (BOTTOM LEFT AND RIGHT).

PAUL LUISE

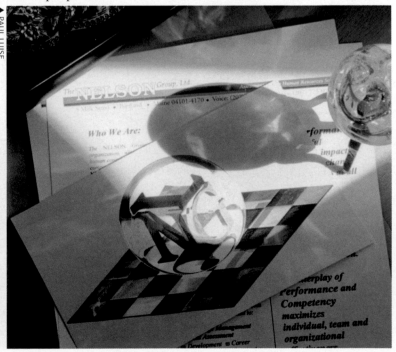

PAUL LUISE

MOON, MOSS, McGILL, HAYES & SHAPIRO, P.A., ONE OF THE PREMIER LABOR AND EMPLOYMENT FIRMS IN THE NORTHEAST, STAYS WITH ITS CLIENTS EVERY STEP OF THE WAY IN REACHING THEIR BUSINESS GOALS. THE TALENT AND EXPERIENCE THE FIRM INVESTS IN THAT COMMITMENT HAVE EARNED IT A NATIONAL REPUTATION FOR EXCELLENCE. ■ THE FIRM REPRESENTS EMPLOYERS THROUGHOUT NEW ENGLAND, AS WELL AS IN NEW JERSEY, NEW YORK, AND PENNSYLVANIA,

in all aspects of labor and employment law (More than 50 percent of the firm's clientele are located outside of Maine). Its clients range from sole proprietorships to multistate and national corporations with more than 100,000 employees, and represent virtually every sector of the economy, from hospitals and other health care providers to manufacturing, transportation, banking, public utility, retailing, hospitality, high-technology, and other service industries.

ADVISING ON THE COMPLEXITIES OF TODAY'S WORKPLACE REQUIRES CONSIDERATION OF BOTH LEGAL AND BUSINESS ISSUES. MOON MOSS PRIDES ITSELF ON BEING A TEAM OF CLIENT-FOCUSED PROBLEM SOLVERS.

Moon Moss attorneys regularly appear before federal and state courts and administrative agencies in connection with labor and employment, complex litigation, and public housing matters.

Training, Counseling, Advising

The firm's practice includes training employers and their employees in the proper handling of labor and employment matters; designing and implementing policies

MOON MOSS OFFERS THE LATEST PREVENTATIVE STRATEGIES FOR THE CHALLENGES FACING TODAY'S BUSINESS LEADERS.

and practices; providing sound, practical advice on day-to-day personnel matters; guiding businesses through governmental audits, inspections, and investigations; conducting internal corporate audits and investigations; assisting companies in safeguarding corporate property and information, including enforcing noncompetition and nonsolicitation agreements

against former employees and competitors; and counseling employers on immigration matters.

The firm's directors are well known for their contributions and dedication to the business community. Moon Moss attorneys regularly organize and speak at conferences and seminars for public and private employers; they also work closely with the Maine Chamber and Business Alliance and local chambers of commerce to educate managers and human resource professionals on subjects such as workplace violence and sexual harassment, as well as rendering advice on pending or proposed legislation. The firm's attorneys often are called upon to write articles informing employers of current developments involving labor and employment issues, and the firm's own newsletter goes out to more than 300 subscribers.

The firm also is well known for its contributions to programs sponsored by the Maine State Bar Association and the American Bar Association.

Many of Moon Moss' clients consider the firm an outsourced human resources department, relying upon the firm for consultation on a daily basis. Moon Moss' extensive experience in all areas of employment law, including alternative dispute resolution procedures, assures a cost-effective approach to resolv-

mental in bringing the Tall Ships to Portland in July 2000. As a founding director and officer of MaineSail 2000, he worked tirelessly to assemble an impressive group of members of local businesses and boating communities to bring about one of the largest and most important tourist events in Maine in decades.

Since 1995, Moon Moss attorneys have edited *The Maine Employment Law Letter*, a monthly publication for Maine employers.

Moon Moss attorneys have been appointed to state and local community boards and advisory committees, and serve on the boards of various community service agencies. Attorneys in the firm have achieved prominence in a wide range of service, educational, and pro bono activities that are a Moon Moss hallmark.

Referring to the firm's slogan—Workplace Guidance and Solutions—Christine Fisher, director of information services, says, "We are singularly focused on today's workplace and the issues facing today's business leaders." At the level of expertise and service demonstrated by Moon Moss, such a focus produces a high national reputation and strong local value. ●

ing all matters. Whether through prelitigation counseling, the negotiation of favorable settlements, pretrial dispositive motions, or victories at trial, the firm's clients have received outstanding results in resolving their employment issues.

Moon Moss also has developed expertise in complex commercial and real estate transactions and other business-related matters, including the acquisition, construction, financing, leasing, sale, and development of office space, shopping centers, and industrial and commercial facilities, as well as residential, recreational, and conservation projects.

Recognition and Service: Local, State, and National

The attorneys at Moon Moss come from a variety of backgrounds, and have practiced at some of this country's largest and most respected firms. They all have one thing in common, a love for the greater Portland area and all that it has to offer. And, while they could practice anywhere in the country, they choose to live and work on the coast of Maine.

The National Law Journal and *American Lawyer* magazine have recognized attorneys at Moon Moss as among the nation's best lawyers

advising and litigating civil rights cases on behalf of management, and among the nation's most influential attorneys of their generation.

A Moon Moss attorney was instru-

1990-2001

1991
I-many, Inc.

1992
Portland's Downtown District

1993
Auto Europe

1993
Maine Employers' Mutual Insurance Company

1994
Senator George J. Mitchell Scholarship Research Institute

1995
MBNA

1995
Princeton Properties

1998
WBACH

1999
Port City Life Magazine, LLC

I-MANY, INC., AN INDUSTRY LEADER IN CONTRACT MANAGEMENT SOLUTIONS, IS AT THE EPICENTER OF BUSINESS-TO-BUSINESS COMMERCE. THE COMPANY PROVIDES SOFTWARE AND WEB-BASED SOLUTIONS FOR MANAGING CONTRACT AND OTHER AGREEMENT-BASED PURCHASING RELATIONSHIPS. I-MANY SOLUTIONS ENABLE COMPANIES TO MAXIMIZE THE QUALITY AND VALUE OF THEIR BUSINESS RELATIONSHIPS. THE FIRM ESTIMATES THAT ITS SOLUTIONS MANAGE MORE THAN $45 BILLION IN CONTRACTED COMMERCE PER YEAR.

The company, founded in 1989 and headquartered in Portland since 1991, has expanded continuously while retaining a stable base. I-many is truly a dispersed operation, with executives located nationwide and business sites opened and acquired throughout the world.

I-many anticipates continued growth indefinitely through development and marketing of effective contract management solutions tailored to specific market segments. Throughout, I-many remains firmly committed to a solid and growing central operation in Portland.

I-many's products are crucial to companies in any contract-intensive industry, without regard to the particular nature of the product or service. The software enables businesses to manage complex trade relationships and facilitate business-to-business e-commerce. It empowers individuals within companies to make better, more informed, and more cost-effective buying and selling decisions.

Success Built on Solutions

The I-many specialty was initially developed in the 1980s, when the business was known as Systems Consulting Company. The company made its mark creating solutions as unprecedented growth in the health care industry replaced simple relationships with highly complex, regulation-heavy contracts between providers, suppliers, state and federal government regulators, insurance companies, and myriad service contractors. I-many's initial contract-management software enabled participants to take command over these increasingly complicated systems.

By the 1990s, I-many was positioned to handle new layers of complexity as they arose, particularly in the area of individual state interpretation of rebate policies and procedures. Today, after more than a decade of successful experience, I-many offers a range of industry-specific systems. Clients include Bristol-Myers Squibb Company; GlaxoSmithKline; PepsiCo, Inc.; Premier, Inc.; Procter & Gamble; and 3M Pharmaceuticals. I-many's software is used by eight of the largest 10 health care manufacturers in the world, as well as by leading consumer goods companies, which process more than $45 billion in sales and more than $6 billion in chargebacks and rebates per year.

Small-Business Initiatives

In 2000, I-many entered the e-commerce world with its Contract and Program Portal. This technology fully automates contract management through the Internet, facilitating management and collaboration with trading partners on contract pricing and eligibility information in real time and in a secure environment.

Another initiative was undertaken by I-many to meet the needs of small and midsize companies that needed an affordable version of the company's software systems. Through its Application Hosting Services (AHS) model, I-many acts as an extension of a manufacturer's information technology department, enabling the manufacturer to reduce disputed claims and questions about disparate pricing, rebates, and similar concerns.

I-many has no problem in matching solutions in new ways to individual needs in a fast-changing marketplace. What has not changed is what I-many does: powering business-to-business contract commerce. ●

I-MANY, INC. IS LOCATED IN THE HEART OF DOWNTOWN PORTLAND.

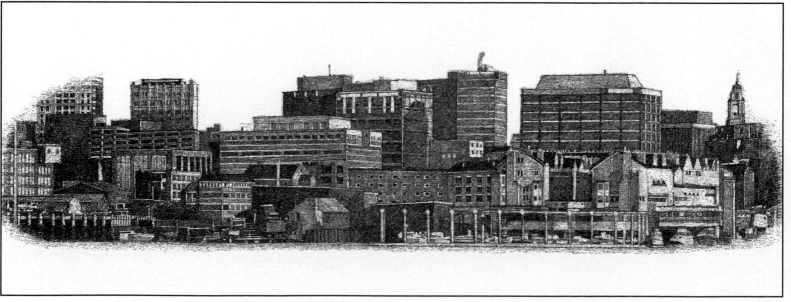

FOR HALF A CENTURY, AUTO EUROPE HAS BEEN A LEADER IN WORLDWIDE CAR RENTALS, WITH AN EMPHASIS ON EXCELLENT SERVICE AND LOW RATES. THE COMPANY HAS BEEN AN ACTIVE MEMBER OF THE PORTLAND COMMUNITY SINCE 1993, WHEN IT EXPANDED ITS U.S. OFFICES. ■ SINCE ITS FOUNDING, AUTO EUROPE HAS BEEN A TRENDSETTER IN ITS FIELD. TODAY, THE COMPANY OFFERS CUSTOMERS MORE THAN 4,000 CAR RENTAL LOCATIONS WORLDWIDE; SCHEDULED FLIGHTS

from the United States to Europe; more than 2,000 three-, four-, and five-star European hotels; chauffeur and transfer services; prestige and sports car rentals; cellular phone rentals; escorted motor-coach tours; and motor home rentals.

Imad Khalidi joined the company in 1990, ultimately becoming president in 1991 and CEO in 1996. Khalidi has led the company into a variety of innovations, including the addition of Destination Europe to its core car rental business in 1995.

Taking Care of Clients

Auto Europe strives to find ways to enhance the conventional concepts of products and services, customer focus, and competitive rates. Auto Europe's rental packages often include a cell phone, preset for a client's use as soon as he or she arrives on the European continent. Clients are equipped with a card listing a variety of numbers they might need, with access codes that often provide rates better than those offered at a hotel. The numbers include Auto

Europe's own toll-free number to provide travelers with any further assistance they might need.

Such details, including a guarantee that a representative of Auto Europe will answer any call within a minute, 24 hours a day, 365 days a year, is part of the company's attention to customer service. The company also makes a practice of informing clients as to the differing taxes and rates of exchange from country to country, helping travelers keep an accurate

grasp on their expenses. Auto Europe is not simply a car rental company; it is a guiding hand, helping to find solutions to almost any possible request or problem.

Khalidi has developed a broad network of relationships in the travel business around the world, and it shows. Those resources are linked, in turn, to the company's service philosophy. "If you think that there is something more important than a client, then you need to think again," says Khalidi. While some of Auto Europe's services are the most luxurious available, the firm guarantees the lowest prices for service, whatever the traveler's class, destination, or needs might be. ●

SINCE ITS FOUNDING, AUTO EUROPE HAS BEEN A TRENDSETTER IN ITS FIELD. TODAY, THE COMPANY OFFERS CUSTOMERS MORE THAN 4,000 CAR RENTAL LOCATIONS WORLDWIDE; SCHEDULED FLIGHTS FROM THE UNITED STATES TO EUROPE; MORE THAN 2,000 THREE-, FOUR-, AND FIVE-STAR EUROPEAN HOTELS; CHAUFFEUR AND TRANSFER SERVICES; PRESTIGE AND SPORTS CAR RENTALS; CELLULAR PHONE RENTALS; ESCORTED MOTOR-COACH TOURS; AND MOTOR HOME RENTALS.

P

ORTLAND, A HISTORIC SEAPORT CITY, IS BEST DISPLAYED IN THE FASCINATING ACTIVITY OF ITS WORKING WATERFRONT, THE ARTISTIC PATCHWORK OF UPPER CONGRESS STREET, AND THE VARIEGATED SMALL-SHOP COMMERCE EVERYWHERE IN ITS OLD-BRICK DOWNTOWN. AND THERE ARE RESTAURANTS BY THE DOZEN. IT'S A FUN PLACE TO BE. ■ PORTLAND'S DOWNTOWN DISTRICT IS THE ORGANIZATION THAT MANAGES THE HEALTH AND ENJOYMENT OF THE ENTIRE AREA, INCLUDING ITS TWO ADJOINING NEIGHBORHOODS,

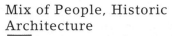

the Old Port and the Arts District, both thriving in their complementary ways. The Downtown District sponsors and cosponsors indoor and outdoor cultural and entertainment events, and coordinates cooperative efforts of downtown's merchants, offices, artists, and residents.

The district organization is also an enthusiastic booster of all things urban. "Our downtown is a big part of the community and its vibrancy," says Barbara Hager, executive director. "Downtown is maintaining its primacy as the place to do business, to see and be seen, to spend your leisure time, to find a gift. Greater Portland's quality of life is enhanced by downtown."

The Old Port and the Arts District

The Old Port has its trademark owner-in-the-store boutique image, with product lines tending toward the unique, exotic, counter-cultural, and handcrafted. Shops are strung together along cobbled streets and brick sidewalks. The Old Port also has a high concentration of places to eat, ranging across the spectrum of possibilities.

The charm of the Old Port includes the thrill of discovery, when the visitor taking a shortcut through an alleyway discovers entrances to stores and eating places there. Short walks pay off in other ways. Since Portland's is a working harbor, pedestrians on Commercial Street and on the wharves can experience some views that are highly unusual today. Fishermen unload, sell their catches, and tidy up their boats. Huge trawlers and giant tankers are berthed within view, luxury yachts pull in and out, and cruise liners are frequent visitors.

The ambiance of the Arts District, centered on Congress Street, is entirely different from that of the adjoining Old Port, but it is a superbly charming experience. The shops offer more urban—but still unusual—cards, shoes, hats, and a seemingly endless variety of other interesting items. The Maine College of Art, Portland Museum of Art, Portland Stage Company, Children's Museum, and numerous art galleries are here, as is Merrill Auditorium, which features symphony and opera performances and the mighty Kotzschmar organ.

Mix of People, Historic Architecture

There is a spectacular mix of people involved in and attracted by all the city's activities. There are kids walking through downtown with tackle boxes, on their way to a day's angling between the boats tied up along the water. There are people in fishing boots, just off the trawler and on the way to the bank to make a deposit. Coffee shop operators display the work of artists whose studios are on the upper floors of the grand old downtown buildings.

The architecture itself is a prominent part of downtown's attraction. Congress Street and adjoining areas are dotted with buildings listed on the National Historic Register, and the entire Old Port is a designated historic district.

Portland's Downtown District works with the city's businesspeople and agencies to make sure the streets are clean and secure, and that the various elements of the urban economy work most effectively together.

The organization also makes sure that downtown life offers maximum enjoyment. Its Old Port Festival,

THE WATERFRONT PROVIDES A RELAXING PLACE TO STOP FOR A BITE (TOP).

DURING THE SUMMER, THE WORK AND THE PRESENCE OF PORTLAND'S DOWNTOWN DISTRICT ARE MOST VISIBLY REPRESENTED BY THE ORGANIZATION'S DOWNTOWN GUIDES, WEARING THEIR UNIFORM SHIRTS AND OUTBACK HATS (BOTTOM).

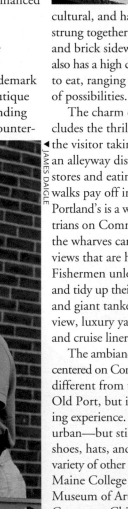

PAULINE DIMINO

JAMES DAIGLE

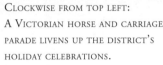

which kicks off the season on the first Sunday in June, is Northern New England's largest such festival. Other unique, large-scale public events in the Downtown District include World Puppets Portland—the international puppetry festival—and the Maine Fabric & Fiber Arts Festival, which showcase the work of a broad representation of artists who live and work in Maine.

Public Events, Public Services

Portland's Downtown District offers outdoor concerts at various sites in the warm weather, as well as Victorian Holiday and other celebrations during other times of year. The organization conducts vigorous collaborations with various artistic associations, as well as commercial ones.

On special occasions, such as the magnificent OpSail event of 2000—a visit by 26 sailing vessels that drew some 440,000 people–the Downtown

District handles all land-side activities.

Portland's Downtown District is a not-for-profit organization, founded as the Downtown Improvement District Corporation in 1992 to provide day-to-day management and marketing services. Although voluntary membership organizations devoted to the benefit of downtown businesses had operated in Portland's Downtown and/or Old Port districts for some years, Portland's Downtown District is a legal business improvement district created by the Portland City Council, and funded by an assessment on property within the defined boundaries.

The district develops and executes strategies in marketing, management, collaboration, planning, and data collection. The organization operates through a full-time staff and membership committees in such areas as transportation and parking, public safety, marketing, and physical environment.

Portland's Downtown District

collaborates with other like-minded groups such as the Portland Arts & Cultural Alliance, Old Port Retail and Restaurant Association, Convention & Visitors Bureau, Greater Portland Chambers of Commerce, Maine Arts, U.S. Coast Guard, Waterfront Alliance, Downtown Arts District Association, and City of Portland.

During the summer, the work and the presence of Portland's Downtown District are most visibly represented by the organization's downtown guides, wearing their uniforms, complete with fanny packs and outback hats. The guides, trained in public safety, information giving, and history—as well as the wealth of things to see, do, and find in the district—patrol the streets in anticipation of spotting visitors who need a little help. The guides have even been known to hold shoppers' dogs while the owners are making purchases. The service is a hallmark of downtown, and of the Downtown District: totally free and always fun. ●

CLOCKWISE FROM TOP LEFT: A VICTORIAN HORSE AND CARRIAGE PARADE LIVENS UP THE DISTRICT'S HOLIDAY CELEBRATIONS.

THE DISTRICT'S MANY STORES AND BOUTIQUES ARE A SHOPPER'S DELIGHT.

THE FARMER'S MARKET IS FREQUENTED BY LOCALS AND VISITORS ALIKE LOOKING FOR FRESH FRUIT, VEGETABLES, AND FLOWERS.

THE WADSWORTH-LONGFELLOW HOUSE, MAINE HISTORY GALLERY, AND MAINE HISTORICAL SOCIETY ARE ALL LOCATED IN PORTLAND'S DOWNTOWN DISTRICT.

JAMES DAIGLE

JAMES DAIGLE

AINE EMPLOYERS' MUTUAL INSURANCE COMPANY (MEMIC) IS A VERY UNUSUAL INSURANCE COMPANY, AND A VERY SUCCESSFUL ONE. IN OCTOBER 1992, MEMIC WAS SET UP AS A PRIVATE WORKERS' COMPENSATION COMPANY BY THE MAINE LEGISLATURE, AND WAS SLATED TO OPEN FOR BUSINESS ON JANUARY 1, 1993. THE DECISION TO ESTABLISH SUCH AN ORGANIZATION CAME AS THE RESULT OF AN IN-DEPTH PROCESS TRIGGERED BY SKYROCKETING INJURY CLAIMS AND COSTS, WITH

the simultaneous flight of workers' compensation insurers from the state.

MEMIC insures about 20,000 of Maine's estimated 27,000 insured employers. Among MEMIC's policyholders, lost-time injuries have dropped 30 percent, and the cost to employers has gone down more than 35 percent.

High Grades for Service

MEMIC is also in a class by itself in another measure, the human one. The company is noted for its measurably superior treatment of injured workers. According to data from Maine's Workers' Compensation Board, MEMIC is substantially more consistent than its competitors regarding on-time payments of benefits to injured workers. State law requires that benefits be received within 14

days of receipt of compensable claims. According to the board, MEMIC is 10 percent better in this regard than other commercial insurance companies that offer workers' compensation coverage in

Maine. In addition, MEMIC was a leading supporter of an expanded Worker Advocate Program to ensure that employees have skilled representation when conflicts over benefits arise.

Despite its remarkable success in these standard areas, perhaps the most unusual thing about MEMIC is the way the company organizes its safety education activities, and how these activities are staffed and managed.

At most insurance companies, safety training is offered to clients when a need is indicated by the level and nature of claims. The insurance company's claims department then directs safety training. Not so at MEMIC. As a mutual organization—owned by its policyholders—MEMIC's board is made up of employers. At the time of incorporation, the new board resisted suggestions that it outsource the actual insurance process to existing companies. Instead, board members determined their own goals and standards for the new organization.

MEMIC spends twice the industry's average cost on delivering safety training to its policyholders. The company recruits trainers from among industry people who know the field, and so has people serving the specific industries from which they came.

WITH THE HELP OF MAINE EMPLOYERS' MUTUAL INSURANCE COMPANY'S (MEMIC) SAFETY TRAINERS, MAINE'S LOGGING INDUSTRY HAS EXPERIENCED FEWER SERIOUS INJURIES (TOP).

MEMIC PRESIDENT AND CHIEF EXECUTIVE OFFICER JOHN LEONARD HAS LED THE COMPANY SINCE ITS INCEPTION IN 1993 (BOTTOM).

CLOCKWISE FROM TOP:
MEMIC HELPS ITS MANUFACTURING
CUSTOMERS CREATE SAFER AND, OFTEN,
MORE EFFICIENT WORKPLACES BY POINTING
OUT SAFETY HAZARDS.

AFTER A WORKPLACE INJURY, MEMIC
HELPS A RECOVERING WORKER TO FOCUS ON
ABILITIES, NOT DISABILITIES. BY TRAINING
IN ACTUAL WORKPLACE SCENARIOS, WORKERS
GAIN CONFIDENCE IN THEIR ABILITY TO
WORK AGAIN.

MEMIC'S SAFETY TRAINERS DON'T
SPEND THEIR DAYS BEHIND A DESK. THEY
ARE IN THE FIELD HELPING CUSTOMERS
PROTECT THEIR MOST VALUABLE ASSET:
THEIR EMPLOYEES.

Insurance Know-How at the Top

Still, an ingredient of MEMIC's success includes a substantial amount of insurance know-how at the top. After spending more than 25 years with the Travelers Insurance Company, John Leonard, MEMIC's president and chief executive officer, arrived at the company in its first year.

Leonard's goal at MEMIC was to establish a new kind of insurance company. His team grasped the most meaningful aspects of the state legislature's 1992 reforms, and crafted a strategy to translate the intent of the law into measurable outcomes. The company established itself as a champion for workplace safety and for the improvement of Maine's economy.

MEMIC's reputation for having changed the paradigm of workers' compensation has spread throughout the industry and into public policy circles. Additionally, the company's financial stature was confirmed when, in May 2000, MEMIC earned an A (excellent) rating from A.M. Best, the nation's top insurance company benchmarking organization.

An Original Philosophy

As with any other company, MEMIC is subject to the cycles of the business economy and other forces beyond its control. Yet the company's continuing high level of success started with the philosophy developed by its original incorporators. Jolan Ippolito, who would later become MEMIC's chairman of the board, stated: "All the old stakeholders thought we would fail. The other carriers thought that we didn't know anything about insurance, and they figured we'd just set up a skeleton company. We thought, 'Why do that? [Other companies] have already proved that they're a sham when it comes to loss control and claims management. Why would we leave it for them to do?'"

MEMIC's performance has earned some unusual accolades. "Though we are a private company, we serve a public purpose, which is to guarantee that employers can buy workers' compensation insurance in Maine," Leonard says. "But, as one public official indicated, 'MEMIC is a case of public policy underpromising and a private company overdelivering.'" ●

SENATOR GEORGE J. MITCHELL SCHOLARSHIP RESEARCH INSTITUTE REPRESENTS A SCHOLARSHIP FUND, A MENTORING AND SUPPORT ORGANIZATION, A RESEARCH INSTITUTE, AND THE EMBODIMENT OF THE DREAMS AND COMMITMENT OF GEORGE MITCHELL, A WORLD-RENOWNED STATESMAN FROM MAINE WHO HAS NEVER FORGOTTEN HOW IMPORTANT ADULT SUPPORT IS FOR A RESOURCES-SHORT YOUNG PERSON TRYING TO SUCCEED. ■ TODAY, THE ORGANIZATION BUILT BY MITCHELL PROVIDES FOUR-YEAR

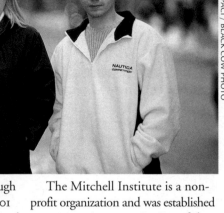

awards of funds and support to 160 Maine high school graduates each year, and, through research, attempts to identify and reduce the barriers to higher education for all young people.

Born in Waterville, Maine, Mitchell was one of five children in a working family whose parents never went to college. All five children were able to achieve the goal of higher education, and Mitchell had reason to feel strongly about setting up the George J. Mitchell Scholarship Research Institute to help as many others as possible.

"College opened doors for him—made many things possible," says Colleen J. Quint, executive director of the institute. "He received help with scholarships, and people stepped in at every stage to mentor and advise."

Campaign Funds Invested

The opportunity for Mitchell to take action on his long-held convictions came with his retirement from the U.S. Senate in 1994. Mitchell received the support of his own contributors to commit $1 million from his now-unneeded campaign war chest

to create a scholarship fund. Through the Mitchell Scholars program, 101 Maine high school graduates received $2,500 grants from 1995 through 1998.

In 1999, Mitchell secured additional foundation funding to establish the institute and expand the program to every public high school in Maine, plus additional students from private and parochial schools or the home-schooling sector. The students are chosen through application of three basic criteria: academic potential; personal service to their schools and communities; and financial need.

The Mitchell Institute is a non-profit organization and was established as a supporting organization of the Maine Community Foundation, which managed the original scholarship program. The Mitchell Institute's mission is to increase the likelihood that more young people will pursue and obtain college degrees. Maine, which has low rates of college attendance and high rates of attrition, is serving as the testing ground for this initiative.

Foundation for Broader Research

Scholarship recipients also become eligible for the Mitchell Institute's support programs, which include a career-based, summer jobs network; a weekend leadership training retreat; community service projects; and mentoring alliances. The programs are focused on keeping the Mitchell scholars in school, giving them career-oriented opportunities and networks, and helping them develop skills they need as leaders.

The success of the overall Mitchell Scholars Program is directly linked to the institute's research efforts. Data collected from the Mitchell scholars is the base for a longitudinal study of barriers and access to higher education. The information also will help test the effectiveness of the institute's scholarship and support programs.

MICHELE SAVAGE AND CHRIS HORNE BOTH FOUND SUMMER JOBS THROUGH THE SENATOR GEORGE J. MITCHELL SCHOLARSHIP RESEARCH INSTITUTE INTERNSHIP PROGRAM (TOP).

EACH YEAR, THE MITCHELL INSTITUTE HOSTS A BRUNCH FOR ITS SCHOLARS. MITCHELL IS PICTURED HERE WITH JESSICA WALKER (BOTTOM).

The research program is a distinctive one: By tracking the Mitchell Scholars through college and 10 to 20 years beyond, the institute plans to evaluate the effectiveness of its scholarship and support programs. The institute will use the information it gathers as the foundation for broader research on Maine students to determine how best to make practical and effective tools for overcoming educational hurdles available to the largest number of students.

Effects to be studied by the institute include some very direct ones, such as what difference the combined programs make in the recipients' success rate, as well as what impact the recipients have when they go back to their high schools to talk with students.

The intent of the study is to learn from the Mitchell Scholars' experience in successfully addressing the problems encountered during the college planning process and the transition to college. The strategies and resources then can be replicated for other Maine students. Further, the information will be a starting point for a broader-based inquiry into the best ways to improve awareness of the benefits of higher education, as well as the best practical tools for obtaining it.

The institute will work with students, parents, and educators in representative Maine communities to explore each group's knowledge of education resources, their personal experiences, and their perceptions about the value of higher education, existing barriers, and the best means of addressing them. The findings will be compared with data from other national, regional, and state studies.

The Mitchell Institute hopes to create a national model by demonstrating how effective use of scholarship assistance and support programs can attract more young people to college, achieve higher college completion rates, and increase community involvement. The institute anticipates that its research will be applicable to other states that hope to attract more young people to college and reduce dropout rates. It may be the only research agenda of such magnitude in the country.

The Senator George J. Mitchell Scholarship Research Institute's work does not treat the recipient as a passive party. Quite the contrary. As Mitchell himself puts it: "We all know remarkable young men and women who work hard in school, who give back to their communities, who come from families that struggle to make ends meet. For many of these students, a college education is more than just a dream; it is a necessity." ●

CLOCKWISE FROM TOP:
THE MITCHELL INSTITUTE HOSTS A VARIETY OF FUNDRAISERS EACH YEAR, INCLUDING THIS ONE IN BAR HARBOR. TED PIETZ AND JOSH KINGSBURY ARE PICTURED HERE WITH MITCHELL.

MITCHELL SCHOLARS (FROM LEFT) DARA KIDDER, ALANA BURNS, AND MICHAEL MASI ARE PICTURED ON THE BATES COLLEGE CAMPUS.

MITCHELL SCHOLARS ARE INVOLVED IN A VARIETY OF COMMUNITY SERVICE PROJECTS, INCLUDING VOLUNTEERING AT RONALD MCDONALD HOUSE IN PORTLAND.

OPENED IN 1995, MBNA's PORTLAND OFFICE IS A VITAL CONTRIBUTOR TO THE SUCCESS OF MBNA AMERICA, A FORTUNE 500 COMPANY AND ONE OF THE WORLD'S LARGEST INDEPENDENT CREDIT CARD ISSUERS. A VISIT TO ANY OF THE COMPANY'S OFFICES ACROSS THE UNITED STATES AND IN ENGLAND, IRELAND, AND CANADA REVEALS AN ORGANIZATION ABSOLUTELY COMMITTED TO OFFERING CUSTOMERS THE FINEST PRODUCTS BACKED BY CONSISTENTLY TOP-QUALITY SERVICE;

offering the very best benefits and work environment to the people of the company; and fostering genuine care and support of the communities where MBNA people live and work.

At the heart of that commitment are the more than 25,000 people of MBNA, including some 4,500 in Maine—some 250 of whom work in Portland. A visit to the Portland office will bring to light two things that define MBNA: innovation and—above all—people who like people.

Innovation

In 1983, less than a year after it had opened its doors, MBNA made industry history by introducing the Gold MasterCard. Featuring higher credit lines, expanded travel accident insurance, and more, the card was an instant success. By the end of that year, more than 100,000 MBNA Gold MasterCard accounts had been opened; fewer than six years later, MBNA would become the first company to issue 1 million Gold MasterCard accounts.

In the mid-1990s, MBNA experienced similar results by pioneering what has since become an industry staple: the platinum credit card. Featuring higher credit lines and enhanced service and benefits, the MBNA Platinum Plus card remains one of the credit card industry's most successful products.

In its first year, MBNA also introduced a new concept to a growing industry. The endorsement of MBNA's credit card product by Georgetown University demonstrated one of the credit card industry's most significant innovations: affinity marketing. The Georgetown agreement enabled MBNA to market credit cards bearing the university name to Georgetown's alumni and students. Their loyalty toward their school generated thousands of credit card accounts, and paved the way for relationships with additional schools, sports teams, professional associations, charities, and other affinity groups. Today, nearly 5,000 groups endorse MBNA loans and credit card accounts to their constituents.

With those endorsements in hand, MBNA turns to another of its strengths: marketing. MBNA Marketing Systems, in fact, is one of the largest telemarketing companies in the world. MBNA's Portland office, for example, takes thousands of applications over the phone each month.

People Who Like People

Since its start in Newark, Delaware, in 1982, MBNA's growth has expanded the company well beyond Delaware's border. In 1993 alone, MBNA founded MBNA Europe; established offices in New York City and Beachwood, Ohio; and opened its office in Camden, Maine. In the years that followed,

MORE THAN 250 PEOPLE WORK IN MBNA'S PORTLAND OFFICE.

MBNA expanded to include offices in Chicago, San Francisco, Boca Raton, and Hunt Valley, Maryland. A short time later, a Dublin, Ireland, office opened, and MBNA Canada was created.

In New England, meanwhile, MBNA continued to grow. Fueled by the size and exceptional quality of the region's workforce, the company opened offices in Portland, Orono, Brunswick, Belfast, Presque Isle, Rockland, Farmington, and Fort Kent, Maine, and in Dover, New Hampshire.

Through all of its evolution, however, one thing has remained constant: MBNA's commitment to its customers, the people of the company, and the communities in which those people work. In 1986, MBNA became the first credit card issuer to offer customer service 24 hours a day, seven days a week. Since its creation, the company has been repeatedly recognized by *Working Mother, Business Week,* and *Fortune* as one of the best companies in the country to work for. And when they are not working, MBNA people are often volunteering for nonprofit organizations near MBNA offices. MBNA even enables them to spend

four hours of paid time each month serving their neighbors in need.

The MBNA Foundation, which today manages all of MBNA's community and education initiatives, was created in 1997. Hundreds of

recipients of its scholarships and grants hail from Maine.

To further help students pursue higher education, MBNA regularly offers part-time employment to those attending local colleges and universities. Nearly a quarter of the people of MBNA's Portland office, in fact, also attend classes at the University of Maine, St. Joseph College, Southern Maine Technical College, Andover College, or Husson College.

The people of MBNA's Portland office have always embraced the company's dedication to the community. Since the office's opening, MBNA people in Portland have actively supported organizations such as Pine Tree Council Boy Scouts of America, Portland Partnership, Wayside Evening Soup Kitchen, Ronald McDonald House, Big Brothers Big Sisters, Portland High School Boosters, Kids First, and Presumpscot Elementary School, where MBNA people often serve as mentors.

Echoed throughout all of the company's offices, commitment to the community is a hallmark of the spirit of the people of MBNA. They like to help, just as they like working together to satisfy customers. That's why they call themselves people who like people. ●

THE QUALITY OF THE CITY'S WORKFORCE WAS A KEY FACTOR IN MBNA'S DECISION TO OPEN AN OFFICE IN PORTLAND.

HEN PRINCETON PROPERTIES TOOK OVER FOUR PORTLAND APARTMENT COMMUNITIES IN 1995, THE PROPERTIES WERE TYPICAL OF THE COMPANY'S ACQUISITIONS—UNDERPERFORMING, POORLY MAINTAINED, AND IN A DOWNWARD SPIRAL TOWARD FINANCIAL, PHYSICAL, AND SOCIAL PROBLEMS. PRINCETON RECEIVES HIGH MARKS FOR THE QUALITY OF ITS RENOVATION OF DISTRESSED PROPERTIES, RESIDENT SERVICE, AND COMMUNITY SENSITIVITY. THAT

record, and the $4 million invested in the renovation of its Portland communities, backs up Princeton's promise to provide a long-term quality living experience.

"We're turnaround specialists," says James M. Whelan, regional manager. "Our specialty is coming in and investing capital for long-term improvement and changing the management philosophy. Our aim is to make the properties an asset to Portland and the community as a whole."

PRINCETON RIDGE OFFERS SUPERB TOWNHOME LIVING JUST THREE MILES FROM THE OLD PORT.

Operations in Four States

A Massachusetts-based parent company, Princeton Properties was founded in 1973. It is a real estate management, development, and holding firm specializing in apartment management. Princeton owns and manages apartment communities in New England and Florida. The company also holds franchise rights for Hawthorne Suites, an extended-stay hotel chain.

Princeton Properties currently owns and operates more than 5,500 apartments and two Hawthorne Suites hotels. In stating the company's mission, James Heriscot, chairman, stated: "We constantly work to protect our investments by attracting residents who share the same level of pride in our apartment communities.

And we closely monitor the condition of each and every property in order to maintain our standards of quality. We recognize that the key to our success is determined by how well our employees perform their jobs, and we strongly believe that their efforts and level of job satisfaction have a direct effect on the company's overall performance."

As the largest private landlord in Portland, Princeton takes its community responsibility seriously. The company's significant investment of capital and talent to renovate, restore, and enhance communities in Portland is a conscious effort to make them an asset to the city and to the community as a whole. The company's performance in this regard has attracted national recognition, including several Pillars of the Industry awards. In March 2001, Princeton Properties was awarded the National Association of Home Builders Pillars of the Industry Award for Property Management Company of the Year.

Furnished Suites a Distinguishing Mark

P rinceton Properties' crown jewels in Portland are its corporate suites—fully furnished apartments designed especially for relocating executives, consultants,

PRINCETON RIDGE'S TWO-BEDROOM TOWNHOMES ARE SET IN A TRADITIONALLY STYLED COMMUNITY OF CLAPBOARD AND BRICK.

DEBBIE JOHANSEN

and professionals who require short-term accommodations. Guests enjoy the comfort of a well-appointed home-away-from-home and the convenience of a complete service package. The suites are the distinguishing characteristic of the company. "We excel at this niche of the market," says Whelan. The company is one of the largest providers of such apartments in New England, maintaining some 600 throughout the company.

Two of Princeton's Portland apartment communities were constructed during World War II by the Army Corps of Engineers to provide housing for the shipyard workers who built the famous liberty ships in South Portland. Forest Park, 220 units along Baxter Boulevard, features elements such as oak and maple floors. Some residents have occupied apartments there for more than 25 years. Princeton Village, located on Brighton Avenue and originally known as Victory Village, has 80 one-bedroom apartments.

The two other Princeton Properties communities in Portland were built along Forest Avenue in the mid-1970s. Princeton Pines has 136 one- and two-bedroom apartments, and is admired for its wealth of open space, beautiful wooded setting, and swimming pool. Forty-one town homes make up nearby Princeton Ridge.

Professionalism Taken Seriously

Princeton Properties endeavors to demonstrate professionalism throughout all aspects of its apartment ownership and management. The staff includes management personnel who have been with the properties and/or in the community for years.

The company's full-time leasing consultants are highly trained, and have earned certification from the National Association of Leasing Professionals. All members of the management team are Registered Apartment Managers of the National Association of Homebuilders, having met standards for experience, education, training, testing, and continuing education. Princeton's full-time maintenance staff is available 24 hours a day.

In coming to Portland, Princeton Properties expresses its sensitivity to the community in the way it treats the residents. "We never forget these are people's homes," says Susan Chester, furnished services manager. "Princeton Properties has made a long-term commitment to these residents and these communities. Witness that we've never sold a community we've purchased." Chester also notes that the company tries to foster a sense of community by hosting ice-cream socials and parties around the pool; a newsletter is published four times a year. There is a successful resident referral program that encourages residents to recommend their friends to live in the communities, with the slogan Good Friends Make Great Neighbors.

Princeton Properties is a business that makes and tends wise investments, and it is a business with a heart. The company's history and current state show how well the combination works. ●

FOREST PARK APARTMENTS ARE RICH WITH CHARACTER AND HISTORIC CHARM.

THE APARTMENTS AT FOREST PARK OFFER POSTCARD WATER VIEWS OF BACK COVE.

W

BACH, MAINE'S CLASSICAL NETWORK, HAS A SPECIAL BOND WITH ITS LISTENERS. THE NATION'S OTHER CLASSICAL STATIONS THINK IT'S PRETTY SPECIAL, TOO—THEY VOTED WBACH THE WINNER OF THE PRESTIGIOUS MARCONI AWARD FOR EXCELLENCE IN RADIO, MAKING IT THE 2000 WINNER OF AMERICA'S CLASSICAL STATION OF THE YEAR. ■ WBACH HAS BROUGHT TO MAINE'S AIRWAVES A UNIQUE, QUALITY SERVICE. BEGINNING

with its original station, WBQQ in Kennebunk, WBACH extended its classical programming to other parts of the state by acquiring outlets in Portland (WBQW) and Rockland (WBQX) in 1998, and Bangor/Bar Harbor (WBQI) in 2001. Today, Maine's Classical Network reaches 85 percent of the state's population and is unifying classical music lovers throughout Maine.

Voice of the Arts

Having the only commercial classical radio stations in the state, WBACH recognizes its special role in exposing Mainers to the world of classical music. A few of the efforts on its stations include weekly Sunday rebroadcasts of Bay Chamber Concerts' live performances from the Rockport Opera House; *The Kids Classical Hour,* a Saturday morning program that introduces children to and educates them about classical music; and the WBACH Summer Concert Series, compris-

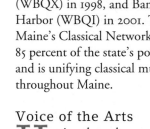

Scott Hooper serves as WBACH's program director and morning show host.

WBACH has a special place in support-ing and promoting all performing arts in Maine.

▲ JACK SAVONA

ing six free outdoor concerts held in Kennebunkport each Thursday evening in July and August. In addition, WBACH is where Mainers tune in to hear live broadcasts of the Metropolitan Opera from Lincoln Center.

WBACH also has a special place in supporting and promoting all

performing arts in Maine. Some of the organizations WBACH has helped promote over the past year include Bay Chamber Concerts, Round Top Center for the Arts, Daponte String Quartet, Portland Symphony Orchestra, Bangor Symphony Orchestra, Portland Stage, River Tree Arts, Maine Music Society, Portland Concert Association, Bates Dance Festival, Oratorio Chorale, Ballet New England, Bowdoin Summer Music Festival, Children's Theatre of Maine, Biddeford City Theatre, Choral Arts Society, Kennebec Per-forming Arts Company, Lincoln Arts Festival, Maine State Ballet, Music in the Meetinghouse, Ogunquit Playhouse, Opera Maine, Portland Ballet, Portland Chamber Music Festival, Portland Community Chorus, Seaglass Performing Arts, Sebago-Long Lake Chamber Music Festival, Portland Museum of Art, and many more.

◄ CONVENTION & VISITORS BUREAU OF GREATER PORTLAND

Community Service

Along with promoting the arts, WBACH assists a wide variety of charitable groups and causes. In addition to organizing and promoting such events and drives, WBACH's stations air a

WBACH IS DEDICATED TO BRINGING CLASSICAL MUSIC INTO THE LIVING ROOMS OF MAINE RESIDENTS.

wealth of issue-specific awareness campaigns on subjects ranging from health and education to alcohol abuse prevention and community safety.

Overall, the four WBACH radio stations contribute approximately $700,000 in public service announcements to Maine charities and nonprofit organizations in a typical year. Each station airs more than 170 public service announcements weekly.

In addition to the arts and charities that receive support from WBACH, the network also uses its airwaves to address issues of local, national, and international importance. For example, WBACH was this year's exclusive broadcast underwriter of the 2001 Camden Conference on Foreign Affairs, a gathering of experts from around the world who met to address issues of national and international significance.

Responsible Business Leader

As a locally owned company, WBACH has a vested interest in the success of all Maine businesses. For that reason, the network's stations have been actively involved in promoting business and commerce throughout the state. For example, WBACH is currently a cosponsor of the Maine Investment Exchange breakfasts, which provide the opportunity for companies to present

their business plans to potential investors.

In addition, WBACH is actively involved in many local chambers of commerce, including those in Ogunquit, Kennebunk-Kennebunkport, Sanford, Biddeford, Portland, Rockland-Thomaston, Camden-Rockport-Lincolnville, and Bar Harbor. WBACH's employees also support their local communities by giving of their time, often in key

leadership positions, to various civic, charitable, and professional activities.

Today, WBACH stands as proof that responsible broadcasting can make a difference within the community. From its small beginnings to its growth as a statewide network and achievement of national recognition, WBACH remains committed to providing the best in quality radio for the people of Maine. ●

WBACH PRESIDENT AND GENERAL MANAGER LOUIS VITALI RECEIVED THE 2000 NATIONAL ASSOCIATION OF BROADCASTERS' MARCONI AWARD FOR EXCELLENCE IN RADIO. THAT SAME YEAR, WBACH WAS NAMED AMERICA'S CLASSICAL STATION OF THE YEAR.

C

AROLYN CIANCHETTE, WHO HAS BOTH THE EYE AND THE HEART OF AN ARTIST, LOVES THE CITY OF PORTLAND. THIS LOVE CAN BE SEEN BY READING ANY ISSUE OF HER MAGAZINE, *Port City Life*. STARTED IN 1999 AS A QUARTERLY, WHICH BECAME A BIMONTHLY IN MARCH 2000, THE MAGAZINE IS AIMED AT REPRESENTING PORTLAND. "THE FIRST THING I DO WHEN I GO TO ANOTHER CITY IS PICK UP THE CITY MAGAZINE AND SEE WHAT THE CITY IS LIKE AND WHAT'S GOING ON,"

Cianchette says. "Our magazine is about the city. It's how I see it appearing to visitors, to locals, and to me."

A Positive Spin on Portland

The flavor of the magazine is important to its publisher. "It's intended to be upbeat, fun to read," says Cianchette. "Light, not literary or controversial. It's meant to be something people look forward to when they see it in the mailbox."

Events around town and people are big in *Port City Life*. Sections on art, fashions, restaurants and recipes, teenagers excelling in and out of the classroom, and technology are also included. There is a travel section and a kids' column, as well as libations, which covers wine, tea, and coffee. Also, there is always a local home interior featured.

"There's so much to write about here," Cianchette says. "People

doing great things and not necessarily great things, contributing to the community."

Designer to Publisher

Cianchette handles or oversees issue planning, story assignment, layout, and graphics. She also sells the advertisements, handles the administration, and hires the freelancers who do everything else. She knows what the issues will be six months in advance, and plans for a year at a time.

This all comes after a career in graphic art and magazine work, but not in owning, starting, and running a magazine. A lifelong Maine resident originally from Biddeford, Cianchette graduated from Simmons College in 1986, married, and went to work as an intern at *Down East* magazine, where she later became associate art director. She started her own graphic design firm in Camden

in 1989, moving it to Portland with a family relocation shortly thereafter.

The magazine idea arose from a personal perception that there was a strong market among active people who take advantage of all that Portland has to offer. In an interview before the first issue appeared, Cianchette put it this way: "This is a fantastic town with so many things to do—all kinds of cultural attractions; lots of good restaurants, and some truly great ones. We have the ocean, lakes, sports teams, recreation options galore. It's really a vibrant area, and we're publishing a quality magazine to reflect that."

Port City Life has a seemingly bottomless well of story and picture ideas about its town. The magazine also has the business record to support the expectation that those ideas will be hitting the mailboxes for a long time to come. ●

PORT CITY LIFE, FOUNDED BY CAROLYN CIANCHETTE (SEATED AT RIGHT), IS ESSENTIAL READING FOR THOSE LOOKING TO TAKE ADVANTAGE OF ALL PORTLAND HAS TO OFFER.

KEVIN BRUSIE

KEVIN BRUSIE

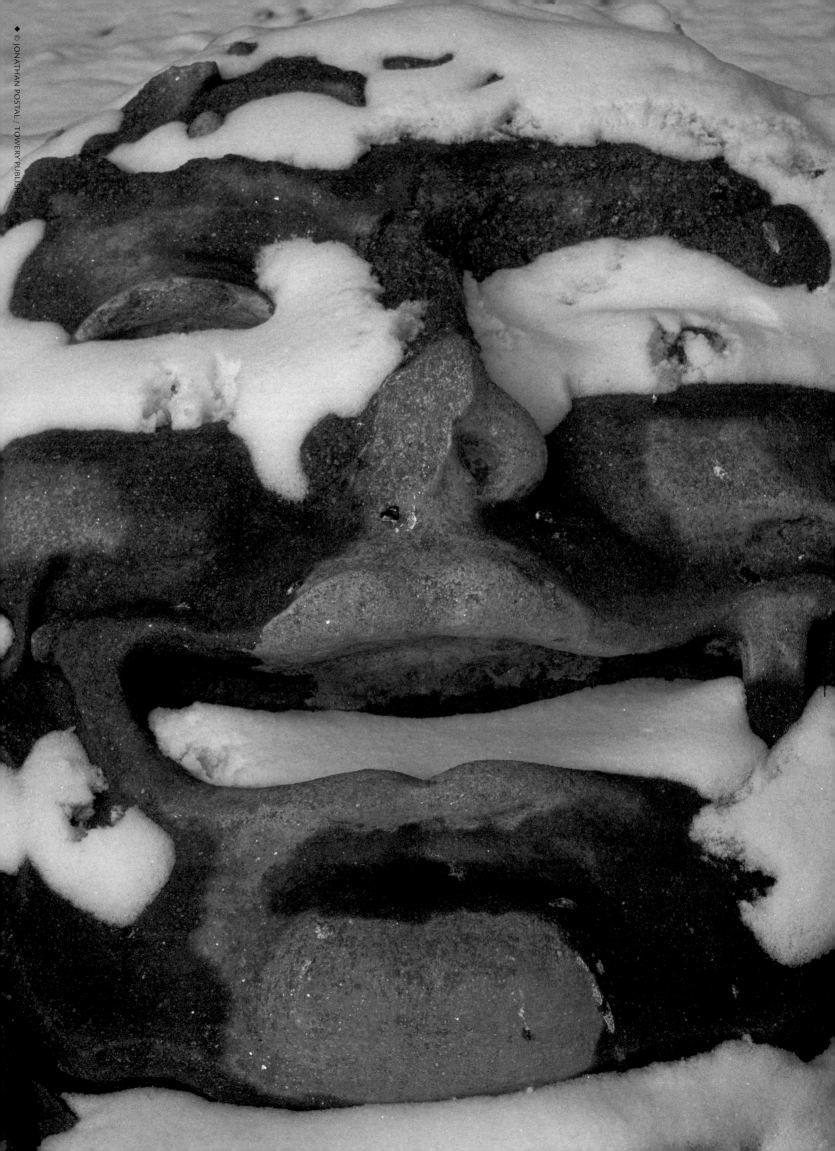

BEGINNING AS A SMALL PUBLISHER OF LOCAL NEWSPAPERS IN 1935, TOWERY PUBLISHING, INC. TODAY HAS BECOME A GLOBAL PUBLISHER OF A DIVERSE RANGE OF COMMUNITY-BASED MATERIALS FROM SAN DIEGO TO SYDNEY. ITS PRODUCTS—SUCH AS THE COMPANY'S AWARD-WINNING URBAN TAPESTRY SERIES, BUSINESS DIRECTORIES, MAGAZINES, AND INTERNET SITES—CONTINUE TO BUILD ON TOWERY'S DISTINGUISHED HERITAGE OF EXCELLENCE, MAKING ITS NAME SYNONYMOUS WITH SERVICE, UTILITY, AND QUALITY.

Community Publishing at Its Best

Towery Publishing has long been the industry leader in community-based publications. In 1972, current President and CEO J. Robert Towery succeeded his parents in managing the printing and publishing business they had founded four decades earlier. "One of the more impressive traits of my family's publishing business was its dedication to presenting only the highest-quality products available—whatever our market might be," says Towery. "Since taking over the company, I've continued our fight for the high ground in maintaining this tradition."

During the 1970s and 1980s, Towery expanded the scope of the company's published materials to include *Memphis* magazine and other successful regional and national publications, such as *Memphis Shopper's Guide*, *Racquetball* magazine, *Huddle/ FastBreak*, *Real Estate News*, and *Satellite Dish* magazine. In 1985, after selling its locally focused assets, the company began the trajectory on which it continues today, creating community-oriented materials that are often produced in conjunction with chambers of commerce and other business organizations.

All of Towery Publishing's efforts, represented on the Internet at www.towery.com, are marked by a careful, innovative design philosophy that has become a hallmark of the company's reputation for quality and service. Boasting a nationwide sales force, proven editorial depth, cutting-edge graphics capabilities, ample marketing resources, and extensive data management expertise, the company has assembled the intellectual and capital resources necessary to produce quality products and services.

Urban Tapestry Series

Towery Publishing launched its popular Urban Tapestry Series in 1990. Each of the nearly 100 oversized, hardbound photojournals details the people, history, culture, environment, and commerce of a featured metropolitan area. These colorful coffee-table books spotlight communities through an introductory essay authored by a noted local individual, an exquisite collection of photographs, and in-depth profiles of select companies and organizations that form each area's business core.

From New York to Vancouver to Los Angeles, national and international authors have graced the pages of the books' introductory essays. The celebrated list of contributors includes two former U.S. presidents—Gerald Ford (Grand Rapids) and Jimmy Carter (Atlanta); boxing great Muhammad Ali (Louisville); two network newscasters—CBS anchor Dan Rather (Austin) and former ABC anchor Hugh Downs (Phoenix); NBC sportscaster Bob Costas (St. Louis); record-breaking quarterback Steve Young (San Francisco); best-selling mystery author Robert B. Parker (Boston); American Movie Classics host Nick Clooney (Cincinnati); former Texas first lady Nellie Connally (Houston); and former New York City Mayor Ed Koch (New York).

While the books have been enormously successful, the company continues to improve and redefine the role the series plays in the marketplace. "Currently, the Urban Tapestry Series works beautifully as a tool for enhancing the image of the communities it portrays," says Towery. "As the series continues to mature, we want it to become a reference source

TOWERY PUBLISHING, INC. PRESIDENT AND CEO J. ROBERT TOWERY (LEFT) TOOK THE REINS OF HIS FAMILY'S BUSINESS IN 1972, MAINTAINING THE COMPANY'S LONG-STANDING CORE COMMITMENT TO QUALITY.

STEVE DAVIS

SORTING THROUGH HUNDREDS OF BEAU-
TIFUL PHOTOGRAPHS IS JUST ONE OF THE
ENVIABLE TASKS ASSIGNED TO TOWERY'S
TOP-NOTCH TEAM OF DESIGNERS AND
ART DIRECTORS, LED BY AWARD-WINNING
CREATIVE DIRECTOR BRIAN GROPPE
(LEFT). MEMBERS OF TOWERY'S EDITORIAL
STAFF CULL THE BEST FROM MATERIALS
SUBMITTED BY FEATURE WRITERS AND
PROFILE CLIENTS TO PRODUCE THE URBAN
TAPESTRY SERIES (RIGHT).

that businesses and executives turn to when evaluating the quality of life in cities where they may be considering moving or expanding."

Chambers of Commerce Turn to Towery

In addition to its Urban Tapestry Series, Towery Publishing has become the largest producer of published and Internet materials for North American chambers of commerce. From published membership directories and Internet listings that enhance business-to-business communication, to visitor and relocation guides tailored to reflect the unique qualities of the communities they cover, the company's chamber-oriented materials offer comprehensive information on dozens of topics, including housing, education, leisure activities, health care, and local government.

The company's primary Internet product consists of its introCity™ sites. Much like its published materials, Towery's introCity sites introduce newcomers, visitors, and longtime residents to every facet of a particular community, while simultaneously placing the local chamber of commerce at the forefront of the city's Internet activity. The sites provide newcomer information including calendars, photos, citywide business listings with everything from nightlife to shopping to family fun, and on-line maps pinpointing the exact location of businesses, schools, attractions, and much more.

Sustained Creativity

The driving forces behind Towery Publishing have always been the company's employees and its state-of-the-art industry technology. Many of its employees have worked with the Towery family of companies for more than 20 years. Today's staff of seasoned innovators totals around 100 at the Memphis headquarters, and more than 40 sales, marketing, and editorial staff traveling to and working in an ever growing list of cities.

Supporting the staff's endeavors are state-of-the-art prepress publishing software and equipment. Towery Publishing was the first production environment in the United States to combine desktop publishing with color separations and image scanning to produce finished film suitable for burning plates for four-color printing. Today, the company relies on its digital prepress services to produce more than 8,000 pages each year, containing more than 30,000 high-quality color images.

Through decades of business and technological change, one aspect of Towery Publishing has remained constant. "The creative energies of our staff drive us toward innovation and invention," Towery says. "Our people make the highest possible demands on themselves, so I know that our future is secure if the ingredients for success remain a focus on service and quality." ●

WITH *THE OPEN CONTAINER*—AN OUT-
DOOR SCULPTURE BY MEMPHIAN MARK
NOWELL—MARKING THE SPOT, TOWERY'S
MEMPHIS HOME OFFICE SERVES AS GROUND
ZERO FOR THE COMPANY'S INNOVATIVE
COMMUNITY-BASED PUBLICATIONS.

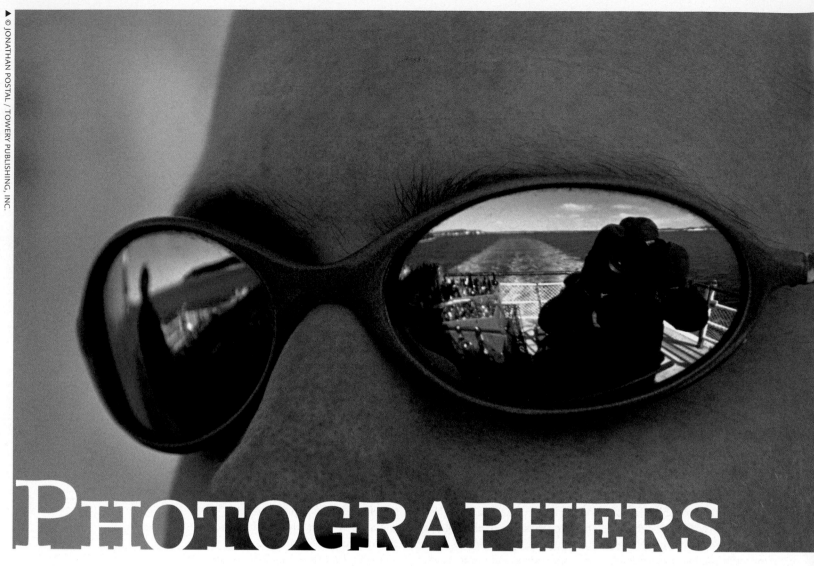

PHOTOGRAPHERS

Originally from New Orleans, **Dean Abramson** owns Dean Abramson Photography and specializes in stock and location photography for editorial, corporate, institutional, and advertising clients. His editorial clients include *Time*, *Newsweek*, *Forbes*, and *U.S. News & World Report*, and his commercial clients include Bowdoin College, Maine Turnpike Authority, Maine Em-ployers Mutual, and Colby College.

Specializing in nature and landscape photography, **Bruce E. Burnham** has photographed for his own My Eyes Photography and for Boothbay Boat Sales. His images have appeared in various New England-based calendars, and he won Best of Show at the Bangor State Fair in 1999 and 2000. He serves as chairman of the Maine Camera Club Council.

Before moving to Maine, **Gordon Chibroski** taught art at the Montana State School for the Deaf and Blind, as well as photography at

the University of Great Falls. In 1995, he covered the America's Cup challenge in California, and he has been a photographer for the *Portland Press Herald/Maine Sunday Telegram* for some 20 years.

Owner of C. C. Church Photography, **C.C. Church** specializes in fine art landscape and dance photography. Originally from Portland, he studied at the Maine College of Art.

A fire photographer for the Freeport Fire & Rescue Department, **Scott D. Conner** specializes in nature and landscape photography. His first published photos appeared in 2001, in a book about the Portland region.

A self-taught photographer originally from Beverly, Massachusetts, **Laurie Dash** works for Illustrations Unlimited, a stock photo business, and specializes in landscape photography. In 1999 and 2000, she won first place in the Portland Camera Club Class A color slide division, and she took second place in 1996, 1997, and 1998.

A member of the Maine Professional Photographers Association and the Portland Camera Club, **Pauline M. Dimino** specializes in area scenic and event coverage photography. She owns Photography By Pauline and offers photographic services that include wedding, portrait, event, newsletter, consulting, sales, slide show, photojournalism, and stock photography.

John Ewing began working for the *Portland Press Herald/Maine Sunday Telegram* more than two decades ago, after spending time at newspapers in Biddeford, Maine, and New Haven, Conn-ecticut. His photographic projects include series on Thoreau's visits to Maine, the Appalachian Trail, Maine's Irish roots in Galway, and the Newfoundland fishing industry.

Stan Farrell is originally from Vassalboro, and he earned a bachelor's degree in mechanical engineering and a master's degree in materials science and engineering at Worcester Polytechnical Institute.

Specializing in black-and-white photography, **Hannah Fettig** sees her photography as a way to learn more about herself and her subjects.

Owner of Fred Field Photography, **Fred J. Field** specializes in photojournalism, portraiture, and picture stories. His work has appeared in dozens of national and international newspapers, *People*, *Newsweek*, and *U.S. News & World Report*, and he has won awards internationally.

A contributing editor to *Vacations* and *Cruises & Tours* magazines, and coauthor of the travel guide-book *Hidden Coast of California*, **Dave G. Houser** specializes in cruise/luxury travel, personality, health, and history photography. He has been a runner-up for the Lowell Thomas Travel Journalist of the Year Award and was named the 1984 Society of American Travel Writers' Photographer of the Year.

in the San Francisco Bay Area. Her work has been collected by museums and public collections in the United States and Europe, and her documentary series, *Home Sweet Home: Caring for America's Elderly*, was recently honored with the *Communication Arts-Design Annual* 1999 Award of Excellence for an unpublished series. Her images have appeared in numerous Towery publications.

Photophile, established in San Diego in 1967, has more than 1 million color images on file, culled from more than 85 contributing local and international photographers. Subjects range from images of Southern California to adventure, sports, wildlife, underwater scenes, business, industry, people, science and research, health and medicine, and travel photography. Included on Photophile's client list are American Express, *Guest Informant*, and Franklin Stoorza.

The York County Bureau photographer, **Gregory Rec** interned at the *Portland Press Herald/Maine Sunday Telegram* in 1995 and at the *Boston Globe* in 1996. In 1997, he graduated from the University of Montana and joined the staff of the *Portland Press Herald/Maine Sunday Telegram*.

Herb Swanson has been a photographer for the *Portland Press Herald/Maine Sunday Telegram* since 1994, and has also worked for the Associated Press and Agence France-Presse wire services. He has worked on three continents, covering stories that range from elections in Hungary to transatlantic sailboat races.

Nance Trueworthy specializes in assignment, location, and stock photography. Her profession takes her to exciting locations in the United States, the Caribbean, and Europe, where she photographs the drama of our natural world as well as famous people in all walks of life. Represented by Liaison International, Stock Boston, and Garden Image, she is published internationally. Her work has been reproduced in books, cards, calendars, and magazines all over the world, and in a Smithsonian museum exhibit, *Ocean Planet*.

Originally from Wisconsin, **Eric Wunrow** specializes in photo-

graphy, graphic design, landscapes, and wilderness sports. His images have sold worldwide in publishing and advertising media, often including text and graphics or illustrations of his own design, and he has explored 80 of the United States' highest mountains. His first coffee-table book, *Mountains of Colorado*, documents 150,000 vertical feet of his trekking.

Other contributing organizations include the Maine College of Art, the Museum of African Tribal Art, Portland Camera Club, the Sunday River Ski Resort, and the University of Southern Maine. For further information about the photographers appearing in *Portland: City of the Eastern Seaboard*, please contact Towery Publishing.

William Hubbell has been a professional photographer for more than 40 years and specializes in corporate communication, architecture, food, and book photography. He has produced six coffee-table books, the latest of which focuses on Maine.

A photographer at the *Portland Press Herald/Maine Sunday Telegram* for more than 20 years, **Doug Jones** also managed Inness Photo Service in South Portland after attending the University of Rhode Island. His work includes a series on Norway's fishing revival.

Once an aerospace photojournalist for NASA, **Dennis Keim** now owns dk-studio and specializes in corporate and editorial photography. His work has been featured in local, regional, and national publications, and his lifestyle photography has appeared in three books: *Huntsville—Where Technology Meets Tradition*, *Huntsville—A Timeless Portrait*, and Towery Publishing's *Huntsville-Madison County: To the Edge of the Universe*.

After studying art in his native Ireland, **James Lemass** moved to Cambridge, Massachusetts, in 1987. His specialties include people and travel photography, and his photographs have appeared in several other Towery publications.

A member of the *Portland Press Herald/Maine Sunday Telegram* staff since 1986, **David MacDonald** has also worked as photo editor and chief photographer at the *Kennebec Journal*, and previously worked in New York City in fashion and advertising photography. He has traveled to Russia four times in recent years, docu-menting everyday life since the fall of the Soviet Union.

A native of Auburn, **Jack Milton** joined the *Portland Press Herald/Maine Sunday Telegram* staff in 1980. He attended the University of Southern Maine and oversees the photography department's computer operations.

Judi Parks is an award-winning photojournalist living and working

Index of Profiles

Library Of Congress Cataloging-in-Publication Data

Mitchell, George J. (George John), 1933-
    Portland : spirit of the Eastern Seaboard / introduction by George J. Mitchell ;
  art direction by Bob Kimball.
        p. cm. —(Urban tapestry series)
    Includes index.
    ISBN 1-58967-000-0 (alk. paper)
        1. Portland (Me.)—Civilization. 2. Portland (Me.)—Pictoral works. 3. Portland
(Me.)—Economic conditions. 4. Business enterprises—Maine—Portland. I. Kimball, Bob.
II. Title. III. Series.

    F29.P9 M58 2001
    974.1'91—dc21

                                                                        2001037540

Printed in Mexico.

Towery Publishing, Inc., The Towery Building, 1835 Union Avenue, Memphis, TN 38104

www.towery.com

Publisher: J. Robert Towery **Executive Publisher**: Jenny McDowell **Sales Manager:** Dawn Park-
Donegan **Marketing Director**: Carol Culpepper **Project Directors**: Candice Gilbert, Mary Whelan
Executive Editor: David B. Dawson **Managing Editor**: Lynn Conlee **Senior Editors**: Carlisle
Hacker, Brian L. Johnston **Project Editor/Caption Writer**: Danna M. Greenfield **Editors:** Jay
Adkins, Rebecca E. Farabough, Ginny Reeves, Sabrina Schroeder **Profile Writer**: James M.
Milliken **Creative Director**: Brian Groppe **Photography Editor**: Jonathan Postal **Photographic
Consultant**: Andrea Nemitz **Production Manager**: Laurie Beck **Profile Designers**: Rebekah
Barnhardt, Glen Marshall **Photography Coordinator**: Robin Lankford **Production Assistant**:
Robert Parrish **Digital Color Supervisor**: Darin Ipema **Digital Color Technicians**: Eric Friedl,
Mark Svetz **Digital Scanning Technician**: Brad Long **Print Coordinator**: Beverly Timmons